Panden

PANDEMIC
OF
DELUSION

Staying Rational in an Increasingly Irrational World

By Tyson Gill

Interlink Books

An imprint of Interlink Publishing Group, Inc.
Northampton, Massachusetts

First published in 2023 by

Interlink Books
An imprint of Interlink Publishing Group, Inc.
46 Crosby Street
Northampton, Massachusetts 01060
www.interlinkbooks.com

Library of Congress Cataloging-in-Publication Data available
ISBN 978-1-62371-795-7

10 9 8 7 6 5 4 3 2 1

Printed and bound in the United States of America

ACKNOWLEDGEMENTS

I would like to acknowledge Michel Moushabeck and the team at Interlink Publishing for believing in this book and bringing it to the marketplace.

I would also like to acknowledge and thank my outstanding scientific editor, Dr. Coren Walters-Stewart, who reviewed the book to ensure that assertions of fact are supported in the scientific literature and that every speculation is plausible and is not contradicted by our best scientific understanding. Her detailed and diligent efforts have been particularly reassuring when putting forth a book that champions facts over belief.

In addition, heartfelt thanks to Jordan Grafman, Ph.D. for his insightful foreword in which he reminds us that neurologists, cognitive scientists, psychologists and many other specialists are hard at work every day and are making dramatic progress in understanding the mechanics of brain function that are ultimately expressed, for better and for worse, in all of our everyday interactions as described in this book.

Finally, I'd like to thank the people who have listened to my talks, read my articles, offered such great encouragement, and stimulated so many ideas over the many years that have taken shape into the form of this book.

CONTENTS

FOREWORD

BY JORDAN GRAFMAN, PH.D.

Beliefs are often based on facts obtained through multiple observations using a scientific method. But beliefs may be susceptible to myths and false information. Too much of the latter can result in delusional thinking, a focus of this volume by Tyson Gill. Although delusional thinking has been with us as long as recorded human history, technology has expanded the rate and shared frequency of delusional thinking. Often delusional thinking has been associated with psychiatric disorders, but it can be even more common in certain forms in neurotypical people. Cognitive neuroscience efforts at understanding the brain basis of delusional thinking has progressed with evidence of specific neurochemicals (e.g., serotonin) and brain areas (the temporal and frontal lobes) having critical roles in inhibiting delusional thinking. Cognitive psychologists have also tried to tease apart the forms of delusional thinking and their causes. Here again, progress has been sub-stantial with certain characteristics of people (e.g., tendency toward magical thinking and reduced influence of stored knowledge to predict the validity of a claim), making delusional thinking more likely. Given the rapid and relatively uncensored spread of all kinds of beliefs on the internet, academic research, while creating a solid scientific basis for understanding delusional thinking, is often ignored by the lay press, and the ordinary citizen may not have access to a clearly outlined approach to combating delusional thinking in our daily lives. This book, *Pandemic of Delusion*, aims to solve this problem by providing the reader with evidence of this pandemic of belief, the skills to dissect an assertion and judge whether it is based on factual evidence, and the insights to engage with others in critical thinking about the beliefs they are exposed to.

Before the advent of the internet, the spread of delusional thinking and false beliefs was slow and, with some trivial and profound exceptions, limited to small groups of people. With the use of various social platforms, delusional thinking and false belief often obtain uncritical acceptance. Sometimes it is difficult to locate the source of the delusional thinking or false belief, but often they are associated with individuals or groups with specific social or political agendas. Most people simply don't have the time to test the legitimacy and validity of this kind of thinking and instead rely on trust. If the information is aligned with your previous thinking, you may explicitly or even implicitly accept the information as factually true or at least as sensible, even without an investigation of the facts. This often serves the nefarious purposes of the purveyor of that information. And of course, understanding the agenda of the purveyor is a part of the process in accepting or rejecting information that you haven't vetted.

Human brains provide the biological mechanisms that allow us to think critically about things. That skill endows us with the ability to refine our thinking about everything from astrophysical theories about the universe to whether that baseball trade was smart or not. While developing the necessary critical thinking to evaluate all forms of thinking and beliefs is occasionally taught in academic settings (sometimes from an early age), it more often is simply learned on the fly in an unsystematic way, or if you are lucky, by dedicated parents, teachers, or mentors. Without the employment of critical thinking by our most famous inventors, scientists, artists, writers, and engineers, most of the achievements that have made human life better for the most part since the Middle Ages would not have occurred. When cultures reject critical thinking, they eventually sink below the intellectual horizon. This book is a remedy for that rejection. So, is this book important and necessary to read? The answer is a resounding yes!

Jordan Grafman, Ph.D. is director of Brain Injury Research; chief, Cognitive Neuroscience Lab, Shirley Ryan Ability Lab; and professor, Department of Physical Medicine & Rehabilitation, Neurology, Cognitive Neurology and Alzheimer's Center, Department of Psychiatry, Feinberg School of Medicine & Department of Psychology, Weinberg College of Arts and Sciences, Northwestern University, Chicago, Illinois.

INTRODUCTION

We are besieged by two global pandemics. One, of course, is the deadly COVID-19 crisis. The other is a crisis of delusion.

The Covid crisis will pass. Vaccinations, prevention techniques, treatments, and natural immunities will see us through it.

Our other pandemic, the delusion pandemic, is in a bigger sense even more dangerous and deadly than Covid. Symptoms began to appear during the Reagan administration in the form of a rejection of facts and science and an embrace of magical thinking and psychic advisors. It incubated and took ever greater hold until it finally exploded into a full-blown outbreak during the Trump era. This pandemic isn't isolated to America, however. We are seeing simultaneous outbreaks of delusion all around the globe.

The extent of this global pandemic is frightening. If unchecked, the consequences will be severe for our continued health and well-being, individually and as a global community. If we had hospitals for delusion, they would be overwhelmed today. And unlike Covid, we have few natural defenses or technological treatments for this pandemic of delusion.

This book is one treatment you can administer to yourself. It is a poke of an anti-delusion vaccine to help your brain resist infection by beliefs that can grow into delusions. Delusions take root as beliefs, and to understand delusion one must start there.

Whether you are a science guru or are scientifically challenged, this guidebook will help you come to a deep, holistic understanding of the science of belief and delusion. It will expose the evolutionary roots of our predilection toward belief, show how our very powers of perception and memory have evolved to facilitate belief, demonstrate how easily our beliefs can be manipulated, and how insidiously beliefs can grow into delusions.

It will go on to show how belief-based thinking not only results in superstition, ignorance, and fear in some, but how it diminishes the reasoning capacity of us all. Our selective abandonment of reason compromises our fundamental decision-making capacity, both in small personal matters and in critical public policy.

Together we will explore an alternative, the discipline of fact-based thinking as manifest in the scientific method. This book will give you the insights and techniques you need to apply scientific rigor to your everyday decision-making. It will help you understand how to verify facts, avoid logical pitfalls and belief-driven biases, and use fact-based reasoning to make important ethical decisions.

Beyond the practical, this book will inspire you by showing how the same very powerful characteristics that make us vulnerable to belief can also help us recognize facts. Hopefully, you will come away with a deep sense of awe and wonder to be a part of our incredible universe based on fact as revealed by science.

Pandemic of Delusion will take you on a wild ride through all the varied landscapes that impact upon facts and beliefs. We will examine a wide range of related phenomena through the lenses of history, psychology, physiology, science, logic, literature, religion, the paranormal, and politics before our journey is complete. All these fields and more influence the way we process facts, beliefs, and delusion. To get a complete and comprehensive picture, our journey must visit them all.

By the end of that journey, you will be better immunized against the rampant delusional beliefs that threaten to infect you every single time you turn on your television or open your web browser. You will feel more confident in your ability to judge purported facts and make sound decisions for you, your family, and your planet.

Organization of this Book

This book is about facts, beliefs, delusions, and science—but it is not written in an academic "science-y" style. It is relatively light, easy reading that anyone can enjoy just for fun. It is really about how we think and the ideas presented here apply to everything we do in our normal day to day activities.

Chapter 1, **Facts,** focuses on the complexities that impact how we think about facts. It compares and contrasts the various kind of facts that we consider in everyday life and goes on to discuss the various ways that we perceive and interpret facts.

Chapter 2, **Beliefs**, looks at beliefs, the antithesis of facts. It examines what beliefs are, identifies different kinds of beliefs, and discusses how and why they are so powerful.

Chapter 3, **Confusion**, digs deeper into the dizzying array of factors that confuse and confound beliefs with facts and examines the underlying functioning of thought, perception, and memory that complicate our ability to distinguish between them.

Chapter 4, **Delusion**, extends the discussion beyond mere belief into the realm of delusion. It discusses various beliefs that grow into delusions and looks at the impact of these strong beliefs.

Chapter 5, **Clarity**, brings the discussion together and sheds some clarity upon all the disparate pieces of the complex puzzle of how we think and provides a more holistic big picture. It focuses on the many ways that our thinking can be changed, toward or away from, more fact-based thinking.

Chapter 6, **Inspiration**, provides a healthy dose of optimism. It offers tangible hope that we can overcome our delusional vulnerabilities and shares a profound sense of the awe and wonder of a real, fact-based appreciation of our cosmos offers.

Chapter 7, **Science**, takes a slightly deeper dive into science that will hopefully get you started on a lifelong journey toward becoming ever more fact-based and fulfilled by a life guided by science.

Chapter 8, **Futures**, brings our journey to a close with a summary and a parting message.

The appendix, **Fallacies**, offers a compilation of logical and ethical fallacies that you undoubtedly encounter every day. Reviewing these at least once increases the chance that you will recognize them when you hear them and thereby become a more fact-based thinker. It also serves as a reference later when you are unsure of the soundness of an argument presented to you.

Finally, a **Glossary** of terms as they are used in this book is presented for your quick reference.

Dear Reader,

The vast majority of us hold some number of casual and even deeply held beliefs. This book challenges our full spectrum of beliefs and their effect upon hot-button issues like politics and prejudices. It is critical not only of religions but of new age thinkers and of believers of all manner of pseudoscientific and paranormal activity.

Therefore, chances are pretty good that this book will at times seem to attack you personally or attack people you love and respect. That is not the intent. But we can't walk on eggshells or we'd have little to talk about and the discussions would be painfully anodyne.

So, when it happens, and it will—when you feel personally attacked because your beliefs are being called into question—try to consider the arguments and observations with some academic distance. Think about how the discussion applies to others with different beliefs that you do not share. In that way, you might find some value in those perspectives that might otherwise be rejected out of hand.

It is my fervent hope and goal, however, that no matter where you are starting from, in the end you will walk away from this journey with new insights and a newfound sense of optimism and wonderment.

CHAPTER 1: FACTS

In order to discuss delusion, we must first establish the baseline of facts and fact-based thinking.

John Adams famously said:

> *"Facts are stubborn things. They cannot be altered by our wishes, our inclinations, or the dictates of our passions."*

And he was right inasmuch as facts will always win out. Facts don't care if you believe them. Climate change is happening whether you choose to believe in it or not.

We ignore or deny facts at our peril. However, because facts are stubborn things does not mean they are obvious or undeniable. On the contrary, facts can be elusive and difficult to recognize when they are attacked or are lost in a sea of misinformation. They can be easily denied and rejected in favor of unfounded beliefs. Even the most clear and indisputable of facts are under constant assault from many quarters.

In this chapter we will define facts and remind you just how vitally important and deceptively uncertain they can be.

A Fact Is a Fact

Why do we need a book about facts? A fact is a fact.

A rock is a rock; a fact is a fact. It seems that facts should be cut and dried, carved in stone, a given. What possible controversy could they create?

Yet, even in modern enlightened society, facts are far from straight-forward. There are many diverse perspectives and opinions about facts that create a staggeringly complex dynamic. Most of us are conditioned at least to some extent to think of facts as mundane, untrustworthy, or even nuisances.

The joke "Don't let the facts get in your way" exposes a pervasive societal tendency. Even distinguishing facts from other claims is often very difficult.

A great many people deny at least some number of demonstrable facts, dismiss facts, and question the credibility of even the very concept of facts. This has real and profound effects on both individuals and on society.

Beliefs compete against facts on a daily basis in all of our lives. Far too often, beliefs win the battle over facts. People defend their beliefs in spite of a lack of facts or even in the face of facts to the contrary. This is often seen as virtue, as evidence of deep spirituality. When confronted with discrepancies between facts and beliefs, a great many people refuse to reappraise their beliefs, instead choosing to question the very knowability of facts in general.

Indeed, facts are in a seemingly unending battle for survival against a relentless, and literally unreasoning, assault by beliefs. And even as we get better at uncovering facts, beliefs seem to be winning the battle.

Defining Facts

Aren't facts just another belief?

They are not.

People often do make confusing sorts of statements like "I believe in facts" or "I put my faith in facts." But these should not muddy the stark distinction between facts and beliefs.

A fact is distinctly different from a belief, and they have absolute definitions. These are not subject to interpretation. A fact is a fact, and that is an independent truth despite what anyone might like to think. A belief is a belief, regardless of preference, perspective, or even personal experience. These are not two sides of the same coin. They are not merely a matter of perspective.

Said another way, if I make the claim that a fact is only a belief, that claim can be shown to be objectively wrong. Conversely, if I claim that a belief is really a fact, that assertion can likewise be proven to be demonstrably in error.

So then, what distinguishes a fact from a belief? The following chart may help to understand this continuum.

ASSERTIONS OF FACT				
ACTUALLY TRUE		ACTUALLY FALSE		
PROVEN FACTS	UNPROVEN FACTS	ERRORS	BELIEFS	DELUSIONS
Validated by objective verification and/or sound logic	*Unvalidated but plausible assertions*	*Mistakenly thought to be true based upon misinformation or unsound logic*	*Held to be true despite a lack of sound supporting edivence*	*A belief that persists despite superior evidence to the contrary*

PURPORTED FACTS

A **fact** is an assertion that is objectively true. It is actually true regardless of whether we realize it or acknowledge it or understand it. As such, it may be proven or unproven.

A **proven fact** is a fact that has been validated by objective verification. This cannot be just any verification but must meet logical and empirical tests of validity. For the sake of simplicity, when the term fact is used in this book it is generally meant to imply proven facts.

An **unproven fact** is simply a fact that has not been proven yet. The trouble is that we can't be sure, until it is proven or disproven, whether it is a fact or an **error**. Until then, it is simply an unproven or **purported fact**.

A **belief**, on the other hand, is an assertion that is held to be true despite a lack of supporting evidence. A definitional requirement is that while beliefs are thought to be true, they are subject to change when new information comes to light.

If a belief cannot or will not be changed regardless of any amount of evidence to the contrary, it is actually a **delusion.** While beliefs may change, a delusion is so strongly held that it does not bend under any weight of evidence or logic to the contrary. Many of the common beliefs we hold to be true are delusions. We only call them beliefs so as not to offend and insult, or as a practical necessity.

There is also a subcategory of delusion called a **bizarre delusion**, which is used to describe a delusion that is particularly far-fetched and well beyond any reason or logic. We will discuss all these in greater detail when we focus on delusion later in the book.

Many assertions cannot be proven or disproven. A great number of these fall under the category of subjective assertions like "I love my mother" or "I have a headache." Given all of this uncertainty, the only practical choice is to maintain a healthy perspective. We do not really need to fuss about proving most everyday assertions. If you assert you love your mother, barring any strong evidence to the contrary, we can merely accept that. If you say you have a headache, it does no harm to accept that as true, barring a repeated pattern of suspiciously convenient headaches.

But because we accept many unproven or unprovable assertions every single day does not give us license to abandon any burden of proof when it really matters. To do so, to become complacent about facts, would be extremely foolhardy.

Science, and any sound decision-making, requires that important decisions be made in the light of proven facts, not based upon beliefs or unfounded assertions. It requires certainty, not wishful or magical thinking. In consequential matters, proof is required, and no assumption of truth should be made until a purported fact is validated.

When we blur the distinction between facts and beliefs when it matters, when we fail to demand legitimate proof of assertions that impact important decisions, we end up with poor or even catastrophic outcomes.

Belief versus Believing

But not all beliefs are false. I have lots of beliefs that are true.
I believe in science for example!

Let's not conflate beliefs with believing. In English we often say "I believe in" to confirm that we acknowledge a particular fact. I certainly believe that the sun will come up tomorrow. Cher believes in love. Hopefully we all believe that black lives matter.

But a belief is very different than believing in something. Just because we believe in something does not make it a belief. By formal definition in this book, and generally in the real world, a belief is a falsehood that people nevertheless believe in.

For example, consider two statements:

Statement 1: I believe the Earth is essentially flat.

Statement 2: I believe the Earth is roughly spherical.

Though they may be similar syntactically, these are not equivalent statements. One is an assertion of fact while the other is an assertion of belief. One is correct, one is false.

Many like to try to create an illusion of equivalence by arguing that assertions of fact are just another assertion of belief. This is aided by the use of the word "believe."

But if a belief were true, we would simply call it a fact. Believing in a fact is not the same as believing in a fiction, and expressing a belief in facts does not legitimize a belief in fictions.

The bottom line here is that for purposes of this book, we use the word "belief" strictly to represent the concept of believing in something that is untrue. For this discussion, don't get too muddled up by the many nuanced and varied ways we use language in everyday comments and discussions.

Probability Facts

If scientists deal in facts, why can't they ever seem to be able to say anything without equivocating?

It's true, scientists can be infuriating. Scientists never seem willing to give a straight answer to any question. They equivocate on every answer and qualify every conclusion. You ask a scientist if water is wet and they'll give you a long, complicated explanation that doesn't seem to clarify it in the least.

Believers are easy. They instill confidence. You can ask them anything and they'll answer simply and with absolute certainty and conviction. This is one reason why beliefs can appear so compelling while scientific explanations often sound so suspicious.

The reason that scientists appear so uncertain is the nature of their discipline. They understand that all answers have a limited context in which they are true. They understand that an answer must be complete and nuanced to be accurate. And in addition, scientists are comfortable thinking of facts as probabilities.

We normally think of facts as assertions that are true. And they are. They are known to be consistent with all known logic and with all other facts, and there is no reasonable expectation that new facts will come to light to contradict them.

But many true facts aren't always 100 percent facts. Many are **probability facts** that can only be expressed as a certain statistical probability. Many things in nature and in physics are probabilities that simply cannot be known in any other terms.

For example, if you ask a scientist if the Hadron Collider could produce a mini black hole that would eat the Earth, they would say yes.

The Large Hadron Collider (LHC) is the world's largest and most powerful particle accelerator. It is located in Europe.

But it would be much more useful to ask what the probability is that the Hadron Collider could produce a mini black hole that would eat the Earth. They would give you an answer like a hundred million billion to one.

For all practical purposes, it is a fact that the Hadron Collider is not going to produce a mini black hole that will eat the Earth. It would be clearly irrational to worry about this happening on the grounds that scientists won't rule it out for certain.

So, even if one cannot say with certainty what the outcome will be in any specific instance, a probability fact is still exactly correct and perfectly true.

Here's an example of a probability fact from science. The atmosphere contains about 21 percent oxygen. That is a fact (although the fraction of carbon dioxide is increasing every day).

That means that if you grab a random molecule from the air, the likelihood that you'll get an oxygen molecule, O_2, is 21 percent. And that is a fact that you can take to the bank.

That probabilistic fact has limitations. It cannot tell you what kind of molecule you will get with any particular attempt, only that you will get about twenty-one oxygen molecules out of every 100 attempts. Not exactly, but about.

🎤 *Just give me a straight answer. If I grab a molecule out of the air, what kind will it be?*

I can't tell you that, but I can tell you that you have about a 21 percent chance of getting an oxygen. That is a fact. Some people express skepticism toward facts when expressed as probabilities. They interpret it as a failure of science, as equivocation, as more confusing qualifications by scientists. Worse, some exploit people's inherent uncertainty about statistics and probability facts to raise unfounded doubts about those facts. Simply put, a probability can represent a fact just as real and reliable as any other.

Before we end this section. I would like to identify another type of fact. I call this variation a **probabilistic fact**. A probabilistic fact is one that has such a high likelihood of being true that we can consider it a fact even though we are never likely to witness it. Here's an example.

I assert that at this moment, as I am typing this line, someone, somewhere sneezed. Do I know that for sure? Can I ever prove it?

The answer to both of those questions is no. However, given the number of people in the world and the frequency at which we sneeze, it is almost certainly true. It can be accepted as a probabilistic fact.

Another example is the Drake Equation. You are probably familiar with this, if not by name. It is the logic that if you look at all of the galaxies, stars, planets, and habitable planets in the universe, it is a statistical certainty that intelligent life exists somewhere other than Earth.

Intelligent aliens exist out there somewhere, that's a probabilistic fact that we can probably safely accept as true.

Symbolic Facts

🗣 *But much of what is really important are ideas,*
not tangible things that can be touched and validated.

Exactly right.

And although this topic seems a bit like an academic discussion in a Philosophy 101 course, let's just touch upon the relationship of ideas to facts.

We normally think of facts as concrete, physical objects like a car or a tree. We even, as pointed out in the previous section, often think of facts as probabilities, like the percentage of oxygen in the atmosphere.

But we also deal every day with things that are real only in our minds. Are these a form of facts? Are there times when we need to think of them as facts, even to apply rules of validation to them?

These include perceptions of emotion like happiness. These include symbolic amalgams, collections of things like our concept of the universe. Or they can be extrapolations like our notion of infinity. They can also be things of complete fancy, like unicorns.

Unicorns clearly do not exist, but the concept of a unicorn does exist as a conceptual symbol in our heads. For our purposes here, let's call these **symbolic facts**. This merely points out that it is a fact that the symbol of a unicorn exists in our brains.

> *Note that when the word "symbol" is used here, it is used in the strict sense of cognitive science to mean the representation of a thing that exists in our brain. Such symbols can represent real things or completely imaginary things.*

These symbolic facts can be important in our lives and can have tangible impact on our lives, so we therefore must not exempt them from appropriate scrutiny and validation when warranted.

For example, human consciousness can be categorized as a symbolic fact. Although intangible, something we perceive as consciousness does exist. If we make claims about consciousness only existing in humans, then we can and should subject that symbolic fact to rigorous tests to prove or disprove those claims.

Such consideration of how we think of ideas can be interesting and valuable, but we must always be clear that just because something exists as a symbolic fact in our brains does not in any way mean that it has any external existence outside of our imaginations.

Symbolic facts are particularly problematic when assessing and comparing those facts. For example, safety is a sort of symbolic fact. Yet, being symbolic, it is very fuzzy and imprecise. What is safe to one person may not be safe to another. Or what is safe enough in one circumstance may not be safe enough in another.

This makes it especially difficult to evaluate assertions about safety. How do you evaluate claims about safety? How do you compare claims of safety? These questions can become very messy.

Logical Facts

🗣 Knowledge isn't all about facts.
It's also about the reasoning we apply to facts.

Absolutely right!

Not all facts are simple things that you can point to or hold in your hands. As we have said, some are probabilistic facts and some are symbolic facts. But still others are **logical facts**. Or, more precisely, facts that are validated largely or entirely through logic.

A logical fact is something that is true based on the valid application of logical reasoning. If A is true and B follows logically from A, then B must also be true.

> *Logic has predicted many major and even extremely elusive facts of nature (like relativity) long before they were validated by experimentation.*

Logical facts don't actually need to observed to be validated as true. We don't ever need to actually see the Hadron Collider generate a mini black hole that consumes the Earth. We know that the probability fact is true based on the established principles of physics.

Quite often great discoveries arise out of the sound logic of physics and mathematics. Mathematics provides us with a system of logic that can be definitively validated. It turns out that the cosmos is pretty darn accommodating about adhering to the rules of mathematics.

Disproving something based on logic is often easier than trying to prove an assertion using logic alone. Without even looking at your latest perpetual motion machine, I can dismiss it as a false claim with confidence. Perpetual motion violates fundamental laws of thermodynamics. The existence of a device that could ignore those laws would overturn all that we know to be true about the universe.

Perpetual motion is disproven purely through simple logic. The problem with logic is that while it works great in the very precise and unambiguous language of mathematics or when adhering to the laws of physics, it can be very difficult to assess sound logic in the very fuzzy and ambiguous form of spoken language.

When spoken language is used, it becomes extremely easy to present misleading logic, and it becomes very difficult to spot misleading or fallacious logical arguments. Despite these challenges, logical facts can be established by applying sound logic even outside of the fields of math and physics, but it does become more difficult to ensure that our logic is sound.

When beliefs are asserted and facts are denied, the weapon is usually bogus logic. By learning to recognize and call out these instances of false logic, you can better remain clear and fact-based in your thinking and decision making.

The appendix summarizes some typical logical arguments that are almost always false. They are called **fallacies**, and arguments that employ them are called fallacious arguments. That is, they present an argument, or even a supposed proof based on logic, but that logic is fundamentally flawed. By reviewing these common fallacy patterns, you can become better at spotting and rejecting them when you hear them.

Lies, Damned Lies, and Statistics

🐾 *Some facts may be probabilities, but you can't ever trust statistics!*

You can absolutely trust statistics… when they are trustworthy. As we discussed, some facts can only be expressed as probabilities. In fact, some physical phenomena only exist in reality as probabilities. Probability facts are described and analyzed through statistics.

The average fraction of oxygen in the atmosphere is 21 percent. That's a validated probability fact expressed through statistics. Yet, when communicated in the jargon of statistics, that probability fact seems untrustworthy, like something intended to fool us.

Our intense mistrust of statistics is not without justification. We have all heard references to "Lies, damned lies, and statistics," an expression popularized by Mark Twain.

That expression reflects the unfortunate reality that statistics seem imprecise and confusing to many people. Since they don't predict individual cases, some can point to specific cases to try to discredit them. It is relatively easy to misrepresent statistics in order to bolster weak arguments or to create the wrong impression. One method commonly used to mistakenly or intentionally misrepresent statistics is by lies of omission, by not telling the whole story behind the statistics.

For example, years ago I was listening to the Dr. Laura Schlessinger talk show on the radio. She was speaking to a guest who threw out the statistic cited by a major women's rights group that 95 percent of women report having been victims of sexual abuse.

To her credit, Dr. Laura questioned that statistic. Immediately, on air, she phoned the researcher to whom that statistic was attributed. The social scientist, a professor in Pennsylvania, was thankful for the chance to discuss this. She said that the 95 percent statistic attributed to her research applied only to a particular high-risk population in the inner city, not to the population overall. She had been trying for years to convince various advocacy groups to cease misrepresenting her research.

Clearly perturbed, Dr. Laura phoned a representative of the major women's rights group that was instrumental in putting forth that misinformation. The representative first tried to justify it, but when pressed she finally argued that "our cause is so important that anything that will draw attention to the problem is justified."

This story is a perfect example of why statistical facts are viewed with such great, and all too often legitimate, suspicion. The fault for this is not with statistics, or with the science they report. Statistics, when reported accurately, are as true as a fact can be. The problem is there is a lack of sophistication among the consumers of statistics that makes far too easy for biased parties to misinterpret or misrepresent statistics to a mass audience that is not savvy in assessing them.

Following is a summary of some of the crimes typically perpetrated against good and decent statistics. We all need to learn to recognize them when we see them:

Misrepresenting the Population

This was the crime against statistics of which the women's rights advocate was guilty. Another form of this offense might be the claim that 75 percent of people turn into ravenous wolves during a full moon. Even if werewolves actually existed, it would almost certainly be the case that the cohort was not pulled from the general population, but from those who have been previously bitten by a lycanthrope.

Ignoring the Distribution

This is a typical crime targeting simple, everyday averages. To be a valid average, the distribution of results must be something close to a "normal" distribution. When the distribution is skewed, the average statistic can be tremendously misleading. An example of a particularly egregious case would be the claim that the average personal wealth of ten random guys over the age of fifty found hanging out in a bar was $19.3 billion—without noting that Jeff Bezos happened to be celebrating his latest space jaunt at that very bar.

Need to see the math?
(193.3B + 9 * 1.17M) / 10 = 19.3B

Ignoring the Denominator

This common crime is conducted by simply choosing to report the numerator without bothering to mention the denominator. For example, one might claim that there were a shocking thirty-one credible cases of voter fraud, without happening to mention that these were out of a billion votes cast over a fourteen-year period.

Inflating through Percentages

When the number of cases is not impressive enough, statistics abusers often choose to report their results as a percentage. For example, they might point out that the risk of dying from a drug reaction goes up by an alarming 50 percent for a particular at-risk group. What they do not mention is that the increase took the total incidence from two per million doses to three per million doses.

Multiple Comparisons

This is the capital white-collar offense of statistics. The way this crime is executed is by performing a statistical analysis that looks at the correlation between a large number of factors and a particular outcome. If the analysis shows that, for example, there is a 92 percent overall correlation, you attribute that 92 percent confidence to one particular factor without mentioning that this was bundled in with many others and that it may not have any actual correlation at all.

Playing to Cognitive Biases

OK, it's true, we are all somewhat guilty of this one. We all present our narrative in a way that we think sounds most convincing. This relatively petty statistics crime can be committed in many ways. For example, relaxing regulatory requirements may increase the risk of a particular activity from 2 to 4 percent. But if we are opposed to the activity, we might reframe that as doubling the risk because it sounds far more dangerous. This may seem like a relatively victimless crime, but it is used so frequently that it has serious consequences.

Blame for rampant crimes against statistics lies not only with disingenuous advocates but must be shared by those researchers who do too little to actively defend the integrity of their scientific findings, as well as we naïve and gullible consumers of statistics. But as with logical fallacies, we can learn to become more savvy consumers of statistical truths. We can learn to sniff out falsely presented statistics. It isn't all that hard to do. Once you begin to recognize these types of misleading representations, they become increasingly obvious and apparent.

You won't always get it right, but the only truly terrible mistake you can make is to allow the abusers of statistics to convince you that statistical facts are not facts at all.

Awareness Statistics

There is one other type of commonly cited statistic that often misrepresents the truth. I call these **awareness statistics.**

You hear these awareness statistics all the time. You hear that X of every Y people know someone who has suffered from cancer, or abuse, or gun violence, or sexism, or ageism, or police brutality, or has been unfairly profiled, or has been burgled, or who uses personal pronouns.

While all of these issues I cited as examples are real and are important, drawing conclusions—both qualitative and quantitative—from these kind of awareness statistics can be very misleading. Worse, these kinds of statistics are often intended to mislead, to exaggerate, and to induce a heightened reaction.

In some situations, awareness statistics can be legitimate. They can tell us how deeply a particular narrative has seeped into a population, or how many people are aware of a particular issue. But that is not generally, or even often, the point of these statistics. Typically, the point of citing such statistics is for them to serve as a surrogate for direct measurement. Rather than directly reporting the number of people who have been injured in motorcycle accidents, we report how many people know of someone who has been injured in a motorcycle accident. The intent is not to measure mere awareness, but to convey an impression of actual accident frequency.

The underlying problem is that awareness relationships in a population are extremely complex, highly uneven, and skewed. Some people have many more relationships than others. We simply cannot correlate "awareness" with actual frequency in any straightforward manner. If a celebrity tweets about their road rage incident, millions of people know of someone who was exposed to road rage. If Nicki Minaj tweets about her friend's testicular reaction to the Covid vaccine, tens of millions of people "know someone" who had a terrible reaction to the vaccine.

Consider the example of sexual behavior. Experts strongly suspect that relatively few men have relationships with a much larger number of women. No one knows the exact numbers, but let's just make up some to illustrate. Let's say that one guy has affairs with ten women during a period of time. Each woman tends to share this information with five close friends. Now, when surveyed, fifty women report that they "know of someone" who has had an affair. It sounds like lots of guys are having affairs, but it's really just that one really horny stud muffin.

So how should we assimilate such awareness statistics? First, be skeptical whenever you hear awareness statistics. Actively skeptical. It is not enough that you merely be aware of their limitations, because they can still be successful in creating a lasting misleading impression despite your academic skepticism. You must not only be aware of their limitations, but actively suspicious of them. You should always ask whether awareness statistics are being presented simply because we cannot measure the actual number directly. If that is the case, you should consider this to be no more than a very unreliable indicator.

But if awareness statistics are being presented even though the actual number can be directly measured, then you should assume that the intent is to manipulate your reaction. If advocates report that 2.5 million people know someone who knows someone who has been murdered, that sounds far more alarming then saying there were 1,000 murders committed. It is their intent to alarm you because the raw numbers are insufficiently alarming.

Finally, resist the urge to accept statistical exaggerations when you support the cause and even when you think people need to be more alarmed. The problem is that the other side can play the same game. Anything you can exaggerate with awareness statistics can be exaggerated by your opponent just as easily. Sixty-five million people know someone who has been a victimized by cancel culture and 27 million people know of someone who was saved by a hero with a handgun.

Stay true to real facts. Don't be swayed by manipulative statistics—especially when you believe in your heart that some exaggeration is warranted. After all, over 45 million people know of someone who knows someone who has been a victim of awareness statistics. Better yet, just don't cite awareness statistics at all unless you are a sophisticated demographer.

Evidence

🗣 *We have lots of evidence that supports our beliefs.*

If you had valid evidence, it would be a fact.

There are many types of evidence, which are essentially validated facts that support a particular conclusion. We are not normally lucky enough to have **conclusive evidence**. That is, evidence that is so powerful that it leaves no doubt. Such evidence cannot be contradicted by any other evidence and points clearly to an unambiguous conclusion.

Conclusive evidence is often **direct evidence** in that it points directly to a particular conclusion without requiring any inferences. But even indirect evidence can be conclusive.

Much non-scientific evidence is **anecdotal evidence**. These are often one or a few incidents, often reported by testimony or hearsay. People often incorrectly cite anecdotal evidence as proof that something is true.

> *Even if we have more than one report that seem to corroborate each other, these are still anecdotal and should not be trusted until they reach the threshold of **statistical significance**. The number required to be statistically significant depends upon the specifics of the sampling.*

Anecdotes are horribly abused, and far too much credibility is attributed to anecdotal reports. Most of the time, anecdotal evidence is simply weak evidence or not evidence at all. And all too often, anecdotal evidence is cited as legitimate evidence to support false beliefs.

Generalizing from anecdotal evidence, or drawing conclusions based on anecdotal evidence, is tremendously unreliable. Back in the 1800s, a snake oil salesman would trot out an accomplice to give testimony in support of his miracle cure. Today we see everyone from television preachers to herbal medicine companies use the same technique of providing anecdotal evidence through testimonials. Most of these claims are intentionally deceitful.

We also see testimonial anecdotes presented almost daily in political theatre. The president points to the crowd to identify a person who has benefited greatly from his policies. In congressional hearings, supposedly wronged parties are summoned to give testimony about how badly they were harmed by the actions of the targeted party. Both of these individuals are put forth as typical examples, yet they may be exceedingly unusual.

The fact that testimonials are so very powerful reflects the unfortunate reality that people cognitively and emotionally attach far greater weight to a one-time anecdotal personal story than they do to conclusive evidentiary statistical analyses to the contrary.

Knowing when anecdotal evidence is simply a rationalization for wishful thinking, a persuasive manipulation, or an outright con job is not always easy. The fact that sometimes all we have to work with is anecdotal evidence makes it that much more dangerous and subject to misuse and abuse.

In many areas, scientists cannot practically conduct a formal study, or it would be ethically wrong to do so. It may simply be an area of study that no one is willing to fund. Therefore, even scientists sometimes have no alternative but to base conclusions upon the best anecdotal data they have.

Likewise, even court proceedings must sometimes rely upon anecdotal evidence, which is slightly different from circumstantial or hearsay evidence.

Anecdotal evidence is essential to making everyday decisions as well. So how do we make the wisest use of the anecdotal information that we must rely upon? First, consider the source and the motive of the anecdote. If the motive is to try to persuade you to do something, to support something, to accept something, or to part with your cash, be particularly suspicious of anecdotal claims or testimonials.

The DealDash commercials are a great example. You hear a woman claim that she "won" a large screen television for only $49. As an anecdote, that sounds very enticing, until you realize how rare that kind of deal actually is. Anecdotal evidence is not always technically a lie, but it can still be a lie of omission and cherry-picking.

Second, consider the plausibility of the anecdote. If the anecdote purports to describe an encounter with ghosts or aliens, someone imagined it or made it up. Just because someone reports something incredible, no matter how credible that person may be, demands more than anecdotal evidence as proof.

As Carl Sagan pointed out:

"Extraordinary claims require extraordinary evidence."

Third, consider the scope of the anecdotal claim. Does it make sweeping generalizations or is it very limited in scope? If the claim is that all Mexicans are rapists because one Mexican was arrested for rape, we end up with a fallacy of extrapolation, which often results from the misuse of anecdotal incidents.

Finally, consider the cost-benefit analysis of the response to the anecdotal claim. If the anecdote is that eating yogurt cured Sam's cancer, then maybe it's reasonable to eat more yogurt. But if the anecdote is that Ed cured his cancer by ceasing all medical treatments, then perhaps that should be considered a far riskier anecdote to act upon.

Despite the rampant misuse of anecdotal evidence, it is often very important. Diseases such as AIDS and Lyme disease have been uncovered by paying attention to limited case reports. While more carefully documented than purely anecdotal reports, case reports are nevertheless not initially statistically significant. In fact, many of the important breakthroughs in science have only been possible because a keen-eyed scientist followed up on what everyone else dismissed as merely anecdotal or anomalous data.

The most powerful use of anecdote is to disprove a negative assertion. For example, if a claim is made that there is no oxygen in the atmosphere, a valid anecdotal report of even one molecule disproves that assertion.

More commonly, anecdotes are best used to simply become aware that something may be possible, but without making any claims as to how likely it is. Good scientists don't ignore anecdotal information, and nor should we. But we do need to be very judicious about how much weight to give anecdotal reports, particularly when they are emotionally compelling.

Assessing Facts

When it matters, though, we are generally smart enough to distinguish fact from fiction.

Clearly, we are not.

It is not only difficult to assess anecdotal evidence, it is also very difficult to assess the validity of facts in general. And just being smart in other ways is not enough.

We all would like to think that we are sufficiently capable of assessing the validity of purported facts, but that is far from the reality, especially with respect to statistical facts. And even when it comes to hard, objective, easily verifiable facts, we do not do well. Studies have explored just how susceptible people are to conflating facts with beliefs.

According to a 2007 Associated Press poll, a third of Americans believe in ghosts and another third believe in UFO visitations. Nearly half believe in ESP. A myriad of other polls give widely varying but consistently high numbers for nearly any popular myth you can think up.

A YouGov America poll shows that 46 percent of Americans believe in supernatural beings. Of those, 22 percent say that demons definitely exist and another 24 percent say that they probably exist. Other countries have their own similar polling numbers.

It would be a mistake to assume that this represents the "crazy" or "stupid" half of the population. The ability to judge the validity of a proposition is not a completely natural skill. It is not merely a matter of being sane or insane, smart or dumb. Rather it is a learned skill that must be refined and practiced to achieve proficiency. Scientists spend many years formally learning and exercising both the techniques and the mental rigor to separate fact from belief. And even scientists, if they are good scientists, do not trust their own judgment in distinguishing fact from belief. They trust only in the process of objective verification established by the scientific method and statistical analysis.

All of the people represented in these polls consider themselves highly sane and rational, quite capable of making fully informed decisions. Yet clearly, individually and as a whole, we are susceptible, at least sometimes, to accepting even the most outlandish claims as facts.

Even if you dismiss and exempt pseudoscience and religion as special cases, there are still innumerable examples of our profound and widespread capacity to accept nonsense. During his four years in office, Donald Trump made over 30,000 false or misleading claims as tallied by objective analysis. To be frank, most of those are more accurately described as outright lies.

Yet, thanks to the combination of belief and the continual reinforcement of Fox News and other "news" sources, the vast majority of his supporters still maintain that they love and trust him because he has "never lied to us." Clearly our capacity for rationalizing away even the most overwhelming preponderance of evidence has no limits.

Intelligence Is Insufficient

🗣 *Yeah, but those are stupid, uneducated people.*

It's not that simple.

Even as we are quick to claim that others are stupid, we'd all like to think that we ourselves are intelligent, discerning, fact-based thinkers. Studies have shown, through objective subject-matter testing, that those individuals who rate themselves highest tend to score lower than those who rate themselves lower. The latter are humbler about their knowledge because they know enough to know how much they do not know.

Few of us can make objective self-assessments. When we think about our own thinking, no matter how bizarre, it seems perfectly rational to us. Even the most undeniably deranged individuals typically cannot see any flaw in their own thinking. And yet most of those people are highly intelligent in many ways.

If intelligence were an effective defense against believing nonsense, America would be doing far better than we do in this department. According to the Organisation for Economic Co-operation and Development (OECD), the United States is the sixth-most educated nation in the world. Even Americans with little or no formal education are exposed to incredible amounts of information.

But despite our education, even the most highly educated Americans are shockingly susceptible to misjudging evidence and accepting beliefs as facts. According to a 2006 study by National Geographic News, only 14 percent of Americans fully accept the fact of evolution. The views of the other 86 percent range from significant doubts to outright rejection.

In mind-boggling numbers, Americans reject or rationalize away mountains of evidence accumulated over more than 150 years and doggedly reserve doubts with absolutely no evidence to call evolution into question. There can hardly be any better litmus test of rational competence than that.

During the first Republican debate of the 2008 presidential election campaign, three of the candidates for president proclaimed that they did not believe in evolution. Many others have repeated irrational denials of evolution. Former President George W. Bush maintained that "the jury is out" on evolution.

If the people who hold or aspire to our highest offices can deny evolution, that is a frightening warning sign with respect to their ability to make fact-based decisions as president. I don't know of anything more terrifying than a person empowered to destroy the world with nuclear weapons and who also has the capacity to dismiss or disregard overwhelming factual information.

The other possibility is that at least some of those candidates do believe in evolution but are also aware of the 86 percent of the electorate who doubt or outright dismiss the reality of it. If they are indeed just playing good politics, then their level of integrity must be severely criticized.

If there is any single litmus test, this should be it. The question of whether the candidates will believe or acknowledge the reality of evolution goes directly to the heart of their decision-making capacity and their personal integrity to be president. If they are able to disregard the overwhelming information that supports evolution, what confidence can we have that they will not just as easily disregard other actual facts that conflict with their worldview or their political expedience?

If they can deny evolution, how confident can we be that they will not then deny, say, the integrity of an objectively free and fair democratic election?

Either their lack of fact-based thinking capacity or their lack of integrity with regard to the truth should exclude all these candidates of any nation from the presidency. In fact, in the years since that 2008 debate, we have seen the rapidly escalating denial of fact by these otherwise highly intelligent public leaders.

But the other stunning thing about this 2008 debate question was the response by the media. Most media commentators came down hard against the legitimacy of the very question with statements like the following:

The candidates' religious views should be out-of-bounds. Their personal views with regard to their faith have nothing to do with how they will function as president.

First, declaring a question of fact to be out-of-bounds simply by protecting it under the umbrella of a religious belief is extremely dangerous.

But secondly, the almost universal position of the media to consider a candidate's stance on evolution to be out-of-bounds reflects the deep and frightening extent to which belief-directed thinking has dominated our culture. It has not only become normal to disregard facts, but it is out-of-bounds to criticize those who do.

Religious folk want to have it both ways. They want complete freedom to claim religious characteristics as virtues, but they cry outrage if anyone attempts to interpret those same traits as a negative. They want it both ways, and they normally get it both ways with the help of a complicit media.

By contrast, the acceptance of evolution in European nations and in Japan is over 80 percent. Studies have measured the acceptance of evolution in China at over 90 percent. Indeed, America is second only to Turkey among the thirty-four modern nations studied in our rejection of evolution. Thank you, Turkey, for enabling us Americans to boast that at least we are not technically the stupidest nation in the world despite our high level of education.

This is even more stunning when you consider that Americans are also among the wealthiest of those nations. As evidenced in data from a 2006 report published in *Science*, the United States is an extreme outlier among world nations in having both high wealth and a high level of evolution denial.

The disturbing implication of our general acceptance of all manner of nonsense is that it demonstrates that adherence to fact is not necessarily enhanced by wealth, education, or information access. In America, with arguably the best of everything, we are among the worst in the world when it comes to assessing truth and facts.

In Chapter 4, Delusion, I will present some case studies that demonstrate how even folks who are clearly quite intelligent can produce sophisticated systems of thought that are simply complete nonsense based upon complete nonsense.

The good news, again, is that through training and practice, even we Americans can all become better at judging, or withholding judgment, with respect to what is truly factual and what is not.

But we first need to place far greater value in facts and raise our societal expectations with regard to espousing and defending them.

Fact Personalities

The simple reality is that everyone has beliefs whether they admit it or not.

Technically true, but as with most things, it's a matter of degree.

One cannot talk very long about light without discussing darkness. Similarly, a discussion about facts cannot proceed along very far without introducing beliefs. Although we are going to focus specifically on beliefs in chapter two, this is a good place to expand upon the ways that people accommodate beliefs alongside facts in their thinking.

Everyone is certainly capable of holding beliefs that are not grounded in facts. But our susceptibility to belief varies dramatically. Some people are very vulnerable to beliefs while others are more resistant. Some hold a large number of very profound beliefs, while others only entertain a few benign beliefs.

Although everyone has a unique personality and no one fits a mold, it facilitates a conceptual discussion to identify three personality types with respect to facts and beliefs. These actually describe the middle and end points of a spectrum with most people falling somewhere in between these three archetypes. Nevertheless, recognizing these distinct stances will help you to better relate to the discussion to follow.

Fact-Based Thinkers
You put your faith in facts. You generally don't believe anything of importance that is not supported by facts or is contradicted by facts. You certainly do speculate about things for which you have too few facts, but you seldom adopt beliefs about them as truths without evidence. You probably self-identify as a scientific thinker and/or atheist.

Belief-Based Thinkers
At least some of your strongly held views are based on belief alone, and these beliefs influence at least some of your important decisions. This doesn't mean that you are completely driven by beliefs. Such a person might have profound difficulty functioning in the world. But what it means is that, while generally grounded in reality, you do have some deeply held beliefs that are not shaken by the absence of facts or by facts to the contrary. You probably self-identify as religious or spiritual.

Belief-Tolerant Thinkers
While you don't have any particularly strong beliefs, you are not willing to outright reject them either. You consider it enlightened and respectful to grant others the right to believe whatever they want and aren't necessarily willing to go so far as to discount the legitimacy or even the truth of those beliefs. You probably self-identify as "open-minded" and/or agnostic.

Regardless of where you currently sit on this spectrum, your position is not fixed by nature or by age. At any point in life, your brain can gradually come to accept more and crazier beliefs, or it can become better at recognizing facts and bogus claims for what they truly are.

The best way to move toward becoming a more fact-based thinker is to expose yourself primarily to people and sources of information that are more fact-based in their thinking and minimize your exposure to belief-based thinking and thinkers. I say this with confidence because, as we will discuss later in this book, the fluidity of our thinking is fundamental to our basic mechanisms of cognition.

Rational Language

🗣 *Despite our beliefs, most of us are perfectly rational.*

We need to be very clear about our language here.

We commonly use many very similar words when we talk about thinking: *rational, rationale, rationality, irrational, rationalize, rationalization, reason, reasonable,* and even *superrational.* Because these words all sound so similar, like different forms of the same words, we can easily misunderstand them. Each form can have a dramatically different meaning than one might expect by extrapolation from another.

Rational describes thinking based upon true facts and sound logic. This is the good kind of thinking. It requires the thinker to be unbiased, fact-based, sane, logical, and as objectively correct as one can be, given the best information available. Note that the threshold here is quite high. It is not enough to merely follow one's own internal logic to reach a conclusion; one must follow independently validated logic and adhere to independently validated facts. One cannot merely feel they are being rational; they must in fact be objectively, measurably, demonstrably rational. A certifiably crazy person may be absolutely convinced they are perfectly rational in concluding that aliens are beaming messages into their brain, but that does not make it a fact.

Rational thinking implies that one is being rational in a particular line of thought or subject-matter area. For example, "That was very rational thinking about climate change." A **rational thinker** is one who generally employs rational thinking. Their thinking can be assumed to be rational. Crazy people can demonstrate rational thinking in certain areas at certain times, but they are not considered to be rational thinkers generally, and all of their assertions should be viewed with higher scrutiny.

The term **rationality** is generally used in the context of questioning a person's capacity to be rational, either generally or at a given time.

Suprarational is a variation that is often used by spiritual or new age type thinkers to describe magical thinking that "transcends" mere logic and reason. It is portrayed as operating on some higher plane of awareness that lies beyond physical laws and constraints.

Superrational is a term coined by cognitive scientist Douglas Hofstadter to describe a subtle, iterative group behavior in economics and game theory. It is sometimes conflated with suprarational.

The word **"reason"** is trickier. In its basic form it is inherently neutral with regard to truth or rationality. It simply describes the cause, explanation, or justification one uses to explain their conclusion or action. But we also use it more generally to describe our rational capacity. The word "reason" also has the benefit of invoking feelings of **reasonableness** or being **reasonable**, that is, amenable to reason.

But to be reasonable in the typical sense only requires that one be fair, moderate, and sensible. Using "reasonable" as a synonym for rational can lower the bar for rationality in the minds of many people who might like to claim that their "reasonable" beliefs are rational conclusions because they are reasonable.

Reasonable people can agree to disagree. Rational people cannot disagree for long after objective facts are revealed.

That leads us to the most inconsistent and confusing of this family of terms, namely **rationale**, **rationalize**, and **rationalization**. To rationalize is to create a rationale, that is, a satisfying connection between an observation and a conclusion. The resulting rationale can be perfectly rational or totally irrational. Rationalization as a verb is the process of rationalizing something. When used as a noun, it normally suggests a bogus rationale.

Rationalization may yield an accurate, fact-based conclusion or an invalid one. One person's rationale for claiming that H_2O (two atoms of hydrogen for every one atom of oxygen) is the formula of water may be based on chemical experiments and spectroscopic analysis. Another person's rationale for believing that demons exist may be that so many believers cannot possibly be wrong. Both are rationales offered to support a conclusion. One of those rationales is valid, the other is not.

When a rationale is clearly an excuse or a denial or a manipulation, it is commonly referred to as a rationalization. If my rationale for stealing that car is that insurance will pay for it anyway, that is a rationalization. We often use the term "**rationalize away**" when the goal is to create some bogus rationale to dismiss or ignore data that contradicts our desired conclusion.

Whether it leads to valid conclusions or merely supports wishful ones, rationalization is part of a broad class of cognitive processes developed as a product of biological adaptation to interpret instincts as useful representations or to deal with cognitive dissonance.

When it comes to beliefs, rationalizing is the process of deluding oneself into thinking that some possibly preposterous idea is sound and credible regardless of the facts of the matter. We rationally reach scientific conclusions, but we rationalize our religious beliefs to convince ourselves that we are rational thinkers.

Self-assessment of our rationality is tricky because if we have rationalized something, then it necessarily seems completely rational to us. In circular fashion, our rationalizations are how we assess whether an idea is sound and reasonable.

We have evolved to be incredibly good at rationalizing. From the evolutionary perspective, it is reasonable to conjecture that it was far more important that we felt certainty in the face of ambiguity or the unknown than that we knew the real facts of the world.

Our current capability to rationalize resulted from tradeoffs between disadvantages and advantages. Rationalization of a gut instinct was explained by Harvard professor Fiery Cushman as the conversion of "hard-won lessons from natural selection" to "useful fiction" for a rational mind. If, for instance, an individual experiences severe brain dysfunction, causing all of their perceptions to be irreconcilable, their ability to rationalize any perceived inconsistencies could allow them to continue to function. But rationalization also facilitates acceptance of maladaptive beliefs that no longer have the same practical and social value they once did.

Our incredibly powerful and nearly unbounded ability to rationalize even complete nonsense puts us all at risk in a modern world in which real facts are too important to ignore. The lesson then is to be very skeptical of our certainty that our conclusions are rational. Few of us can distinguish between our own perfectly rational conclusions and rationalized nonsense. The only way to ensure that our conclusions are truly rational is to make sure that they are based on valid evidence, sound logic, and correctly interpreted statistical analysis.

Core Principles

🗣 *I rely upon my core principles, not mere facts.*

Fact-based thinkers have core principles also.

Stressing the importance of facts over belief is a profound core principle in itself. In this book we assert two specific guiding principles that we will return to over and over again. The first is:

> *Decisions based on fact are inherently better than decisions based on belief.*

That core principle is an inherent underpinning of science. Science is, in fact, essentially an expression of, and implementation of, that core principle. Not everyone shares this principle. On the contrary, many think that only decisions derived from faith-based beliefs can result in the best outcomes.

We challenge that.

While we can certainly contrive or cite specific decisions based on beliefs, even egregiously false beliefs, that prove to be good decisions, that does not in any way detract from the truth of our scientific core principle that decisions based on fact are inherently better than decisions based up on belief.

One cannot disprove a general rule by exception. Exceptions are expected and accounted for as part of any valid generalization. Just because there are some cases in which decisions based on belief turn out to be a good thing, doesn't mean that decisions based on fact are not inherently, and in most cases, better.

For example, decisions based on random chance may sometimes turn out to be better than decisions based on fact. Does that mean that one should consider random choices as an equally sound method for making decisions?

Clearly random choices are not as good as informed choices. There is no reasonable scenario in which a full knowledge of the relevant facts does not provide the opportunity at least for a more well-informed decision.

In the fictional Batman universe, there is a villain named Two-Face. Two-Face used to be an idealistic and passionate district attorney named Harvey Dent. Harvey struggles through terrible challenges in trying to up uphold the law and ultimately suffers a cruel physical disfigurement that drives him insane.

In his great disillusionment and pain, he becomes Two-Face, a criminal with a rigid personal dogma colored by a view of the world as inherently random, a world where it doesn't matter what you want or choose or struggle to achieve. From that starting point, his deranged mind rationalizes that only random choices could be correct.

As Two-Face, he therefore makes all his important decisions based on the flip of a coin. Heads I set you free, tails I kill you. Sometimes those decisions turn out well for Harvey; other times they don't. But based on those occasional good outcomes, one could hardly argue that the flip of a coin is a sound basis for decisions, which often flew in the face of fact and reason. More often, the flip of a coin allowed Two-Face to commit awful crimes while absolving himself of responsibility for that decision.

Similarly, just because there may be cases where a decision based on belief turns out well does not make belief a wise basis for decisions.

Before I close this section, I will at least introduce our second core principle. It states:

> *The more we allow our minds to accept belief as fact, the more our ability to distinguish between fact and belief becomes compromised.*

This second principle of fact-based thinking is also not widely shared or even considered, but the implications are sweeping and profound. We will discuss this at length from many different perspectives in upcoming chapters.

We Are Not Vulcans

But in a fact-based world, what place is there for instinct, emotion, compassion, principles, and other things that make us human?

Facts and emotions are not mutually exclusive.

I often hear people express worry and reservations about a strong emphasis on facts. One commonly voiced concern is that, if we overly focus on facts and logic, we will all turn into Mr. Spock from *Star Trek* and sacrifice all of our humanity and compassion to become robotlike, emotionless and unimaginative Vulcans (although that's an unfair stereotype of Mr. Spock's complex personality). But let's look back at an iconic human who might be viewed as an excessively fact-based guy.

Joe Friday was the main character on *Dragnet*, a long-running television show that aired through the 1950s and again in the late 1960s. It was actually based on an earlier radio series and was later adapted as a feature film.

Joe was a stoic and almost comically stuffy police detective who was impervious to extraneous information and for whom only facts and evidence were relevant to a case. One could hardly call him exciting or imaginative, but his dogged, relentless pursuit of the facts always guided him unerringly through a sea of unsupported claims and accusations to arrest the real criminal.

When a female witness would express suppositions and suspicions, Joe would cut her off mid-sentence and say, "Just the facts, ma'am."

That line became part of everyday verbal culture for a generation of Americans. It may actually have done some harm, associating a passion for facts with a stoic and deadpan personality. But Joe understood that the only way to arrive at truth was to focus on "just the facts."

Joe relied on facts, but that did not mean that he didn't use his gut, his experience, his instinct, his intuition, his ability to discern patterns, and his imagination to uncover those facts. When it came time to make an arrest, however, he was able to put everything else aside and make a decision consistent with all the facts and only the facts of the case.

And that was a good thing. As a detective, Joe Friday had a narrowly defined duty. His only mission was to find the objective truth of the crime as dispassionately as he could. The ethics of his role in the justice system allowed no room for accusations based on biased, unfounded, or unproven suspicions or speculations.

For Joe, given his sworn duty to collar the real criminal, all that mattered was to establish the facts and to reach the correct conclusion based on the facts of the case. If he failed in that, if he ignored or overlooked any facts in the case or introduced his own biases, it would surely be thrown out in a court of law.

It was the job of the court to further validate his facts and conclusions. A court of law has an obligation to consider the true facts of the case. If there is a jury, the judge will often instruct the members to only consider the facts and to disregard any unsupported claims or arguments.

But it is also the job of the court to consider other moral and ethical factors as well. In the end, having reviewed all the facts, it is up to the judge or jury to render a humane verdict. To whatever extent allowed by law, judges and juries should apply their own common sense, their own ethical guidelines, and their own sense of compassion to reach a sensible decision. The court only requires that the jury actually consider the evidence and not render some verdict in advance based on belief or ignorance.

There can be no justice, no correct decision, if facts are ignored, overlooked, or dismissed. However, facts do not dictate our response to them. Once fully aware of all relevant facts, we are then free to make any decision we wish. We can choose to apply our humanity, our principles, our passions, and our compassions however we feel is right.

Facts don't detract from our humanity. Adherence to facts does not turn us into some caricature of Mr. Spock, the emotionless Vulcan from *Star Trek*. Nor does it suppress our humanity or our compassion. We are still free even to make a decision that flies in the face of all those facts—as long as we understand that we are doing so and understand the real factual consequences of that choice.

When Facts Are Lacking

*But beliefs, true or not, are often the only way to
motivate people to do the right thing.*

The end does not justify the means.

Sometimes, lacking any facts sufficient to make a proper informed decision, you have to proceed with insufficient facts. But that doesn't mean that
decisions based on belief, particularly when facts to the contrary exist, should
be encouraged or applauded.

Consider a report I once watched on a cable nature channel. It showed
dramatic video of rescuers trying to save a deer that had been caught out in
the middle of a frozen lake. The poor deer could not stand up on the ice, let
alone walk off, because her hard hooves were practically frictionless on the
slick surface. The deer was rapidly freezing to death.

The rescuers were faced with a life-and-death decision. Should they risk
walking out onto the ice to reach the distraught deer? They did not know if the ice
could hold their weight. They could easily end up dying along with the animal.

Before I tell you what really happened, let's imagine that one rescuer had
a dream just the night before. In it, he was standing out on an icy lake waiting
for something, for some unknown purpose he was yet to discover.

Now, standing at the edge of the frozen lake, it comes to him—the dream
was a revelation. He is destined to save that deer.

> *"I can reach him," he tells his fellow rescuers with confidence.
> "I believe I was meant to save that deer."*
>
> *With that, the man boldly strides out onto the icy surface,
> reaches the deer, and manages to drag the exhausted animal to the
> safety of the snow-covered bank.*
>
> *"It's a miracle," his fellow rescuers proclaim upon hearing of the
> dream.*

But it was dumb luck, not a miracle, that the man did not crash through the
ice. There was simply no evidence, empirical or reasoned, that the ice would
hold him, let alone with the added weight of the deer.

In this hypothetical case, a belief-based decision luckily produced a good outcome. But that does not make belief-based decision any more reliable than flipping a coin. A far better path would have been a fact-based decision. But in the case of the stranded deer, the rescuers had too little information to make an informed decision and too little time to gather sufficient information.

Given the urgency of the situation, they had several choices.

First, they could have abandoned the deer, judging that the risk to themselves did not outweigh the life of the deer. Second, they could have done their best to obtain more data, to gradually push a heavy weight out on the ice in order to determine a safe path, even knowing that such delay to test the ice could cost the deer its life.

Third, they could have chosen to act on the principle that the life of the deer was worth the calculated risk. They could have chosen to attempt the rescue, even knowing that it might cost one or more of the rescuers their lives.

Any of these choices would have been fundamentally superior to a decision motivated by a belief in personal destiny based on a dream. If one of the rescuers had died in the attempt, it would have been the result of a choice made with clear recognition of the risk. If, despite the risk, the attempt succeeded, isn't that far more heroic and noble than a success driven by some misguided belief in destined infallibility?

You'll be happy to hear that the actual event was even more spectacular than these hypothetical stories. KWTV News helicopter pilot Mason Dunn maneuvered his chopper blades to physically blow the terrified deer into the shoreline. He knew the facts, he understood the risks, and he made a personal moral decision to accept those risks. He made that choice under no delusions. Dunn was a real hero. In 2006 the Oklahoma State Legislature passed a resolution honoring Dunn for his many feats of heroism as a news helicopter pilot.

Facts and Self-Interest

Cute story about the deer, but what of it? Regardless of the motivation, the rescuer would have succeeded or died in the attempt either way. At least belief gave the deer a chance.

There is a fundamental difference.

Had the man who was motivated by a dream known that his dream was a mere coincidence, and that he was not truly fated to save that deer, he might not have been willing to accept the true risk.

A bigger issue is that belief generally only serves the interests of those who would seek to motivate us to act against our own best interest in order to profit themselves. If I were the deer out on the ice, it would certainly be in my own self-interest to convince the rescuers to believe that they could not fail, to trick them into ignoring the true risk, and to attempt to rescue me regardless of the danger to them.

Now consider that our dilemma does not merely involve the life of one little deer. Suppose we are talking about accepting the risk of going to war, a hazardous workplace, dangerous drugs, or ignoring climate change. We could replace the deer with any number of risks for which others, often wealthy and powerful and influential, stand to profit by deceiving you into accepting an unknown and unacceptable risk. These people benefit by concealing the true risks and convincing you to accept false claims or assurances. They rely upon your inability to distinguish true facts and to serve their self-interest by ignoring your own self-interest.

Beliefs are the primary tools of those who seek to oppress. Only by creating a culture that accepts or at least tolerates belief can political and economic oppressors convince a permanent underclass to ignore facts and to actively support their own oppression.

In 1917, the muckraking author Upton Sinclair published *The Profits of Religion*. In it, Sinclair exhaustively documented the essential role of religion and belief in general in establishing and maintaining corporate economic oppression over the masses. The book is just as timely and relevant today as it was back in his day.

Facts are the enemy of those with an agenda to mislead. Misinformation and suppression of information are their primary weapons to push back against facts. To defend ourselves against such self-interested exploitation, it is imperative that we be practiced in recognizing unfounded beliefs and in making important decisions in full awareness of the relevant facts.

Opinions Are Not Facts

❦ You may call it a belief, but I call it revelation.
You have your facts, and I have my facts.

It sounds like you are trying to muddy important distinctions. Daniel Patrick Moynihan, a long-time senator from New York, may be best known for this quote: "Everyone is entitled to their own opinion, but not their own facts."

In 1988, Moynihan attributed the quote to Alan Greenspan, who may have heard it from James R. Schlesinger in 1973 who may have heard it passed down from Bernard Baruch back in the 1940s. Some have joked that it is perhaps the only popular quote not traceable to Mark Twain.

In any case, the sentiment has definitely passed the test of time. It is still as true today as ever. Perhaps more so. Although believers insist that their beliefs are real facts, simply calling a belief a fact, no matter how forcefully, and with however much passion and conviction, does not make it a fact. As we have said, that requires objective validation.

A belief may not always even qualify as a valid opinion. In any case, it seems like we used to be better at separating fact from opinion. But, in today's vast swamplands of misinformation, the distinction seems muddier than ever.

In the introduction of his 2007 book, *The Assault on Reason* former Vice President Al Gore wrote:

> *"The persistent and sustained reliance on falsehoods as the basis of policy, even in the face of massive and well-understood evidence to the contrary, seems to many Americans to have reached levels that were previously unimaginable."*

I think it's fair to say that today, after four years of Donald Trump and his confederates in the administration and legislature, many of us Americans would give anything to return to the relatively sane and rational leadership of 2007. This is no accident. For a long time, long before Trump, conservatives engaged in a campaign to muddy facts. They realized that facts got in the way of their agenda, so they set out to discredit them.

In their 2010 book, *The Merchants of Doubt*, Naomi Oreskes and Erik M. Conway documented the long and successful escapades of a group of scientists led by physicist Frederick Seitz, one of the creators of the atomic bomb. Seitz and his colleagues offered their services to big business to create misinformation, sow doubt, and generate uncertainty over a wide range of business liabilities exposed by legitimate science.

Seitz and these others successfully manipulated public opinion by planting unwarranted doubts about acid rain, ozone, pesticides, secondhand smoke, and many other important and highly profitable atrocities right up through and including their work to discredit climate change.

To achieve their ends, they merely employed a relatively small but effective bag of tricks. Most were used to create the illusion of controversy, to make it seem as if settled science is actually in doubt. Most of these techniques are still used liberally today and still seem to work just as well as ever. Perhaps one of their most effective tactics was to convince us that a fact is merely one-person's opinion, and an opinion is a type of fact.

An opinion is not a fact.

A more recent innovation in the field of fact-muddying was introduced in 2017 by political consultant Kellyanne Conway who popularized the concept of "alternative facts." This was nothing more than yet another attempt to muddy science and facts so that they become equivalent to beliefs, deceptions, opinions, and other unfounded claims.

Meanwhile, conservatives who found facts inconvenient were busily at work on a parallel track. They incessantly repeated their outrage at the "biased liberal media" that was so unfair to them and their corporate backers.

Like the doubt-peddling about science, this fake bias campaign was also wildly successful. It pressured objective media into giving undue deference to conservative nonsense so that they could prove that they did not have liberal biases.

One day I was listening to a science show on NPR. By way of introducing a discussion of evolution, the host went way out of his way to point out rather gratuitously that of course many people also believe in creationism. He did this to reaffirm NPR's unbiased reporting, but it also had the effect of suggesting that there is a comparable factual equivalence between the two positions.

Evolution is exhaustively documented with evidence from every known field of human study. Evidence from geology, comparative anatomy, anthropology, genetics, biochemistry, paleontology, and dozens of other fields all exhaustively support the reality of evolution. Despite concerted efforts to create doubt, there is not a bit of credible evidence to contradict the fact that evolution happens.

On the other hand, creationism is supported by a few stories in an ancient allegorical book. To give the impression that there is any equivalence whatsoever between these two ideas is ludicrous and harmful, and shame on NPR for being bullied into suggesting that there is.

The success of their media pressure campaign caused conservatives to direct those same tactics against academia. They cried out like a murder of crows suddenly cawing at the same time that universities, like the media, all have a liberal bias and are actively engaged in liberal indoctrination. It is probably fairer to suggest that people who seek out higher education tend to be liberal and that an objective, uncensored education tends to make people more liberal.

That campaign was largely successful as well, and many colleges and universities have overcompensated in their efforts to demonstrate that they do not have a liberal bias.

Unfortunately, all too often what is required to prove that your school does not have a bias against conservatives is embracing and legitimizing nonsensical conservative beliefs and biases. This is an affront to education, undermining the entire educational mission.

We do not need to go as far as Afghanistan to tour the Taliban schools. We only need look at the deplorable state of yeshiva schools in New York State to see that we need to be very, very careful about how far secular society allows itself to be bullied and shamed into normalizing nonsensical ideas that harm us all.

Even in our normal suburban public schools, belief infringes upon fact-based education, through overt interference as well as more subtle pressures. When I taught high school, I learned the hard way what many American teachers attest to have learned. It is wisest just to avoid the parental outrage and skip over the chapter on evolution.

You may be entitled to your own opinions, but others are not required to accept them, and should certainly not be forced to teach them—or not to teach the truth.

CHAPTER 2: BELIEFS

The previous chapter defined and discussed facts and affirmed their vital importance in critical decision-making. It also discussed some of the ways that facts are under continual assault from many quarters, most notably by beliefs.

Beliefs are the natural enemies of facts. Beliefs are used to justify actions that are based on lies, misinformation, manipulation, fantasy, wishful thinking, or are simply baseless. This is antithetical to fact-based thinking, which demands that decisions be based upon verifiable objective reality. And beliefs pave the road to delusional thinking.

Facts and beliefs can coexist in our minds, but they cannot exist independently. They affect each other. Belief-based thinking necessarily corrupts fact-based thinking. And fact-based thinking comes unavoidably into contention with beliefs.

This chapter will examine this complex interaction in greater depth and make the case that beliefs are both infectious and toxic and that they unavoidably compromise our essential rational capacity.

Pseudoscience

I watch a lot of shows on television that look at the actual science behind many strange phenomena.

Those shows are pure entertainment, and harmful entertainment at that. There is a broad category of beliefs, collectively referred to as pseudoscience, that make a pretense of plausibility to pretend that they are worthy of scientific investigation. They sometimes purport to have some logical or factual basis but are most often supported only by unsubstantiated and highly dubious anecdotal evidence.

One of the earliest instigators of our modern pseudoscience movement was a 1968 book by convicted fraudster Erich von Däniken called *The Chariots of the Gods?* It made many debunked claims arising from the premise that extraterrestrials were viewed as gods in ancient times. His books, typically classified as nonfiction, have sold over 63 million copies and have inspired many derivative works along the same lines.

Unfortunately, there is a lot of this nonsense to be seen, and any amount is too much. There are scores of series on YouTube and elsewhere that claim to depict legitimate paranormal investigation. Particularly unfortunate is that the networks that promote most of this stuff are those that purport to be educational, with deceptive names like Science Channel, Discovery Channel, and the History Channel—with the latter featuring a "documentary" series by von Däniken called Ancient Aliens that ran for 18 seasons.

These shows all follow the same basic formula. They find some "unexplained" situation. They present a lot of handheld footage of regular people somberly retelling rumors, so-called scientists setting up their detection gear, and tense moments as they try to identify noise in the static. They bring in experts to legitimize their investigations. They interview people about how they feel apprehensive or fearful about whatever it is. They spend a lot of time setting up "scientific" equipment and flashing shots of needles on gauges jumping around. They speculate about a wide range of possible explanations, most of them implausibly fantastic. They use a lot of suggestive language, horror-film style cinematography, and cuts to scarily produced clips. Each episode invariably ends with no evidence but a lot of very strong suspicions. They end up determining that while they can't say anything for sure, they can say that there is indeed something very mysterious going on. They promise to bravely keep investigating—don't miss the next episode.

These shows do tremendous harm. They legitimize the paranormal and trivialize real science. They turn the tools and trappings of science into cheap carnival show props.

The following is a partial list of pseudoscientific or popular myths, currently or once widely held, that violate fundamental principles, lack any evidence, rely upon implausible logic, have been exposed as hoaxes, or simply do not pass any rational sniff test:

- Acupuncture
- Aliens, alien abductions, and UFOs

- Angels and demons
- Astrology and horoscopes
- Auras
- Big Foot, Loch Ness, and Yeti
- Cars that run on water
- Channeling and séances
- Precognition, clairvoyance, and clairaudience
- Creationism and intelligent design
- Crop circles
- Crystal and pyramid power
- Demons and devils
- Dianetics and Scientology
- Divining and dousing
- Ghosts and hauntings
- Levitation and mind over matter
- Life after death
- Lizard people
- Lucky talismans and unlucky omens
- Miracles and curses
- Neurotheology
- Numerology and tarot cards
- Ouija boards
- Out-of-body experiences
- Palmistry, tea leaves, and other fortune tellers
- Perpetual motion
- Possession
- Prayer and prophecy
- Psychic or faith healers
- Rapture/end of days
- Reincarnation and souls
- Saints and visitations
- Telekinesis and telepathy
- The Bermuda triangle
- Voodoo and witchcraft

All of these various pseudoscientific and related beliefs are devoid of any basis in reason or fact. Moreover, none of these have passed even the most casual tests of reproducibility and validation. Scientific researchers have not closed-mindedly ignored these but have exhaustively investigated all of them. At some point, it is reasonable for scientists to refuse to entertain the legitimacy of recycled pseudoscientific claims that will not go away.

Yet each of these has startling numbers of believers. Some fade from general acceptance but others gain in popularity. There is always a steady flow of pseudoscientific myths purporting to have some degree of rational justification.

I myself received formal training in some of these, eager and hopeful to find some bit of truth in them. In one course that supposedly trained us to read human auras, we were told that there was a factual scientific basis that supports the existence of auras. Instructors showed us Kirlian photographs and taught us how to defocus our eyes and split our vision on the area above the subject's head.

This practice would indeed create the illusion of a halo. But what was actually happening was hardly metaphysical. The forced defocusing causes the eyes to perceive two separate overlapping images, the result of visual parallax. You can easily reproduce this yourself by simply moving your thumb close to your eyes. You see two of superimposed thumbs. If you experiment and practice a bit, you can cause these to create the illusion of a halo around one. You can even imagine you see colors in it.

It is the same for all of these pseudoscientific beliefs. If they seem incredible, it is because they indeed lack credibility. People want to think they are highly perceptive, that they can see auras, and they are easily fooled into believing just that. Virtually everyone in that class came away feeling highly spiritual to be one of those rare perceptive individuals who can perceive auras.

People provide many rationalizations to justify their belief in pseudoscientific ideas. Here are some typical ones illustrated using leprechauns as a placeholder. You can substitute any other pseudoscientific belief and you'll hear the same rationalizations:

- *I saw a leprechaun so no one can tell me otherwise.*
- *Someone I trust told me that they saw a leprechaun.*

- *Belief in unicorns and fairies is just stupid, not rational like leprechauns.*
- *The idea that leprechauns do not exist is just a theory after all.*
- *The idea that leprechauns do not exist is just flat-earth thinking.*
- *There have been so many leprechaun sightings that there must be something to it.*
- *Scientists cannot prove that leprechauns do not exist.*
- *Scientists have no explanation for all the leprechaun sightings.*
- *Any legitimate scientist has to admit there is a possibility that leprechauns exist.*
- *There is a scientist who believes in leprechauns, so therefore there is no agreement even within the scientific community on this question.*
- *The government is covering up the existence of leprechauns.*

We need to say: enough already. These pseudoscientific beliefs and the television shows that exploit them are not just good fun. They are highly corrosive to our intellectual fabric, both individually and socially.

There would be a way to do this responsibly. These shows could investigate unexplained reports and dispense with all the paranormal theatrics and refuse to even consider paranormal explanations. They could provide actual explanations rather than merely open the door to paranormal ones.

MythBusters proved that a show that sticks to reality can be fantastically entertaining and popular. These other shows could exhibit the same respect for reality and the public good, but they do not.

Fantasy Science

🗣 *A lot of science sounds like fantasy to me.*

We do have to be careful.

We are all familiar with science. But a great many books that are considered science fiction should really be relegated to the science fantasy genre. Many science fiction novels and movies depict completely implausible future science. This often includes novels that win prestigious science fiction awards such as the Hugo Award. When a book is promoted as a "Hugo Award winner" it suggests that the science presented therein is plausible. Often it is not.

It is my opinion, at least, that science fiction should be limited to scientifically plausible fiction. It should explore things that might plausibly happen. A lot of great science fiction has already come true since the time of its writing. Great science fiction predicts things that are in fact extremely likely to come true, even inescapable, even though few people could see it coming when the work was written.

The Star Trek communicator is a great example of science fiction. The Star Trek teleporters are clearly science fantasy.

Why bother making this distinction?

This is important is because science fantasy promoted as science fiction leads many people to develop an unrealistic confidence in the potential of science. They can dismiss real problems like climate change because of an unrealistic fantasy that science will eventually find an answer. Mixing science fiction with science fantasy can even cause some people to think of science as magical, as if the supernatural is simply science we have not yet discovered.

Faith Healing

🎙 *My grandmother prayed for her cancer to be cured and she went into remission.*

Faith healing and the power of prayer are strong pseudoscientific beliefs that generate a lot of sympathetic reactions.

People pray for a cure and they sometimes are cured. Is this proof of God? Clearly it is not. Some of these remissions would have naturally occurred anyway. But moreover, every study in which the patient is not aware that anyone is praying for him or her has failed miserably. Clearly, the power of prayer only works if the person knows and believes in it.

The power of prayer tells us more about the power of belief than it tells us about the existence of a god. In fact, you can substitute God with any belief in anything. No matter what the placebo is, it will work just as well. In South America, shamans dance, chant, and blow smoke. In Africa, sangomas throw stones and exorcize demons. Elsewhere, a Reiki healer might pass their hands over the believer to transfer psychic energy or an acupuncturist might stick them with little needles. All these things can work just as well. Even most modern doctors understand this and walk a delicate line between giving their patients the probabilistic facts of their case and enabling a false hope in some placebo treatment.

Belief can also work the other way. If a Haitian witch doctor convinces a believer that they have been cursed with voodoo magic, they can actually become sick or even die. Studies have shown that in many cases placebo antidepressants work just as well as our most powerful pharmacological treatments. They have clearly shown that just the belief that one is receiving morphine can have the exact same effect as actually receiving morphine. Believing you just drank alcohol can make you drunk as a skunk.

The placebo effect is really the "belief" effect.

Belief can affect our thinking, our outlook. Presumably there are cases in which the cause of depression is truly chemical and this could not work, but in others, depression may simply be more like a perceptual bias that can change as easily as switching between seeing a witch or a vase in a visual illusion.

But where does this lead us? Clearly it is good to believe in something that may make us feel healthier and more positive. In doing so, we are making good use of our innate physiology of belief. Does it mean that belief in general is good? Does it mean that we should embrace religious beliefs? Is this an exception to our general proposition that "decisions based on fact are inherently better than decisions based on belief?"

This is truly a difficult question, but it seems to me that most modern physicians are doing the best they can. While not condoning magical treatment over real, proven medical treatment, they try to be as encouraging and positive as possible. They're not hitting the patient over the head with dire facts, but they are still as honest as they can be when asked direct questions. If the patient requests drugs that have no medical benefit, many doctors will prescribe them anyway knowing that the patient's belief that it might cure them may do just that.

More than that, it seems to me that we should learn to do a better job of giving the patient fact-based things to believe in. Give them real support systems, real interaction with people who have overcome their illness, real evidence and appreciation of the power of attitude. For attitude can be changed in many ways, deliberately or accidentally. We need to become better at scientific techniques that readjust patients' outlook, attitude, and emotional state so as to give them the best chance possible to heal. Toward that end, it may be that we can learn some things from faith healing.

Benign Beliefs

🗣️ *What if some people believe in leprechauns, what harm does it do?*

Not all beliefs are equally harmful, but all do some harm.

There are some harmless beliefs and some that are actually healthy. Clearly it is good to have a belief in oneself, to have healthy confidence and optimism. It is good to have belief in other people, to start with an assumption of goodwill and trust. It is a good thing to believe in the hopes and dreams of mankind. It is good to believe that your mother truly loves you. These are good beliefs to hold, even if they are often at least partially unfounded.

But those optimistic subjective outlooks and assumptions are only beliefs in the very mildest sense. When it comes to pseudoscientific or other beliefs that fly in the face of objective reality, these are no longer completely harmless and benign.

Of course, no one should tell Grandma that her dead husband is simply dead. No one should dash the hope that a terminal cancer victim finds in prayer. But we should nevertheless be cognizant of the fact that these such beliefs are not good for mentally healthy people, and we should not condone their use except as a form of palliative care.

The reason that such beliefs, as harmless as they may appear, are not benign is because they unavoidably force our brains to rationalize them. Every time we exercise our ability to rationalize beliefs, I contend that we get better at it. Each new belief makes us that much more susceptible to rationalizing stronger and less benign beliefs.

The essentially simple contention that what we accept today extends the range of what we are willing to accept tomorrow is consistent with a growing body of scientific research. In their 2017 paper entitled "Biological and cognitive underpinnings of religious fundamentalism" published in Neuropsychologia, the authors found that Vietnam veterans who suffered damage to particular regions of the prefrontal cortex exhibited religious fundamentalist thinking characterized by reduced cognitive openness and flexibility. Their research also supports the view that intensive or prolonged exposure to rigid thinking can induce similar changes to the prefrontal cortex.

Rationalizing beliefs not only compromises the rational capacity of individuals, it also has a synergetic effect on society. Our acceptance of a belief adds one more straw of legitimacy to it and allows others to rationalize it more easily. That reinforcement feeds back upon ourselves.

The end result is that each benign belief we accept diminishes the rational capacity not only of ourselves but of society as a larger thinking organism.

Infectious Toxins

Let people have their beliefs. If they make them feel better, what harm does it do?

Let me tell you what harm it does.

This is actually the prevalent mainstream view of modern society today. This belief-tolerance is shared by most regular people, most influencers, and even most scientists. It sounds reasonable and broad-minded. Expressing tolerance toward belief will not normally incur criticism—but criticizing or judging beliefs sure will.

Beliefs are considered a personal thing. If a person needs or wishes to believe in something we consider nonsense, who are we to judge, let alone criticize or interfere, with a purely personal belief?

There are two very serious problems with this view:

1 *Beliefs are infectious, they spread from person to person very quickly and we have few natural defenses to resist them.*

2 *Even in small doses, beliefs act as a cumulative toxin, incrementally compromising our ability to resist even more toxic beliefs.*

Beliefs are like mercury. We may tolerate small amounts in our shellfish because, well, shrimp is so damn tasty, but we have to know that no amount is good for us. Like a heavy metal toxin, even the smallest dose cumulatively compromises our belief immune system, making us incrementally more susceptible to more serious infections.

And here is the terrifying thought. Belief is so very infectious that none of us can avoid exposure and none of us are 100 percent immune. This is especially true thanks to the powerful transmission vectors of modern information technology. And once infected, belief so insidiously infiltrates and compromises all our normal healthy thinking that we can no longer reliably assess our own mental health. If enough of the world is compromised by a pandemic of delusion, how can we ever hope to get better?

That may sound like an overreaction. And at this point in the book, these assertions are simply put forth without proof based on evidence or logic. However, we will get to the cognitive underpinnings of our pandemic in due course.

Costs and Benefits

🗣 *But many of our guiding beliefs do a lot of good!*

But does that good outweigh the harm?

To be fair, one cannot simply ignore all the comfort that faith-based beliefs provide. One cannot dismiss all the charitable works motivated by belief and all the social improvements championed by people of faith. There can be no doubt that people of faith frequently act on altruistic principles and are motivated by their beliefs to accomplish great good.

But these positives should not make us embrace or even become belief-tolerant with regard to unfounded beliefs in general. Nor should it cause us to simply throw up or hands and accept them. Before accepting beliefs as an imperfect but necessary part of our accepted thought process, one must weigh any good they do against three critical considerations:

1   *The adoption of beliefs, no matter how benign they may seem, does some harm.*

2   *One must weigh the benefit of beliefs against their harm.*

3   *Before one accepts the harm caused by beliefs, one must consider whether those beliefs provide the only mechanism to achieve the desired benefits.*

We will discuss each of these considerations in due course. But, as a preview of coming attractions, we will show that beliefs cause far more harm than believers recognize or admit, that the harm often outweighs the benefits, and that there are other ways to achieve the same benefits that do not require acceptance of those harms.

We have already conceded that decisions based upon beliefs can sometimes result in good outcomes, but we also pointed out that this does not mean that beliefs are generally a good basis for decision-making. Similarly, we have acknowledged that systems of belief and faith do a lot of good in the world. However, one cannot look at benefits in isolation without assessing the costs, the negatives associated with gaining those benefits.

Adopting beliefs to achieve some good outcome carries undesirable consequences along with it. These undesirable side effects may not be worth the cost. Yet any benefits and costs are seldom subjected to even the most cursory risk-assessment analysis.

In the theory of risk assessment, there are two factors to consider in determining how to respond to a suspected risk. The first factor is the likelihood that the risk might occur. The second is the severity of the consequences if it does happen.

Low Risk/Low Impact
This category includes risks that have little likelihood of actually occurring and do not result in particularly severe consequences if they do occur. They are generally not worth fussing about. What may actually constitute the greater risk is spending too much time or resources on such a risk while ignoring more severe risks.

> *A belief that the pyramids were built by aliens might fall into this category. Few people actually believe it and it doesn't cause much direct harm if they do.*

There is still fundamental harm, however, in accepting any belief, no matter how low the direct impact may be.

High Risk/Low Impact
This category includes risks with a high likelihood of occurring, but a very low severity. For example, there might be a very high probability that an employee could catch a common cold from a colleague in the workplace. If that happens, the cold is expected to be relatively harmless. Perhaps the employee will be out sick for a day or two. It would certainly not be worth any draconian measures to isolate each employee in their own sterile environment in an attempt to avoid spreading germs.

> *As applied to beliefs, this would represent a minor mistaken belief that spreads quickly but doesn't matter much. For example, millions of people watched a viral YouTube video showing a golden eagle swooping down and carrying away a child. Yes, the video was faked, but a mistaken belief that it was real probably caused little more harm than some parents keeping their kids away from golden eagles.*

Low Risk/High Impact
This category includes risks with a low probability of occurrence but a high severity when they do. Earlier we had fun with the example of the Hadron Collider. The possibility that it might generate a mini black hole that would consume the Earth would be considered by most to be a high-impact risk. However, the likelihood of that happening is infinitesimally small, if possible at all. Therefore, we hardly need worry about it.

> *Many dangerous beliefs fall into this category. For example, the possibility that a political opponent is a satanic baby-eating pedophile is about as likely as a black hole eating the Earth. If true, the consequences would be severe. But in this case, the far bigger risk is that someone might actually believe it to be true and act to stop it.*

High Risk/High Impact

The most concerning type of risk is the high-impact, high-probability risk. We know that the risk of global warming is extremely high. It is happening, it can be seen. The risk is virtually 100 percent, but let's grant those with an agenda their concession and call it only 90 percent likely. If that 90 percent chance comes to pass, the result could mildly be characterized as having a high impact. In the best-case scenario, the ecosystem of the Earth will become wildly imbalanced causing unprecedented death, destruction, and suffering. If the worst-case but still very plausible outcome occurs, the fragile atmosphere of the Earth could rapidly turn our planet into another Venus, too hot to sustain any kind of life ever again.

> *The renowned British scientist Stephen Hawking repeated exactly this dire warning at a 2006 international conference in Beijing.*

Clearly global warming is a high-probability, high-consequence risk. Any reasonable risk-assessment analysis must conclude that it poses an unacceptable risk.

If the threat of climate change is real, then the consequences even of mere hesitation are unimaginable. If the threat is not real, then the consequences of taking action are negligible, even beneficial for other reasons. The cost-benefit calculation of action is clearly favorable. The cost of inaction is unacceptable. Yet we largely ignore it.

Part of the reason we are able to dismiss and rationalize away even the direst threats to our very survival is our capacity to accommodate belief, to rationalize belief over fact. That does not come naturally. You don't become a climate change denier through mere ignorance. You must be compromised, acclimated, prepared to accept beliefs regardless of the consequences of doing so, by long-term belief poisoning.

It comes down to the tolerance for belief that we build up with every innocent belief we accept as true. Every little belief we adopt, that we even merely tolerate, conditions us to accept even more obvious and dangerous beliefs.

To do a cost-benefit analysis of organized religion as a belief system, one has to assess both the level of benefit and the level of harm. Does religion yield a net benefit to society, or does it do net harm? To be fair, one should not exclude new age and paranormal thinking in this as well, but we generally pick on religion here as it represents an institutionalized belief. This is where reasonable people disagree wildly.

Religious supporters will focus on the benefits and claim that the good it does far outweigh the damage. They will point to religious charities, to supportive clergy, and to the throngs of people who find comfort in their faith.

Opponents of religion will claim that it has done far more harm than good. They will point out that religious dogma has dominated most of our last two thousand years and has produced repression, stagnation, torture, and war.

The cost-benefit analysis of belief in general and religion in particular is not clear. Or if it's clear to some, it is nevertheless disputed vigorously with no resolution in sight. We need to approach this from a different perspective.

Beliefs and Morality

🗣 *Without religion there would be no morality.*

There would be no morality, but there would still be ethics.

We cannot hope to judge whether the good done by religion outweighs the harm it causes in any manner that would sway either side. Therefore, perhaps we can arrive at a more compelling and convincing argument by moving on to the last step of our cost-benefit analysis:

> *Before one accepts the harm caused by beliefs, one must consider whether those beliefs provide the only mechanism to obtain the benefits it offers.*

If religion is the only way to achieve those desirable benefits, then perhaps it is reasonable to accept any negative side effects associated with it.

But if those same benefits are also achievable through secular means that carry fewer negative side effects, then it would be unnecessary to accept religion along with all of its negatives. In this case, the primary benefit of which religion claims it is the sole and necessary source is morality. Without religion, they say, without the guiding light of belief, there would be no morality. By inference, without religion, we would descend into depravity and chaos.

This is an assertion that can be easily validated or invalidated. We need only look at people who have no religion as ask whether they are moral. Or, more properly, we need only ask if they are ethical.

Morality is the form of ethics practiced by religious people. It is distinctly different from secular ethics.

According to S.I. Hayakawa in his indispensable reference guide Choose the Right Word, *the words "moral" and "ethical" were once nearly synonymous but have recently diverged in meaning. Moral is now generally used in a religious context while ethical is usually used in a more secular context.*

We talk about the morals of a priest or saint but the ethics of a lawyer or legislator. Moreover, morals have come to mean "personal conduct as set by an external code or standard" while ethics refers to "just and fair dealings with other people, not by the application of an external standard but by a pragmatic consideration of all aspects of a situation in light of experience."

Religion is certainly not a necessary part of human experience. We can live quite happily and ethically without it. There are millions of atheists for whom it is not necessary. It's difficult to measure accurately, but a 2013 demographic study by Ariela Keysar estimated the number of nonbelievers to be 450 to 500 million worldwide. In France, as one example, the fraction of nonreligious in the population is estimated at 41 percent. All of these people are quite happy and ethical without the moral guidance of religion.

Believers still never cease trying to claim "moral" behavior as their most powerful reason for being. They conduct "scientific" studies, for instance, showing that religious people are more charitable. But charitable giving is not a valid surrogate indicator of enlightened ethics. In fact, these studies fail to mention things like most of that giving is to their churches, and that typically only 10 percent of the money received by those churches goes to charitable causes—and that their charity often has proselytizing strings attached.

People without faith are every bit as charitable, as compassionate, as socially conscious as people of faith. To deny that is to accuse the vast majority of Asians and 41 percent of French citizens of having low moral character.

It is simply not objectively true to insist that nonbelievers have no foundation, no basis for ethical behavior, and no motivation to engage in it. Most atheists are driven by **humanist principles**, an ethical and social consciousness that arises not from authority but from deep within their own humanity.

Religious adherents like to claim that without God, we cannot have any true moral or ethical principles. But humanists do hold many powerful values very dear. It is not even remotely true that atheists have no principles beyond opposition to religion. Atheists, who are virtually all also humanist in their value system, adhere to a deep set of values.

Prominent humanist Paul Kurtz compiled the following set of humanist principles. It is long. But I am going to reprint it here because it is so vitally powerful and important:

> *We are committed to the application of reason and science, to the understanding of the universe, and to the solving of human problems.*
>
> *We deplore efforts to denigrate human intelligence, to seek to explain the world in supernatural terms, and to look outside nature for salvation.*
>
> *We believe that scientific discovery and technology can contribute to the betterment of human life.*
>
> *We believe in an open and pluralistic society and that democracy is the best guarantee of protecting human rights from authoritarian elites and repressive majorities.*
>
> *We are committed to the principle of the separation of church and state.*
>
> *We cultivate the arts of negotiation and compromise as a means of resolving differences and achieving mutual understanding.*

We are concerned with securing justice and fairness in society and with eliminating discrimination and intolerance.

We believe in supporting the disadvantaged and the handicapped so that they will be able to help themselves.

We attempt to transcend divisive parochial loyalties based on race, religion, gender, nationality, creed, class, sexual orientation, or ethnicity, and strive to work together for the common good of humanity.

We want to protect and enhance the Earth, to preserve it for future generations, and to avoid inflicting needless suffering on other species.

We believe in enjoying life here and now and in developing our creative talents to their fullest.

We believe in the cultivation of moral excellence.

We respect the right to privacy. Mature adults should be allowed to fulfill their aspirations, to express their sexual preferences, to exercise reproductive freedom, to have access to comprehensive and informed health care, and to die with dignity.

We believe in the common moral decencies: altruism, integrity, honesty, truthfulness, responsibility. Humanist ethics is amenable to critical, rational guidance. There are normative standards that we discover together. Moral principles are tested by their consequences.

We are deeply concerned with the moral education of our children. We want to nourish reason and compassion.

We are engaged by the arts no less than by the sciences.

We are citizens of the universe and are excited by discoveries still to be made in the cosmos.

We are skeptical of untested claims to knowledge, and we are open to novel ideas and seek new departures in our thinking.

We affirm humanism as a realistic alternative to theologies of despair and ideologies of violence and as a source of rich personal significance and genuine satisfaction in the service to others.

We believe in optimism rather than pessimism, hope rather than despair, learning in the place of dogma, truth instead of ignorance, joy rather than guilt or sin, tolerance in the place of fear, love instead of hatred, compassion over selfishness, beauty instead of ugliness, and reason rather than blind faith or irrationality.

We believe in the fullest realization of the best and noblest that we are capable of as human beings.

These humanist affirmations hardly paint the picture of a secular community devoid of ethical principles. On the contrary, most find them far more compelling than simplistic Bible teachings.

In Lawrence Kohlberg's stages of moral development, he identified a hierarchy of six stages of moral development, in order from the most rudimentary to the most sophisticated. They are as follows:

> *Stage 1: Obedience and Punishment Orientation*
> *Stage 2: Individualism and Exchange*
> *Stage 3: Good Interpersonal Relationships*
> *Stage 4: Maintaining the Social Order*
> *Stage 5: Social Contract and Individual Rights*
> *Stage 6: Universal Principles*

With its essential focus on obedience and punishment, religious morality is largely at the lowest stage of moral reasoning. In all fairness, most modern religious people of faith are motivated to do good works by higher stages of moral reasoning as well, but nevertheless, the underlying motivation is always a fundamental belief in obedience to the Word of God and the fear of punishment in the afterlife.

In contrast, as is evident in Paul Kurtz's humanist affirmations, humanists function largely at the level of universal principles. While they often make ethical decisions based on earlier stages as well, they certainly have no fear of eternal punishment factoring into their motivations.

Clearly then, religion (and belief in general) is not the only route to ethical behavior. It is not required to motivate ethical behavior. In fact, Christian morality is arguably inferior to secular ethics.

According to a recent Pew survey, people who attend church at least once a week are more likely to say torture is often or sometimes justifiable. Christians in fact are always measurably ahead of the rest of the country when it comes to waging war or condoning brutality and violence. Indeed, evangelicals supported President Bush and his fabricated Iraq war more strongly than any other demographic.

And Christian support for brutality extends even to torture. A Washington Post/ABC News poll showed that 72 percent of non-religious people believed that the CIA treatment of prisoners amounted to torture, while only 39 percent of evangelicals agreed. When asked if they supported treatment that amounted to torture, the numbers came out as follows:

Demographic	Approve	Disapprove
Evangelicals	69%	20%
Protestants	75%	22%
Catholics	66%	23%
Non-religious	41%	53%

Clearly, in this at least, religion is not required to instill ethical values. In fact, it apparently does considerable harm.

If false beliefs are not the only source of ethical behavior, then it would be irrational to accept the negatives associated with the adoption of a deeply held belief system that is completely irrational. If religion is not the only route to ethical behavior, then there is no necessity that we accept the negatives it carries along with it.

Accept religion or accept depravity is a false choice.

Deeply Held Beliefs

🗣 *You can dismiss my beliefs all you like, but they are profoundly real and meaningful to me and to many other believers.*

Your passion for your beliefs only makes them more harmful. Our society overall, and even we atheists, have largely bought a bill of goods sold to us by the religious community.

It is the flimflam that "deeply held" beliefs are more sincere, more legitimate, less crazy, and more irreproachable than any old ordinary beliefs. Often these are also marketed under the labels of "sincere" or "cherished" or even "deeply cherished" beliefs.

We have all been manipulated into granting an undeserved level of respect and deference to beliefs when they are immunized by these adjectives. This deference is not only undeserved, but it excuses some of the most damaging practices by those espousing these deeply held beliefs. We tend to push back on beliefs until someone proclaims that they are deeply held, sincere, and cherished. Then suddenly it becomes taboo, insensitive, and disrespectful to criticize them. In fact, we often accept that such deeply held beliefs should be exempted from or even protected by the law.

Well, unless of course it's a deeply held, sincere, and cherished belief fervently important to Muslims. In that case it's obviously sick and crazy.

Emotions govern beliefs. A person's centrally held beliefs form that individual's identity; therefore, they are held with strong emotional fervor. Any contrary evidence is rationalized away. Consequently, changing people's beliefs is not as simple as showing that there is conflicting evidence.

Take for instance the vehemence by which "deeply held" beliefs were defended by Katie Geary of the Becket Fund for Religious Liberty:

> *"Groups that insist on insulting others' deeply cherished beliefs are the truly immature ones here. Little do they realize how juvenile they appear to the 'fairy tale' believers they so ardently wish to cut down."*

That's quite a dressing down, and this is only a small sample of her attack against any criticism of deeply held beliefs. However, as the Humanists of

Minnesota pointed out, it is often impossible to see any difference whatsoever between deeply held beliefs and plain old bigotry.

It was her deeply held beliefs that inspired Kim Davis, former county clerk for Rowan County, Kentucky, to refuse to grant marriage certificates to gay couples in defiance of the law.

Cherished beliefs led right-wing conservative leader Kevin Swanson to publicly call for the mass execution of gay people.

Deeply held beliefs led the owners of Hobby Lobby to claim religious exemptions so that they could be free to discriminate. Likewise, it was his deeply held belief that abortion is murder that led anti-abortion extremist Scott Roeder to shoot Dr. George Tiller in the head.

It was also sincere beliefs that prompted John Salvi to bomb a Planned Parenthood clinic, killing two and wounding others. These are just a handful of extreme examples. But to point to sensational incidents does a great injustice to all of the routine, totally unsensational harm perpetrated every day by those with deeply held beliefs.

In her book *Breaking Their Will: Shedding Light on Religious Child Maltreatment*, Janet Heimlich documents the shocking abuses that routinely harm children all around the world, all motivated by deeply held beliefs and enabled by a reluctance to push back against them.

These examples illustrate the danger of all of those "harmless" beliefs that we are told we must respect. These should be cautionary examples that point out the danger of letting ourselves get taken down this path of deference to belief, deeply held or not. In fact, I could go on updating this book daily with ever more troubling examples of deference to religious beliefs, when they are characterized as sincere, bleeding over into how we think about secular matters.

A more recent example is Stewart Rhodes, a Yale Law School graduate and founder of the Oath Keepers, who is accused of fomenting the January 6, 2021, attack on the US Capitol. In "The Case Against the Oath Keepers," Jeannie Suk Gersen wrote for *The New Yorker* that Rhodes's "sincere belief" in Trump's "big lie" may be invoked as a defense. Gersen wrote:

> *"Some jurors may find it difficult to convict Rhodes and others of seditious conspiracy if they find that sincere views about reality informed the defendants' purpose."*

This is merely one more example of how deference to religious beliefs infects secular matters. If we give deference to a heartfelt religious belief, you don't have to be a Yale Law School graduate to demand that same consideration be accorded on secular matters. And how can fair-minded people, already conditioned to believe such considerations are proper in religious matters, not be moved to support them more broadly? How do court rulings supporting a religious belief that making wedding cakes for gay couples is wrong, then not then rule that insurrection based on a strong, heartfelt belief is also protected?

Any time we give any special deference to those more benign beliefs, even limited to religious ones, we necessarily make it that much more difficult to criticize and curtail the more destructive ones applied more broadly. In a world that is fundamentally based in fantasy, logic offers little assistance in drawing such lines. Our deference to innocent little deeply held beliefs moves us directly to allow carve-outs that condone and institutionalize bigotry, prejudice, violations of civil rights, and yes—even insurrection.

We don't accept the notion that racism or terrorism or homophobia are any more legitimate if these beliefs are claimed to be deeply held, sincere, or cherished. Similarly, we should not be bamboozled into accepting this same justification for the acceptance of or favoritism toward religious beliefs.

Respect for Beliefs

This discussion has crossed a line! When you disrespect my deeply held values, you disrespect me!

That is a manipulation intended to make any criticism out of bounds.

We must always be respectful of individuals as human beings and be respectful of all the ways in which they have earned and deserve respect. But does that mean that we must show respect for all of their beliefs? If we disrespect certain of their beliefs, do we necessarily disrespect the believer? Are we not allowed to judge the legitimacy of any belief for fear of disrespecting the believer? To avoid disrespecting anyone, must we pretend that any belief is worthy of respect?

By its very definition, a belief is not based on any supportable fact. What grounds then does it have to demand respect? What position should we take regarding a sincere belief in witches, in leprechauns, or in Bigfoot? Must we respect those beliefs to avoid disrespecting the believer? If I doubt the reality of alien abductions, do I disrespect that person who fervently insists that they were abducted? If I criticize a government policy, does that mean I criticize the entire country? Does it mean I hate the nation and all its people?

Why would beliefs be any different? Should we respect beliefs just because they are widely held? If so, should we accept the belief that Muslim suicide bombers will be rewarded in the afterlife, or that evolution is a myth, or that Noah literally filled an ark with two of every animal? Or should we simply respect your beliefs? Is it OK to ridicule, dismiss, or patronize the obviously silly beliefs of others, but not OK to view your beliefs with the same disrespect?

Maybe, to avoid all these hurt feelings, we must show respect for all beliefs, regardless of how demonstrably ridiculous they are proven to be. Are all ideas, regardless of their merit, equally worthy of respect? If so, what grounds upon which to measure respect does that leave us?

Those are a lot of rhetorical questions that have clear answers. All beliefs are not equal, and all beliefs are not deserving of respect. To pretend to respect them, even to avoid disrespecting the believer, would result in nothing less than an abdication rational thinking.

The better path is to recognize that criticism of particular beliefs is not necessarily criticism of the believer and does not typically reflect any animosity toward them.

People deserve respect. Ideas and particular beliefs do not.

Proof by Numbers

🗣 *If my beliefs make me wrong, so are a billion other people.*

Yes, they are.

A belief has no basis in fact. That is true by definition. There is no empirical evidence to support a belief. Any such perceived evidence would have to be rationalized in some fashion by the believer to convince themselves that their belief is not crazy. Worse still, there may be a lot of evidence that contradicts one's belief. The mind must work hard to rationalize all of that evidence away somehow.

The strongest rationalization that one can find to support beliefs might be some rational sounding logical argument, but even this would fall apart under scrutiny, and it would be difficult to rely upon that as a foundation to rationalize that one's belief is perfectly sane.

What is left? What else is there to support rationalizing that a belief is reasonable, that we are not crazy for believing it? All that is left is the agreement of others. The only confirmation possible is the support and acknowledgment of others to reassure the believer that they are perfectly rational.

Do you see what I see? Good, I'm not crazy then.

This is why belief-based ideas are by nature not a personal thing. As a syndrome, beliefs require the acknowledgment of others to be sustained.

Religious believers tend to form very large groups, not because their ideas are rational but because they are so irrational that they cannot be sustained without large numbers of fellow believers to legitimize those beliefs.

They tend to be ever active to expand their numbers, evangelizing, proselytizing, and sending out missionaries to convince others to adopt their thinking. Every person who becomes a believer adds one more "fact" to the legitimacy of their fragile, unfounded belief system.

This syndrome also makes them tend to be militant, even to declare war on nonbelievers. Is this because they are evil people? No, it is because every nonbeliever is one more fact that contradicts their belief system. If those troublesome facts cannot be converted, they must be dismissed, discredited, or destroyed.

Evangelism, superiority, and self-righteousness are almost inevitable artifacts of the belief syndrome.

> *I visited Mongolia shortly after the country opened up to Westerners. I figured that I'd be one of the first Americans to visit. Wow, was I wrong! By the time I visited, the country was already besieged by American missionaries. On the plane trip back, filled with returning missionaries, I spoke with the missionary next to me. He seemed very open-minded. He told me that they didn't try to force any particular religion on the Mongolians. They were free to choose any (Christian) faith they liked!*

My only thought was that it was such a shame that these missionaries assumed that any of their Christian belief systems were superior to ancient Buddhist philosophies and that they apparently missed the rare opportunity to learn anything from the Mongolians they were privileged to visit.

So, it is no surprise that those who cling to beliefs require and create a lot of fellow believers to join them and reinforce those beliefs. To then point to those large numbers as some sort of proof of legitimacy is circular. Moreover, it violates the "argument from numbers" fallacy of logic.

As we have seen, large numbers of people believe almost any silly pseudoscientific myth that we can list. But even those believers who invoke a proof-by-numbers argument to defend their own beliefs would not accept a proof by numbers argument as adequate proof in those other cases. Even worse, we know that mass delusions are quite real. Just because a delusion affects large numbers of people does not make it any less a delusion.

We will deal with this last point in greater depth in Chapter 4, Delusion.

The Rubber Rebuttal

🗣 *You militant atheists are the ones who desperately need the confirmation of others to support your fragile worldview!*

Yes, I know: I'm rubber, you're glue.

I hear this a lot. It's actually a very common tactic to turn any criticism back on the source. Donald Trump carried this schoolyard style defense to ludicrous extremes.

I was stunned to hear this particular logical jujitsu espoused by author and radio talk show host Thom Hartmann. Thom is a progressive and normally fact-based thinker whom I respect greatly. Yet he has claimed on at least several occasions that atheism is a "religion" that holds an unfounded belief that God does not exist. He put forth the argument that atheists become "fanatical" in pushing their "belief in no belief" on others so that they can reaffirm their unfounded belief that there is no God.

I find this to be an amazing assertion and dramatic evidence of how rationality can fail even the most intelligent of us when compromised by belief. (Thom has indicated he does hold religious beliefs.) It seems ludicrous to me at least that one could argue that the party whose position is confirmed in every conceivable way by reality should require the reaffirmation of others. That is like the schizophrenic accusing the psychiatrist of being the deranged party for not acknowledging the delusions of the patient.

Further, to say that atheists are "fanatical" in pushing their "belief in no God" upon others is like accusing the scientist passionately trying to communicate the dangers of global warming of being a religious zealot. I see little historical evidence of "fanatical" evangelism by atheists to compare with that of believers. Quite the opposite, atheists as a whole have been incredibly tolerant of belief-based propositions put forth as truth by others, often through extreme measures.

Once I found myself defending evolution in the face of a very determined group of coworkers who insisted that evolution is a myth and that biblical creationism is a literal truth. To my amazement one of my coworkers accused me of engaging in "flat-earth thinking" by stubbornly clinging to my false belief in evolution. This is a great example of how any argument can be fallaciously turned around upon the person who might more legitimately make the same claim of the other.

> *When Donald Trump was accused of propagating the "big lie" that his failed reelection campaign was rigged, he immediately started to accuse his opponents of supporting the "big lie" that the election was legitimate. He used this same tactic over and over when legitimately criticized.*

It's a transparently thin defense, but it is very persuasive to folks who are open to and eager for any rationale to support their beliefs. The "I'm rubber, you're glue" logic is formidable in creating doubt and confusion, but like all other logical fallacies it must be tested against actual facts and logic.

And, again, religious believers are the ones making the extraordinary claim. It is up to them to prove it. Atheists do not need to prove it is untrue and do not need the affirmation of others to reinforce that view. Any efforts by atheists to promote atheism are not remotely comparable to the massive and obsessive ministry of religious believers.

Compartmentalization

It is unfair of you to try to paint me as irrational because I hold some sincere, heartfelt beliefs that you do not share. I can quite clearly separate my beliefs from my rational decision-making in real-world matters.

Except you cannot keep them separate.

In an episode of the talk show *Real Time with Bill Maher*, the host held up an issue of *USA Today* and pointed out a front-page headline that read, "Most Say They're Touched by Guardian Angels."

As he points to the headline, Bill says:

> *"If you're asking me why Americans can't solve problems, I would say that this is a good reason."*

One of his guests, political commentator Andrew Sullivan, made the following impassioned rebuttal:

> *"To say that people that believe in faith cannot intelligently then say economics is a different issue and I cannot actually apply reality-based reasoning to this because it is a different category of area is insulting."*

Bill responded:

> *"There is a connection, excuse me Andrew, between magical thinking and not thinking clearly about practical issues. Sarah Palin is a Pentecostal; they believe the Holy Spirit can heal, so why would you need health care insurance?"*

To this, Andrew countered:

> *"Yes, in that respect I think you're absolutely right. Those people that believe for example that economics, science, facts, history are*

all subject to magical thinking, the same magical thinking of their religious beliefs are crazy. They shouldn't be involved in a rational process. But there are plenty of people of faith who actually do believe in angels and do believe in saints and do pray and do believe God is part of their lives but are also grown-up enough to know that when we talk about economics, I'd like to know the facts. When we talk about foreign policy, I'd like to know what is going on in the real world. That there is a difference between heaven and Earth and can deal with Earth on secular terms and our faith on religious terms. It's the confusion."

This interchange nicely summed up the danger of our illusion of **compartmentalization**. The thing that Andrew Sullivan doesn't understand was summarized by James Randi, the famous magician and pseudoscience debunker:

"Magical thinking is a slippery slope."

James Randi warned us all that once you start to believe a little bit, it becomes easier to believe a bit more. Before very long, you are no longer able to tell the difference between belief and fact. Every belief that you adopt requires you to rationalize that belief, making it much easier to rationalize even more beliefs and become comfortable with even more bizarre belief-rationalizing patterns of thinking. Eventually, even matters of reason and fact must necessarily become compromised by those same patterns of belief-friendly rationalization.

For anyone to insist that they can handle it, that their beliefs are compartmentalized, that they do not compromise their reason, is to step onto a slippery slope into self-delusion. It is like alcoholics who insist that they can handle just a few drinks and it doesn't affect their judgment one bit.

Is compartmentalization possible at all?

Yes certainly, to some extent. But we cannot trust our own compromised judgment to self-assess our limits. To believe that we, like Andrew Sullivan, can compartmentalize just fine, thank you, is the height of folly. In fact, his view almost certainly demonstrates an already compromised capacity for objectivity.

We should not rely upon compartmentalization or assume that our rational thinking is not compromised by our beliefs. Few of us are able to avoid the impact of belief on our thinking. Even alcoholics or pot smokers or drug addicts can handle certain jobs while under the influence. But for them to claim that these cause no impairment of their reason are simply foolish or already seriously compromised.

But let's assume Andrew Sullivan is special. Let's grant that maybe he is capable of perfect compartmentalization. I have long praised former president Carter for his demonstrated capacity to compartmentalize his personal religious life from his highly data-driven and scientific approach to governing.

But few of us are Jimmy Carter.

Even if Andrew Sullivan is as exceptional as Jimmy Carter, it would still be socially irresponsible of Andrew Sullivan or anyone else to deny and dismiss the danger of cross-contamination. It would be irresponsible to dismiss the compromising effect of belief rationalization upon rational thought. It would be like scoffing at concerns over drinking and driving because I can drink and drive just fine, thank you.

Let's be honest. The real reason that believers like Andrew Sullivan claim compartmentalization is because they want to believe their beliefs while still thinking of themselves, and be thought of by others, as a perfectly rational thinker.

Compromised Thinking

It's unfair to question my rationality just because I'm a person of faith.

It is perfectly fair and reasonable.

If you were ever a juror on a court case, the judge would have given you specific instructions to follow in considering the testimony of the witnesses. You might have been instructed as follows:

> *If you find that any statement made by a witness is not fully and completely the truth, you can legitimately regard all testimony by that witness as suspect.*

This is an important directive. It acknowledges that any evidence of prevarication or inaccuracy legitimately calls all of the testimony of a witness into doubt.

Perhaps they were simply uninformed about one isolated fact that they got wrong. But that should still raise doubts about their level of knowledge in all areas.

It is possible that the witness was only motivated to lie in one particular area and that the rest of the testimony is truthful. Nevertheless, their lie about one fact legitimately calls their veracity in all areas into doubt.

Similarly, if someone holds beliefs, then they clearly demonstrate compromised rationality at least in that one area. It is then perfectly reasonable to question the rationality of their thinking in all areas.

Of course, the level of skepticism in all these cases should be proportionate to the severity of the mistake, lie, or belief. But one cannot espouse beliefs and then try to claim that their conclusions on other matters must not be questioned.

CHAPTER 3: CONFUSION

In Chapter 1, we reviewed some important characteristics of facts and reaffirmed the importance of recognizing facts and ensuring that we make well-reasoned decisions based upon them.

In Chapter 2, we discussed various beliefs and identified some of the dangers of adopting beliefs and of basing important decisions upon them.

Now we'll examine some of the factors that further confuse the two and aggravate the conflict between them. These confounding factors muddy the distinction between facts and belief, resulting too often in erroneous conclusions, decision paralysis, and even delusional thinking.

Too Many Facts

🗣 *The problem is not too few facts, the problem is that we have too many! Who knows what to believe?*

I agree!

In "The Rime of the Ancient Mariner," poet Samuel Taylor Coleridge's stranded sailor lamented:

"Water, water everywhere, nor any drop to drink."

That seems like an apt description of our situation today with regard to information. We are deluged with purported facts, and sometimes it feels that we are drowning in them.

There are so many contradicting facts about practically everything that it can be impossible to know which competing facts to pay attention to.

Facts should be the basis upon which truth is known. Today, however, facts seem to be used far more effectively to support beliefs, misinformation, and lies than to reveal truths. Because there are so many facts, it is easy to dredge up misrepresented, misleading, and partial facts than to manufacture outright lies. Indeed, those who wish to sell us nonsense don't often bother to tell lies anymore. They instead tell technical truths that are lies by context, omission, or distortion.

Nowhere is this new perversion of facts truer than in politics. Today, politicians like Donald Trump incessantly cite completely misleading facts to support their bogus claims and outright lies. Even if the majority of people do not believe these "trumped up" facts, they nevertheless conclude that all facts are suspect and that no facts can be trusted. This tangibly undermines the level of rational thinking of our entire culture and leaves us without a sound basis for making good decisions as a society.

In his excellent op-ed, sociological theorist William Davies pointed out that "they [facts] seem to be losing their ability to support consensus." According to Davies, there is clear agreement that "we have entered an age of post-truth politics." This post-truth age is not fueled by assertions of faith, but by assertions of fact. As Davies further points out, "Rather than sit coolly outside the fray of political argument, facts are now one of the main rhetorical weapons within it."

Facts have become the new bullshit. We claim to care about facts, but only because, as with the Bible, we can always find something in them to support our beliefs and prejudices and self-interest. Our abundance of data seems to only serve to diminish and undervalue it, to make it increasingly vulnerable to manipulation and misrepresentation. The sheer volume of it makes it very difficult to say anything with certainty without some other bit of data seeming to contradict it.

And this perversion and misuse of facts is not just true in politics, but it has become the new normal in all walks of life. All too often journalists and pundits do not pursue facts to reveal truth but rather invoke them to gin up excitement and viewership ratings. This makes great theater, but it does little to advance the important questions that we face. It instigates and perpetuates conflict rather than help us reach a sound, fact-based consensus.

Even scientists, our gatekeepers and guardians of fact, all too often emphasize only those facts that advocate for their desired outcome rather than serving the far greater goal of advancing science as a quest for truth.

Lawyers have their own brand of facts. Their goal is not to clarify the truth of the matter in question but to offer facts only as far as they serve to persuade, to win the case for their client.

We see debate as a powerful tool for arriving at truth. But, like lawyers, debate mostly focuses on winning the debate, not on arriving at truth. We see this painfully exhibited on debate-style talk shows in which smart debaters score points rather than arrive at a fact-based consensus.

Despite all these challenges, abandoning facts is simply not an option. Allowing the manipulators to turn all fact-based thinking into rationalization games and data manipulation exercises is not an option because good decisions simply cannot be made without sound facts. If we allow facts to be coopted by magical thinkers, by self-serving politicians, or even by well-meaning advocates, we might as well put the psychic hotline staff in charge of our fates.

What is the answer?

We must reclaim facts. We must become smarter consumers of facts who are no more likely to be fooled by the bogus facts cited by manipulative politicians or corporations any more than we are by laughably ambiguous Bible citations and interpretations. We must learn to recognize valid data and sound conclusions amid all the cherry-picking. We must learn to treasure and respect fairly presented facts as diamonds among all the heaps of rubble and fool's gold that we have to sift through every day.

Our overabundance of data should make us value—and demand—sound analysis and conclusions based on valid and relevant data all that much more.

Surrender is not an option. We either learn to swim in an ocean of facts or we drown in it.

Soft Fuzzy Facts

🗣 *Becoming smarter consumers of facts is all well and good, but most of real life is not about facts. It's about subjective assessments that must be made in the absence of facts or independently of them.*

We agree on this as well.

Most of our vitally important questions are not as scientifically clear as measuring the speed of light. We have to deal with real-world problems that lie outside of the so-called hard sciences of physics, chemistry, biology, astronomy, geology, and meteorology.

Many answers must be found in the **soft sciences** including sociology, psychology, and economics. These are important sciences that in many ways have a far more difficult job than the hard sciences. There are many unavoidable reasons for this:

1   *The soft sciences deal with human beings, and studying human subjects requires strong ethical constraints.*

2   *It is often simply impractical to study human behavior over the long term and under controlled conditions.*

3   *Because self-reported data is so unreliable, drawing predictive conclusions from survey studies is exceedingly difficult.*

Even though it can be very difficult to obtain reliable data from the soft sciences, they do nevertheless manage to do a great job in giving us the best information we can feasibly obtain.

Much of the research conducted by the soft sciences involves trying to determine why people do what they do. Toward that end, the primary tool of researchers are survey studies that either ask subjects directly about their motivations or indirectly by asking questions from which inferences can be made.

Unfortunately, despite the hard work of social scientists, asking people why they did what they did, or why they are doing what they are doing, or why they are going to do what they are going to do, frequently yields incomplete and misleading information. Not only are there myriad reasons why people intentionally or unintentionally misrepresent, but it is doubtful that many people are even aware of the complex factors that motivate them.

Many decisions are made subconsciously based upon a multitude of complex neural network associations. These associations need not be rational. These connections don't need to be internally consistent to one another or related to the actual outcome in any way.

Studies have suggested that we make most decisions subconsciously. Technology can detect a thought being generated prior to our awareness of it. The outcome of a decision (e.g., deciding to press a button) can be encoded in brain activity of the prefrontal and parietal cortex and detected with functional magnetic resonance imaging as much as ten seconds before awareness of the decision. Only afterward, when we become aware of the decision, does our brain contrive some post-facto rationale, creating the illusion of conscious decision-making. Only in our post-rationalizations and post-analyses do we impose some logic to our decisions to make them feel sensible or to justify them to ourselves and others, by concocting a basis—desires and beliefs—that could have produced the outcome.

Therefore, the reasons we come up with, and report to researchers, are largely made up at every level to sound rational to ourselves and to those we are communicating to. Our subconscious decides it likes that particular car model for a host of reasons, not all of which even seem relevant. We are not even aware of most of them. But when asked, or brains have to come up with some logical-sounding reason. So, we say honestly, "Because it's green." Unfortunately, the fact that it's green probably has little or no actual predictive value.

The effect of this is that the reasons we give for our behaviors are rather arbitrary and seldom very predictive. The truth is, we usually can't hope to understand our own incredibly complex neural networks, let alone the neural networks of others. Yes, sometimes we can identify a strong neural network association driving a particular behavior, but most determinative associations are far too diffuse across a huge number of seemingly unrelated associations.

The situation gets infinitely worse when we are trying to analyze and explain group behaviors. Most of our shared group behaviors emerge from the weak interactions between all of our individual neural networks. The complexity of these interactions is virtually unfathomable. The challenge of understanding why a group does what it does collectively, let alone figuring out how to influence its behavior, is fantastic.

If you ask a bird why it is flying in a complex swirling pattern along with a million other birds, it will probably give you some reason, like "We're looking for food," but in fact it is probably largely unaware that it is even flying in any particular pattern at all, let alone why.

So why point all this out? Do we give up? Does this imply that a rational civilization is impossible, that all introspection or external analysis is folly?

Quite the contrary, we must continue to struggle to understand ourselves and others. Truly appreciating our complexity is part of that effort. This effort, although imprecise and inefficient, does have tremendous value. Sometimes, pollsters or marketers do have great success putting their finger on the next big thing by conducting polls and surveys.

But to do better at this, we must abandon the constraints of logic that we impose upon our individual and group rationalizations and appreciate that we are driven by neural networks that are susceptible to all manner of illogical programming. We must take any self-reporting with the same skepticism we would to the statement "I am perfectly sane." We should be careful of imposing our own flawed rationality upon the flawed rationality of others. Analysts should not assume undue rationality in explaining behaviors. And finally, we must appreciate that group behaviors can have little or no apparent relationship to any of the wants, needs, or expressed opinions of those individuals within that group.

Today we routinely perform complex decision making and predictions with computer-based neural networks. In these systems, if the inputs are accurate, we can probably trust the performance of the artificial intelligence over that of humans for specific tasks, and explainable AI metrics shed some light on how the outputs are produced. This is why it is the highly complex skills, like medical diagnosis, have the most promise for radical advances using machine intelligence. The computer can perform complex pattern recognition, using objective evidence.

Human biases, beliefs, and mistaken perceptions can have an influence on the output if they are introduced in the data.

> *Most of us are familiar with the highly publicized problems of apparent bias in facial recognition systems. When their outputs were analyzed, by demographic group in contexts that would lead to consequences like being falsely accused of a crime, many facial recognition software programs have higher rates of misidentification for non-white faces and "faces with traditionally female characteristics."*
>
> *But such problems are far easier to eliminate in computer systems than in humans. Part of the solution is to train those systems with data that are representative of the population and unbiased.*

It's possible for humans to improve as well. We can clean up our human neural networks by exposing them to sound facts and logic, free from beliefs and biases.

Emergent Beliefs

But true faith serves a far greater purpose: to reshape humanity in the image of God.

You could not be more correct!

That sentiment is so true that it merits an entire section. The expression of simple beliefs at the population scale is almost certainly a driving force of religion and other institutionalized belief systems.

I am eternally fascinated by **swarm intelligence** and **emergent behaviors**. These terms describe the phenomenon by which individual organisms, following only simple logical directives without any wider intent or awareness, contribute to highly complex and far-reaching behaviors that "emerge" or arise out of their collective activity.

The most observable examples of swarm intelligence include bird flocking, animal herding, fish schooling, bacterial growth, and ant colonies. Ants, as one easily observable example, collectively create extremely complex bridges and nests, even though no particular individual organizes that activity or is even aware of it.

The amazingly complex creations of ants emerge from very simple logical primitives such as "if another ant is on top of me, stop moving." From this kind of deceptively simple behavior, ants collectively exhibit astounding feats of mass migration, swarming, tactical warfare, nest construction, and engineering. However, if that very basic behavior were to change in a significant number of ants, then their ability to create bridges and nests could collapse, and perhaps their species would as well.

What intrigues me most about this sort of swarm intelligence is the intriguing certainty that we humans collectively exhibit our own highly complex emergent behaviors. Even though none of us may intend it, even though few of us are even aware of it, each of us nevertheless contributes to the emergent behaviors of our collective population, just as if we were merely cells in some greater human super-organism.

Therefore, the most fundamental ways that we think about things likely do contribute rather more directly than we imagine to the large-scale behavior of our species.

We must accept it as a compelling assumption that if enough of us engage in belief-based thinking or in fact-based thinking, our collective behavior might likely change dramatically.

This is analogous to generating a complex fractal image based on a triangle versus one based on a hexagon. The resulting images will be dramatically different in character. Another similar analogy is crystal growth. A crystal grown from copper acetate is green and monoclinic whereas a crystal grown from copper sulfate is blue and triclinic.

Belief is not then merely some tiny, personal thing. It can have a profound impact on our emergent behaviors as a society. Religious believers seem to intrinsically agree with this hypothesis. They affirm, both implicitly and explicitly, their trust that if enough people adopt their personal beliefs, large-scale social behaviors that they desire will emerge.

But atheists do not agree that emergent behaviors driven by belief are good for us. They intuit that behavior emerging from the acceptance of fantasy can only result in bigotry, intolerance, gullibility, susceptibility to manipulation, disregard for the planet, and even warfare. We consider it likely that belief-based thinking can only produce destructive swarm behaviors like gun violence, terrorism, torture, and jihad.

Therefore, we atheists should trust that there are no benign religious beliefs. We should never doubt that our simple rule of logic, that we believe in facts and reason, not in gods, serves our species far better on the grand collective scale. We must trust that our respect for facts and humanist ethics, when expressed through a sufficiently large number of individuals, will indeed result in emergent behaviors that are more ethical than dogmatic, more fact-based than fantasy-based, and more focused on our lives and our planet right now rather than life ever after. We must trust that fact-based thinking will better give rise to the more enlightened swarm intelligence that we so desperately need if we are to survive as a species.

Until it Happens to You

You can't understand because you never experienced what I experienced. If you had, you'd know that there is much more to the world than science can explain!

But it has happened to me.

Polls validate what we already know from personal experience: that the vast majority of people have experienced things that they cannot explain, things that no one else seems to be able to explain. If not them directly, then they most likely know a close, sane, reliable friend who experienced some event that seems to defy any sort of rational or scientific explanation:

A beloved grandmother relates the story of how the spirit of her deceased husband came to visit her one night, of how he kissed her on the cheek.

An aunt tells a chilling tale from her childhood of how she refused to say her prayers one night, and a terrible clawing and scratching threatened her from outside the room, and of how it stopped when she started to pray.

A lifelong friend tells of how she shared her apartment with the spirit of a previous occupant who became upset whenever she had a male visit her, turning lights and music on and off in agitation.

The night you watched a UFO zig and zag in totally inexplicable patterns in a clear, moonlit sky.

A scoutmaster relates the story of the night during which some nightmarish presence lurked around their campsite.

The morning your wife knew with absolute certainty that her brother would be in an accident that day, only to call to warn him and find out it had just happened.

The night you had an out-of-body experience during which you flew out across the city, an experience that at the time you knew with certainty was not a dream.

The mystical fortune-teller in India who knew things about you that he could not possibly know and predicted the initials of the wife you would meet years later.

It might be surprising to learn that all of the events above actually happened to me or to those close to me. These are just a few of the "unexplainable" events from my own life. It's relatively easy to dismiss the stories of others. But when they happen to you and those close to you, they are not so easy to discount.

So, I do get it.

Sure, maybe some neuropsychologist would explain away all of these stories as some kind of mini-psychotic episodes. Maybe a paranormal investigator would fail to find sufficient data to support them in a controlled environment. Maybe Harry Houdini would pull up the tablecloth to reveal a hidden switch or James Randi could demonstrate the sleight of hand that was used.

But when they happen to you, or to those you trust, they change your view of the world. Even if all those other events can be explained away, that doesn't disprove what you saw and heard. It ignores the real world to suggest that we should simply dismiss strange events, that we should just dismiss anything that doesn't fit into our limited understanding. In fact, that is the opposite of what science values.

In science, new breakthroughs are only made through precisely the opposite behavior. New discoveries are made by people who notice that little out-of-place detail, that unexplained dot on a chart.

The difference is that a scientist welcomes that new piece of unexplained information as a great opportunity for inquiry, a rare chance to learn something new, to expand the scope of human knowledge.

That is precisely why scientists like Dr. Carl Sagan spent many years eagerly investigating any remotely credible report of a paranormal event. Not out of a narrow-minded compulsion to explain it away, but out of a childlike curiosity and excitement that it might actually be true—on the small chance that it might open up entire new worlds of inquiry.

Like the escape artist Harry Houdini who spent much of his life seeking out proof of the occult, Dr. Sagan never found any evidence of the paranormal. Nor did Randi, despite offers of lucrative rewards. This was disappointing, but not in the least surprising.

However, what a scientist will never do (a good scientist at least) is to accept a proposition as fact without validation. If they cannot explain a report or observation, then they let it remain unexplained until new data sheds light upon it. A scientist would rather not know than make up an answer. A scientist would rather keep that door open, reserve judgment, admit "I don't know," rather than so frivolously discard a potential treasure trove of real discovery.

Ghost Story

But when confronted by the unknown, we have to develop
some working hypothesis. We cannot just ignore it.
We have to act on some assumed basis, wrong or not.

Very true, but that response should be a rational one.

We often do have to respond, take some action, even when we have no explanation for what we are responding to. As one case study, I'll relate an actual ghost encounter experienced by myself and my partner Marcie:

Marcie and I were managing a large apartment complex to cut expenses while we went to college. The first day we moved in, the handyman named Ed took us on a tour of the basement.

Now, you have to picture this creepy basement. At one time the apartment complex was a long row of separate buildings. Since then, the basements had been joined by knocking jagged holes through the brick walls, forming a veritable labyrinth overstuffed with vintage furniture and miscellaneous odds and ends like your grandparent's attic. It was sparsely illuminated by the shadowy flickering of swinging light bulbs.

I was following closely at Ed's heels learning all the guy stuff I needed to know, while Marcie mostly followed along behind. After the walkthrough, Ed gave me the key, telling me that he had the only other key to the basement. Tenants were not allowed down there.

When we got back to our apartment, still full of unopened moving boxes, Marcie was quiet and pale. She eventually shared what she had seen. As she had followed along in the basement, she had the strange feeling of being watched. As she walked past some old bed frames, she saw her. Marcie looked up to see a woman, wearing 1930s clothes with her hair in period style looking over at her sternly. Her looks said, "I'm not sure I like you being here in my basement."

The woman was semi-transparent, and as Marcie tried to process the presence of the woman, she realized that she had no lower half.

She ran to catch up with Ed and me.

We quickly pushed that incident to the back our minds. After all, what else was there to do?

But soon after, we started hearing footsteps in the living room from our bedroom at night. Our parakeet would confirm some presence with tentative chirps of fear. Moreover, small objects started to disappear from our apartment during the night.

Many a night Marcie would wake me up to investigate the sound of footsteps, but I never found anyone or anything. Needless to say, we compulsively checked the locks and windows to make sure that no one was entering our apartment.

Then Marcie had a second sighting while doing laundry in the basement. She looked up to see a man squatting next to the washer. He was intent on cleaning something with a rag, his arm making circular motions as if cleaning the rim of a bicycle wheel.

When she stopped to take in the man, he turned his head toward her and grinned…

Marcie dropped the basket and never went back down into the basement again. I did all the laundry from then on but never saw any ghostly figures personally.

I share this story to acknowledge that we do have experiences that we cannot explain. Even scientists do. To deny that would be a denial of our experience.

But the difference between rational and superstitious thinking has entirely to do with what assumptions we make about these experiences and how we respond to them. Just because my girlfriend and I had the experience we did, and since we could not explain it, are we then at liberty to claim that it is proof of anything we care to imagine?

Does this story prove there are ghosts? Perhaps I made up the story to make a point to you, the reader. I assure you I did not, but I could be lying. Or perhaps my girlfriend made it all up to avoid having to do laundry. Perhaps our imaginations simply ran away with us. Perhaps vagrants were hanging out in our basement.

Is it likely that ghosts were walking through our living room at night, invisible yet making loud footsteps, in order to steal various small items by passing through walls with those solid objects in hand?

Or is it more likely that footsteps from somewhere else were transmitting through the sprawling old structure?

Isn't it at least notable that I only heard footsteps after being awoken from a deep sleep to the suggestion of footsteps in the other room?

For lack of a better word, we used the word "ghosts" to describe what we saw and heard. Based on that, can we now claim that we have proof of life after death?

As a good student of science, I was quite excited about the ghosts. If they really existed, what a find! I had dreams of Nobel Prizes in hitherto unimagined fields of physics. Just imagine what I could learn!

I used to go into the basement hoping to find the "ghosts," just on the exceedingly unlikely chance that there was actually some basis in reality to our experiences. I had a whole interview planned to help me learn who and what they were and how they did the things they did.

Scientists investigate methodically.

Marcie was affected by her Jehovah's Witness upbringing. She inherited the fear of the unknown that comes from belief-based thinking. So she jumped to the worst assumptions, fearful that these ghosts were dangerous, when in fact it would have been just as legitimate to assume that they were friendly, perhaps even protecting us.

I told my ghost story to my research advisor at the time. I had a close relationship with my chemistry professor, the person whose example had taught me to analyze difficult problems in a logical and objective manner. I was confident that if anyone could provide a fresh and rational analysis of my ghost situation, it was him.

As I related as much of the story as had passed by that point, I sensed my professor stiffening, shuffling. Eventually he cut me off with some vague comments about demons and evil. I never mentioned the story to him again and he never inquired about it. My research advisor illustrated the fact that none of us, even very smart scientists, are immune to superstitious thinking.

Now, decades later, I still can't explain what really happened. And I'm fine with that. Scientists don't like not knowing something, but they are far happier not to know the truth than to accept a falsehood, as comforting as it may be. To accept the idea that we were visited by ghosts would be too easy, too lazy. It would be to simply adopt the popular myth.

In 100 years, it might become quite popular to blame such sightings on techno-cloaked alien visitors who are observing and learning about the human race. Perhaps scientists of the future will be called blindly stubborn not to accept the obvious truth that such "ghost" sightings are actually malfunctions of their alien cloaking technology.

I may not know what happened in that apartment complex, but I am quite confident that the answer is quite mundane.

There Is Always a Trick

You have disproven your own thesis. If you cannot explain your ghost story, perhaps you are blinded to the fact that some things exist that are beyond the bounds of your science.

Unless you realize that there is always a trick.

At times, we are all tempted to believe in the divine or in the supernatural. Indeed, it can seem narrow-minded to dismiss the seemingly inexplicable stories related by sensible, credible people we trust. Sometimes we ourselves experience things that seem to defy any rational scientific explanation. These experiences seem to prove that there must indeed be more to the universe than reason can explain. It can be hard to push back on the logic that our inability to find a scientific explanation proves that there must be a supernatural one.

And lastly, many of us, including me, would really, really love to live in a world brimming with magic and mysteries.

Whenever you are tempted to entertain belief in something supernatural or paranormal, just remind yourself of one invariably true anchor to reality: There is always a trick.

I'm reminded of a formative event back in the 1970s when I went to a performance by the charismatic magician Doug Henning. Between big illusions like making live tigers disappear, he would walk out to the edge of the stage and do sleight of hand magic. In one such interlude, he held up a newspaper and showed it to us, turning each page so we would remember the layout. He then proceeded to methodically tear it into smaller and smaller pieces. As he did so, he kept his teasing narration going. It went along the following lines:

> *You think you see it tearing, you think you hear the sound of paper ripping apart, you think you see me holding two separate pieces. All your senses are convinced that I'm tearing up this paper, but I am not.*

He continued to rip the paper into shreds and stack up the pieces, in full view, into a little folded-up pile. Then he began to unfold it and show us the full newspaper perfectly intact once more. As he paged through the "reassembled" newspaper, he continued his teasing:

> *There is no magic, this is a simple trick. Obviously, I could not actually have torn up the paper. But the trick is the magic and the magic is in the trick.*

Doug Henning was brilliantly messing with the audiences' minds there, but what I learned from him is that there is always a trick. You can be totally baffled by something inexplicable, but you can be assured of one thing—there is a trick. You just don't see it right now. And importantly, you can still be amazed by the trick and—even knowing it is only a trick—astounded every bit as much as by true magic.

Knowing there is no magic, nothing supernatural, no God, does not need to make the world one bit less exciting and inspiring. Quite the opposite. You can feel even more amazed knowing that the real explanation must actually be so clever, so masterfully executed, that one imagines that only some supernatural story could possibly explain it. The trick is *so* amazing that it is easier for us to consider some magical explanation rather than the real one.

Years later I watched one of those television shows that exposes magical tricks. In that episode, the magician and his gorgeous assistants make a minisub appear and disappear again, right on stage. It was astoundingly, compellingly real. Surely there could be no conceivable way that such a feat could be accomplished without true supernatural intervention.

But after the commercial break they simply showed the same performance as shot from a side angle. It suddenly seemed stupidly crude and simple, so pathetically obvious that one could not imagine anyone even attempting to fool anyone with it, let alone anyone actually being fooled by it.

It was incredibly disappointing to see that trick exposed. It was ruined forever. I vowed to never again watch one of those shows. I want to be amazed. I want to experience that awe and wonder over and over. Yet I still know there is always a trick. All it takes is to shift the camera ever so slightly and the trick becomes ridiculously obvious.

The "good magic" that magicians or fantasy novelists or movie makers offer us does not excuse the "bad magic" of hucksters, con-artists, priests, rabbis, imams, televangelists, psychics, and other charlatans. These promoters of the supernatural do not trick us to entertain us. Unlike magicians, they do not admit or acknowledge that they are tricking you to entertain you. They want you to actually believe them in order to manipulate and exploit you. Some do it, they believe, for our own good. But, good intentions or not, they tangibly damage our capacity to reason.

We can choose not to ruin an entertaining illusion by pulling back the curtain to expose the trick. But magicians do not believe or tell others that stage magic is true, and we certainly do not base life decisions upon a conviction that you really witnessed a woman being sawed in half and then reassembled.

There is no equivalence between our choice to suspend our disbelief in an entertaining magic trick or ghost movie and our choice to suspend disbelief about the idea that a psychic can predict the future or that some god influences the present.

Counterintuitively, it is often the smartest of us who are most susceptible and gullible with regard to magical thinking, and most likely to influence others. I recall when, at the height of the crop circle craze, one network interviewed a "scientist" who had investigated the circles. He proclaimed that he had studied the markings extensively and could see no earthly method by which they could have been produced. Therefore, he concluded in stentorian tones, they could only have been created by an extraterrestrial (or supernatural) force.

Of course, two local guys eventually came forward and showed how they pulled a roller along to create the crop circles. Their revelation was as obvious and mundane as the minisub disappearance trick. But the ego of that scientist led him to conclude that if he could not see the trick, the only explanation must then be a supernatural one.

Even Sir Isaac Newton, one of humanity's most brilliant thinkers, was compromised by similar hubris when he assumed that if he, Sir Isaac Newton, could not explain the stability of planetary orbits, it could only mean that God must intervene. Even legendary scientists can fall prey to magical thinking.

So, when confronted by things you cannot explain, just remember: There is always a trick. Let that certain knowledge make you more confidently skeptical regarding religious and supernatural claims, confident enough to simply reject them out of hand, even when they seem to defy rational explanation and even when very smart people cannot explain them and endorse supernatural explanations.

But in doing so, don't be any less awed and inspired by the perfectly explainable but nevertheless amazing magic in the world.

How These Things Get Started

🗣 *Some paranormal events may turn out to have rational explanations, but certainly they all cannot.*

They can and do.

In 1991, we learned how two bored guys in rural England created crop circles on a lark. We also saw how quickly the entire world was ready to accept that as proof of alien visitations. We also know that despite their mea culpa, many people still persist in disbelieving them and instead believe that, like the Nazca Lines in Peru, those crop circles are proof of alien visitors.

There is indeed no end to the crazy stories that go around and just won't die. My uncle was saved from a bear by Bigfoot and has the scars to prove it. This guy on TV was molested by aliens—his story was checked out by a team of scientists. My grandmother was kissed by her dead husband, and she wouldn't make that kind of thing up. The Virgin Mary appeared to a homeless guy in the Bronx who had no reason to lie. Forty-seven cows mysteriously died in Iowa after a Haitian witch doctor got snubbed at a truck stop and cursed the town—couldn't be coincidence. Everyone knows that old house is haunted by a woman who was murdered by her lover in the forties. That was the day my dead pet returned to save my life!

Given that there is absolutely no possibility that any of these stories are actually true, one has to wonder how they ever get started in the first place. How is it reasonable to believe that there are mundane explanations for all of them? Surely some of them must be true, especially when multiple people report the same thing. And, well, who in the world would start such crazy stories?

Well, the crop circles guys did.

And I would.

In fact, I did.

One summer during college I was rooming with my longtime buddy, let's call him Bob. As I walked back to our place late one sweltering night in Wisconsin, I was feeling particularly bored and fanciful. The nighttime shadows helped work my imagination into a receptive frame of mind, and as I walked past the window of a local craft store, I was struck by these handcrafted dolls on display in the window. Now, like many people, I do admit to being generally spooked by dolls, and as I looked at this one particularly creepy looking doll bathed in old-time streetlamps, I got inspired to mischief.

I took off running and got myself plenty winded by the time I reached our building. I intentionally stumbled and crashed as I climbed our stairs and pounded on our door with desperate urgency. Bob opened the door to the sight of me in very convincing panic-stricken terror. I rushed into the room and made him drag my terrifying story out of me. I told him I had been walking past this store and noticed this doll and suddenly I felt an eerie presence, like some evil spirit, and without warning this doll leapt into the window and clawed at me. I panicked and ran all the way back to the room, the entire time feeling like some malevolent demon was chasing me.

Bob's reaction was all I could have hoped for. Though frightened, he valiantly insisted that we go back that very night to face this demon. I reluctantly agreed to show him where the store was but refused to get closer than the end of the block. I watched from down the street as Bob heroically inched forward, craning his neck tentatively to glimpse this demon doll. Suddenly he jerked, bolted, almost got hit by a passing car as he stumbled into the street, ran all the way back to and past me, shouting breathlessly "I saw it, dude! It was hideous!"

In retrospect I should have owned up to my prank right then and there. But Bob was so pumped up I decided to tell him in the morning. By the next morning I had forgotten all about it, and anyway Bob had already left to go somewhere before I woke up. I was reminded of my folly of the night before when Bob returned and proudly related how he had gone to the craft shop, paranormal investigator-like, to sleuth out the origins of this demon doll.

The owner told him that by the greatest (actually worst) of coincidences, the dollmaker, a lady by the name of Ramona Audley happened to be paying a visit at that very same moment. Bob politely confronted Ramona and asked her whether she knew that she was crafting possessed dolls. Ramona apparently nearly went into a terrified state of shock, and I later learned that the dolls were removed from the store window that very day.

Ramona, I did you wrong and I'm so sorry.

It gets worse. When Bob told me what he had done I was mortified. That poor Ramona Audley! I never intended to frighten her or the shop owner! But how could I tell Bob the truth of my prank now that he had done this? How could I make him feel like such a dupe? I settled for hoping that this whole debacle would just blow over.

Needless to say, it did not just blow over. It took on a life of its own like Godzilla emerging from the ocean to wreak havoc. For the next several decades, whenever Bob introduced me at any kind of gathering, he insisted that I tell the doll story. I would refuse, feigning intentionally ambiguous reluctance. But Bob would invariably take over and tell the story on my behalf, prefacing it with a lengthy introduction about how he would never believe this story from anyone else in the entire world except from me. My sanity and integrity were (undeservedly) just that irreproachable.

Dear reader, if you could have admitted to making up such a story, you are a better person than me. To make matters even worse, Bob is a naturally gregarious guy who interacts with a lot of people. Who knows how many people he has told this story to, who have in turn related it to many other people, who all swear that they were assured that this story came from an impeachable source? Every year that went by, during which I hoped that the story would be finally forgotten, every time I failed to disavow it, the myth became that much more entrenched.

My dolls truly had become demons. I did eventually try to tell Bob the truth, but that never seemed to dampen his belief in the story.

I felt like Houdini must have felt when he tried to assure Arthur Conan Doyle and his wife that all his magic tricks were just tricks. Houdini even went as far as revealing some of his tricks to the Doyles as proof.

They never believed him either. Instead, rather than give up their deep belief in spiritualism, they apparently rationalized that Houdini was now trying to fool them, to conceal his real magic with simple tricks. Just as Bob maintained his belief in Ramona's dolls, the Doyle's continued to publicly tout Houdini as proof of their magical spiritualism.

I wish I could have warned those crop circle guys about the life of its own that their prank could take on. How unkillable it could become. Even after finally coming clean, I still live in perpetual dread of seeing my bogus story reenacted on some paranormal reality show. Lots of people are probably more willing to believe that I lied about it not happening than believe that I simply made it up as a silly impulsive prank. After all, what kind of person would make up such a story?

Umm, yes, that would be me.

And that, my friends, is just one way that these things are born and take on a long life of their own. It is not all that incredible, just kind of sad.

Brainwashing

*Surely, you're not suggesting that anyone with even
half a brain would believe such a crazy story!*

All of us are susceptible to suggestion of all sorts, up to and including brainwashing.

Brainwashing exploits the natural malleability of our memories and perceptions. It is the technique of intentionally and methodically instilling beliefs into a person so that they become totally convinced of their truth.

Experts in brainwashing as performed by certain governments and cults will tell you that, given enough time, anyone can be brainwashed. Anyone. A prisoner can be made to believe that his captors deserve his true allegiance, or an ordinary, rational person can be made to believe that he was handpicked by God to be a martyr.

Many people have some level of belief that only the weak-minded can be manipulated so easily. That is a belief that the people who are adept brainwashing find very helpful. They assure us that those who believe they are immune are usually the easiest to brainwash.

That universal attitude reminds me of the hilarious scene in *The Woman in Green*, one in a series of Sherlock Holmes films starring Nigel Bruce and Basil Rathbone. Holmes and Watson visit the Mesmer Club to investigate the possibility that hypnosis is being used to commit crimes. Watson indignantly tells Holmes that hypnosis is poppycock, and at any rate it only works on dim-witted fools. It could never work on a strong-willed man of science like himself. Predictably, within a few moments, poor Dr. Watson has been hypnotized and made to do ridiculous things.

Of course, Holmes proves to be immune to hypnosis—but then again, he is the one and only Sherlock Holmes.

If, like Dr. Watson, you at least accept that brainwashing works on those other dim-witted people, how does it work?

The trick, the experts will tell you, is to first make the subject feel included in the group—special, protected, understood. A climate of trust must be created, but beyond that it must be a climate of mutual understanding and us-versus-them that outsiders just can't share.

From there, it's easy. You simply move the person in tiny increments, each a perfectly logical and rational little step away from the last. If you believe that, then you must surely believe this as well. It follows logically, does it not?

In that way, in tiny little steps, the person moves methodically farther and farther from their starting point. Eventually, somehow, those little steps have taken them to a belief that they never would have accepted if viewed from their original starting point. But now, from way out on that limb, it all now seems inescapably obvious and logical and sensible to take just one more little step farther out there.

As their beliefs gradually morph, their perceptions and memories morph along with them, reinforcing and validating their new beliefs.

Realize that brainwashing is only the intentional implementation of techniques to quickly modify thinking. You may not believe it works, but many other, less intensive versions that utilize the same principles undeniably work very well. These include education, indoctrination, socialization, marketing, and many others.

Regardless of the technique, the targeted person will find some way to provide, what is to them at least, perfectly logical and rational reasons for their previously unbelievable new belief. Our brains are quite capable of rationalizing practically anything to make it seem sensible to us.

Before you know it, a person can be made to believe with all their heart, as confirmed by all their perceptions and memories, that Jesus died for them, that some other group is out to oppress them, that alien abductors are picking them up, or that tax breaks for the wealthy will benefit them too.

The only prevention is to not allow yourself to be exposed to these inputs and to expose yourself instead to healthier and more fact-based "training facts." If you believe yourself to be too strong-willed to be affected, you're easy prey.

If you expose yourself to brainwashing in any of its forms, you will be influenced whether you realize it or not, whether you agree to it or not.

I once had a friend who wanted to immerse herself in a particular religious community in order to study them for her thesis work. It was a religious community that preached concepts she found both silly and offensive. I cautioned her to be extremely cautious because mere repeated exposure will necessarily make her increasingly more and more comfortable with their teachings. She discarded that advice. I hope she did not end up becoming a convert.

When I spent some time in the Middle East, I detested being woken up before sunrise by that hideous blaring call to prayers blasting from cheap horn speakers. But over time you get comfortable with it. Eventually I probably would have grown to enjoy it. Our tastes in everything from music to vegetables to gods are similarly malleable.

We often say we're "getting used to it" or "the idea is growing on me," or "I've grown accustomed to it." All of these are really just ways we recognize, without fully realizing, that our neural networks are being modified through repeated exposure.

This is a valuable adaption. It makes evolutionary sense that we become comfortable with, even enjoy whatever situation we may find ourselves in. But this same adaptation also makes us incredibly vulnerable to changes in our thinking, even when that thinking is unfounded and destructive.

Seeing Is Believing

🗣 *I may not be able to trust my neural network, but I can trust my own eyes!*

Actually, you cannot.

When you perceive something, when you see it or smell it or hear it for yourself, it makes a tremendous impact.

But I saw that ghost and I heard those disembodied footsteps.

I saw that newspaper torn apart before my very eyes.

We all saw a submarine appear and then disappear from stage!

We tend to give unquestioned credibility to our perceptions or to the eyewitness testimony of others.

My trusted friend was attacked by dolls!

But while our senses normally serve us well, they are incredibly unreliable.

There are numerous experiments that demonstrate clearly how easily our senses can be fooled. Of course, we can generally trust our senses well enough for most things. But for important things, we cannot assume undue reliability.

For most of our history, eyewitness testimony was instrumental in sending innocent people to jail or even to death row. It was only after the advent of DNA testing that we began to appreciate how often absolutely convincing eyewitnesses are completely wrong. Thankfully, the science of DNA testing has both exposed and partially replaced our unfounded reliance upon eyewitness accounts.

One reason that our perceptions are so very unreliable is because our brain heavily filters incoming information. Studies estimate that our low-level filters shield us from as much as 80 percent to 90 percent of sensory stimuli. Our visual processing centers, for example, filter extraneous information through selective attention and specialized processing networks based on cues like faces, eyes, self-propulsion, synchronous movements, sudden changes in speed, patterns of approach or avoidance, and orientation. Our other senses are likewise filtered. This makes practical sense, for if we did not have these adaptations, we would never be able to focus or concentrate on anything over all the distractions.

To prevent overload, our subconscious sensory gatekeeper decides what information to pass along to our conscious awareness and what to toss out.

Dysfunction of our sensory gatekeeping has been shown to be critical in several psychiatric disorders. But how does it decide what to toss out and what does it pass along? The following seem to be likely perceptual filters:

It tosses out anything that it considers irrelevant.

It tosses out anything that might make us unnecessarily uncomfortable or afraid.

It tosses out anything that conflicts with our biases.

It passes along anything that confirms our biases.

Our perceptual filters not only impact what we see and hear but also our interpretation of what we see and hear. Do we see a witch or a vase in that silhouette? Do we hear a goat or a baby's cry? Our interpretation is deeply influenced by our state of mind and our biases.

The takeaway here is that our very perceptions are heavily filtered through the belief-colored glasses of our unconscious. It's like we only hear about the world through a sycophantic subordinate who only tells us what we want to hear.

And this does not even consider the many, many perceptual illusions that can exploit quirks of our pattern-recognition systems to create false pictures in our minds. Is it any wonder that eyewitnesses are so often completely certain and so often utterly wrong?

You have undoubtedly familiar with the word "blind spot." A blind spot is when you cannot see something even though it is right in front of your eyes. This concept derives from the physical phenomenon of the real blind spot we have on the retina of our eyes. The retina is the surface of the back of our eye that is covered with little light-detecting rods and cones. But in the location where the optic nerve connects, there are no rods or cones. This creates a physical blind spot in our vision, a zone that we literally cannot see. But if that is the case, why aren't we constantly aware of this?

One reason is that we have two eyes. Each one is able to cover the blind spot of the other. This doesn't tell the entire story, however, because if we close one eye, we still can't detect any blind spot without a lot of very careful observation.

What also happens is that our brains process our visual signals to fill in these blind spots. It "guesses" what is there based on the rest of the visual field. Clearly our brains are very good at video signal processing and manipulation.

In fact, our brains are so good that if you put on a special pair of mirrored goggles designed to flip your vision upside down, your brain will very quickly correct and flip it right side up. If you take off the goggles, you'll see everything upside down for a while until your brain adjusts.

Research is continually learning more about how extensively what we see, and presumably all that we sense and perceive, is processed by our brains. For example, recent studies have shown that our vision is highly "stabilized" by our brains. This can result in as much as a fifteen-second lag between actual updated of parts of the image that we believe we are seeing in real time. Our brains "fill in" much more than merely our blind spot. In fact, studies suggest that does not so much show us real-time imagery as it hobbles together a best-guess composite at any given time. It is shown to ignore, for example, gradual changes that don't trigger a "refresh."

My speculation about all this is that, given the pretty safe assumption that all brain functions are evolved variations of common underlying primitives, all of our senses and perceptions are not so much accurate, real-time perceptions as they are like pulling up short-term memories. We don't so much see and hear and taste as we normally think of it, but rather we recreate these perceptions in real time.

You can see this for yourself by looking up a video that demonstrates the McGurk effect. In these demonstrations, you see a person clearly repeating a word like ba, ba, ba. They then switch to an image of the same person repeating fa, fa, fa while keeping the ba, ba, ba as the audio. Despite knowing this, we cannot help but hear fa, fa, fa clearly and distinctly. Our brain doesn't hear sounds as much as it recreates the sound it believes it is hearing based on a broader pattern recognition and matching process.

The point of this is to highlight how marvelously powerful our brains are in modifying and even fabricating our perceptions in real time. However, that's also a frightening thought because it raises the question of how much can we then trust our senses. If our brains control what we perceive and our beliefs filter those perceptions, then our beliefs control our very perceptions.

Sometimes, perception may conflict with a person's beliefs about the nature of the world. For example, one might see street art that appears three dimensional, yet simultaneously know that no depth truly exists. It can be truly disconcerting to reconcile our perceptions with our understanding of reality.

More importantly, our beliefs effect not only our perceptions but our attitudes toward what we think we perceive.

Pattern Recognition

🖋 *You seem to be trying to reduce human beings to mere machines.*

Machines, maybe. Mere machines, definitely not.

Humans are far more than machines, but analogies to machine function can nevertheless provide insights. And anyway, don't sell machines short.

Computers can do amazing things. For a computer, it's a rather trivial matter to compute millions of tax statements and produce exact results. This is something that no single person could accomplish even if they dedicated their entire lifetime to the task.

On the other hand, there are things that the human mind can accomplish with ease, so easily that we are unaware of even doing anything, that are incredibly complex and difficult tasks for a computer.

Most of these things fall under the general category of pattern recognition. Pattern matching is all about spotting sometimes very sparse bits of a pattern and imagining a complete picture based on them. There is arguably no better instrument for recognizing patterns, abstract as well as real, than the human mind.

To be fair, however, computers are challenging humans even in this regard. Facial, speech, gait, and a myriad of other pattern-recognition algorithms are accomplishing astounding results.

A human can glance up into a tangled, shadowy jungle and immediately discern the presence of a tiger despite all the best efforts of that predator to camouflage, blend, sneak, and hide. In fact, most animals can spot patterns in shapes, forms, and movements, to identify entities that threaten or are crucial to their survival, based on only low-level processing of the smallest number of visual cues.

Animacy perception is a type of fast, automatic visual processing, that takes place at a very low level in our brains, and is present in infants only a few months old. It is tuned to recognize cues, like self-propelled motion, that identify something as alive. Infants already understand the concept of inert and animate objects—it has been shown that they are surprised when inanimate objects move on their own.

For animals, the ability to recognize patterns in complex environments was key to survival and reproduction; we evolved to be veritable pattern-recognition machines. Facial processing and animacy (or agency) perception are evolutionary traits that are advantageous in social interactions and in detecting threats. It allows us to quickly determine if that shadow in the trees is a potential mate or a deadly predator.

Natural selection, the survival of those with traits that improve their chances of survival, favored those with the ability to recognize patterns quickly (with low-level rather than high-level processing) and accurately (with specialized networks in specialized areas of the brain). On the whole, we humans, and much of how we think and behave, can be understood as pattern-recognition processes. These processes have severe limitations and weaknesses, however.

It is these very strengths and weaknesses of our pattern-recognition systems that causes us to be susceptible to belief. One problematic "feature" of our pattern-recognition system is our evolved tuning to favor false positives.

False Positives

We can produce patterns out of practically nothing. When we look at a handful of stars in the sky and see a man pulling a cart as he pours water from a vase, we are showing off our ability to imagine patterns based on incredibly sparse data. This perceptual acuity brings with it the problem of false positives.

> *A false positive is when we detect a pattern that does not exist. A false negative is when we fail to detect a pattern that does exist.*

We are so good at spotting patterns, especially when we expect to see them, or when we fear them, that we inevitably detect patterns even where none actually exist—patternicity (or apophenia) is the general tendency to find patterns and connections unrelated information. This tendency in visual perception is called pareidolia, and related types of patternicity, like over-attribution of agency and anthropomorphism (over-attribution of human traits) are common. When we see an angel in the clouds, a ghost on weather-worn barn siding, or Mother Mary in the mold on a peach, we are experiencing apophenia.

These perceptions quickly become reality to us, part of our actual experience. We don't recall seeing some mold that looked like Mother Mary, at some level we recall only seeing Mother Mary and that reinforces our belief that her actual existence is supported by our personal experience.

We see the patterns we believe we will see, and those perceptions reinforce our mistaken beliefs. If you are told that witches exist and that they look like little goats in the dark, you will quickly spot them and confirm that belief.

It's interesting that so many paranormal sightings are influenced by cultural differences. Years ago, we didn't see angels, we saw demons. What changed? Did demons stop visiting us because of some great influx of angels? Or perhaps did our cultural interest just change?

It's interesting that people of other cultures and other religions don't see angels. Apparently, angels only appear to believers.

What about UFO sightings? Why is it that aliens never seem to crash land in countries that have no popular culture of alien visits? Perhaps they are able to maneuver their disabled space vessels at the last moment to crash only into countries with people who believe in them.

Why is it that Hollywood always seems to be one step ahead of the next influx of alien tourists? Apparently, each new species of alien to arrive on Earth visits movie special effect artists first before they expose themselves to the public.

As we have pointed out, our brains are essentially pattern-recognition machines. Almost everything we do is a form of pattern recognition. And evolution has tuned our pattern-recognition neural networks to err strongly on the side of false positives. To maximize safety, a significant bias on the side of false positives was an evolutionary necessity. Over-attribution tendencies are a reflection of processing biases toward the least costly error.

Let's return to our tiger in the woods example. Imagine back when we were evolving as animals. There were real tigers in the forest that were a mortal threat to us. Therefore, our neural networks were trained to recognize even the vaguest hint of a tiger in the trees as a real tiger. It did not much matter if we imagined a hundred tigers that were only shadows or leaves blowing in the wind. What was critical was that we not miss even one real tiger, no matter how cleverly it concealed itself.

If we detected a tiger where there were only shadows, no great harm was done. But if we failed to detect a tiger where there was one, we were tiger chow.

The evolved tuning toward false positives also appears to be stronger when it comes to anything that might threaten us or distress us. Certainly, a fear of dying and a fear of the afterlife can threaten and distress us sufficiently enough to create unfounded perceptions.

❧ Everything I see proves what I am saying!
All the evidence is clear and all around us if you just look!

That's the problem exactly.

Cognitive scientists often discuss various forms of cognitive bias. Confirmation bias is just one well-known type of many. There are far too many to list here. Recognizing cognitive biases in all their forms is really important.

But learning about cognitive biases effectively focuses mainly on symptoms, not their underlying causes. In order to better overcome biases, we also need understand the mechanisms that give rise to them.

Confirmation bias impacts everything we do today. For example, a study was done of a popular and highly regarded British psychic. This stage performer does those shows where the psychic "reads" members of the audience. Afterward, audience members were interviewed and asked to estimate what percentage of her readings turned out to be correct.

Their estimates were very high, reporting perceived accuracy in the 80 percent and 90 percent ranges. A review of transcripts put the actual accuracy rate of the psychic guesses down in the 20 percent range.

This soft-wiring of our neural networks on the side of false positives not only underpins confirmation bias, but also many of our cognitive biases and has huge ramifications in our social and interpersonal interactions.

False positives almost certainly reinforce our unfair generalizations, stereotypes, and prejudices. We selectively recognize generalizations in everything. This not only exaggerates the number of incidents, but by excluding other types of incidents that conflict, it exaggerates the perception of the prevalence of that pattern.

If I am sensitive about my hair, I almost certainly detect far more perceived insults about my hair than are objectively real. I also tend to dismiss compliments, creating the impression that all I receive are insults.

This is true of any *ism that impacts us, whether it be sexism, racism, or any other form of bigotry or hostility. And let me be very clear. All these things do exist and do happen, but I'm making the observation that any given individual almost certainly detects many false positives that are not really incidents of it and overestimates the overall fraction of comments that are attacks.

This expands on our usual assessment that I am "sensitive" about something. Such prosaic sensitivity can be seen as another symptom of these underlying mechanics. Our understanding of the false positive bias of our neural networks helps us understand how and why this happens and make us better able to accept it in others and defend against it in ourselves.

This is important because our exaggerated perceptions based on false positives have huge repercussions for individuals and for society. They cause us to react negatively in situations where such a response is actually counter-productive. It also exaggerates our feelings of anger and hostility, which not only produce unfortunate behaviors and emotions, but those false positives reinforce our pattern-recognition brains to recognize even more extreme false positives. Our biased perceptions and our memories of those false perceptions serve to reinforce our biased neural network in a self-reinforcing feedback loop. Soon we see our *ism everywhere, we hear it in every comment, see it in every glance, and respond with depression and anger which make it still worse.

These same mechanisms play a critical role in our one-on-one interpersonal interactions as well. If our friend or spouse says something we find bothersome or offensive, we quickly become attuned to it and start to see it in every nuance of expression and hear it between the lines in every comment. This reinforces our neural network to become even more sensitized toward it, detecting even more false positives. We can soon get to the point where there is nothing you can say, or even not say, to the listener that is not further evidence to support their feelings. We can quickly become surrounded, even paralyzed by all the imagined tigers in the shadows.

False Corroboration

One show described how over 1900 people have filed sightings of a Loch Ness monster that scientists cannot explain. Something must be out there!

Back to those harmful pseudoscience "investigation" shows again. First, most of the images they present of Nessie, when not faked, are clearly things like flotsam and light reflections. Hardly unexplainable.

But more importantly, the shows suggest that those 1,900 reports are independent, corroborative reports. They are not. These are corrupted, polluted accounts by people reporting what they have been conditioned to look for by previous accounts and descriptions.

These reports should all be held suspect in the same way that, in any police investigation, eye-witness accounts are considered corrupted if they have already heard someone else's account of an incident. And, as we will discuss in the next chapter, even our memory of those incidents becomes corrupted.

Once we are attuned to a pattern, our pattern recognition systems make a lot of false positive identifications. Once someone points out a particular set of stars, we see a big dipper easily. Once someone publicly reports that a shriveled peach looks like Mother Mary, large numbers of people see her face clearly in the mold. Once Hollywood special effect artists create a flying saucer for a movie, huge numbers of people "corroborate" sightings of them in the real world.

My wife and I moved to Puget Sound. After someone pointed out a seal in the water, we started to see a huge number of seals. Most were dogs, logs, or ducks.

Over 1,900 people may have reported Loch Ness monster sightings, but these eyewitness accounts are not independent and they are not corroborative. These are a form of mass suggestion. These people are like us with our seal sightings, except they feel that their potential monster sighting is worth reporting. And all these reports serve as "evidence" for future paranormal investigation shows that cite this as a compelling and persuasive number of accounts.

Misty Watercolor Memories

🗣 *First you tell me I cannot trust my perceptions, next you'll tell me I can't even trust my own memories!*

Well, um, yeah.

Our perceptions are easy to fool, and our perceptions produce our memories, meaning that sometimes our memories are based on mistaken perceptions. That mistaken perception might morph many times in the recalling so that it eventually has little relation even to the original mistaken perception.

While it is disturbing that our own perceptions are so unreliable, it is even more disconcerting to appreciate how unreliable our memory is. Just as experiments that test our perceptions prove them to be incredibly unreliable, experiments that test our memory prove just how easily it can be fooled. It's relatively easy to plant false memories.

In one typical experiment, subjects are shown some pictures. Just prior, as part of their introduction, the researcher mentioned in passing some items that were not actually in the pictures. Subsequently the subjects report great confidence in having seen those suggested items in the actual pictures. It is disquietingly easy to implant clear and vivid memories through simple suggestion.

It turns out that memory isn't really like a videotape recording. We don't really store video or audio footage in our brain archives. Retrieving a memory is more like producing a docudrama. We have a rough memory of the script outline. From that we pull in stock footage from different memories and put it together to recreate that memory the way we imagine it must have occurred. We don't recall memories as much as we recreate them.

In the process of producing our docudrama memories, details are changed. All the stock footage isn't exact. Even more, no docudrama is free of bias. Each time we recall a memory, we apply our current knowledge, feelings, and biases to that new production.

To make memory even more unreliable, each time we recall that memory, we produce a newly revised mental docudrama, and that new docudrama refreshes our memory of the original. It is like a new docudrama based on the previous movie. With each one we drift further from the original memory. But each time we recall it, our certainty in our memory becomes stronger. Before very long, the memory of which we are absolutely certain could have drifted wildly away from the original.

Just by repeating something enough, we lose our ability to distinguish it from an actual memory. It is true that if we say something enough, if we hear it enough times, we start to integrate it into our memory. When that happens, it becomes something we are sure we know for a fact from personal experience.

I know that I have had that experience. There are some stories I have told that are composites of other stories. I have told these not to mislead, but just to combine elements into one easily relatable example. After some time, I have noticed that I have found it very difficult to recall whether that incident actually happened as I remembered it, or whether it was just a composite version I had created.

The idea that memories are so unreliable is extremely disquieting. After all, what are we but our memories? All the atoms in our bodies are replaced after a short time, but our memories are what give us any sense of continuity. If we cannot rely upon our memories, who are we?

On one occasion I was waiting for a date in front of a restaurant near my apartment in lower Manhattan, when Lucy Liu walked up and stood next to me. She was waiting for someone as well and we exchanged pleasantries.

Oh wait—that never actually happened.

In fact, once I impulsively related this story to a group of friends. As I did, I had a growing feeling of uneasiness as if something was wrong. Then one of my friends said, "Hey that's the story I told you!" It then hit me that I was remembering her experience. I was so mortified that I tried clumsily to cover up for my humiliation.

I had had the actual experience of waiting outside that same restaurant several times to meet dates. I had had actual experiences of encountering other celebrities in NYC. I was obviously familiar with Lucy Liu from television and movies. The presence of my friend who told me that story probably triggered a temporary conflation of all of these to produce a false memory.

This kind of thing happens all the time, but we are not usually made aware of it in such an embarrassing fashion. You see, we do not recall events like a tape recorder. Rather our memories are recreations that are never recreated exactly. They are full of errors and omissions and are colored by our biases, fears, hopes, and needs at the time we recreate them. Each time we recreate it, the memory becomes more entrenched. If my friend had not been present to point this out about Lucy Liu, I may well have further integrated her story even more vividly into my own memories.

As marvelous as our memories are, they are extremely unreliable. But that is difficult to accept. After all, our memories form the basis of who we are and all we think we know. To question our memories is to question our own competence, our own sanity, and even the very foundation of our self-identity.

Yet we must be skeptical of memories, particularly our own. Most of our memories are not as falsifiable as a misremembered encounter with Lucy Liu.

There is no one to call us out on most of the memories that form our experiences and define us as who we are. Most of our memory glitches aren't exposed on a witness stand or in a chance social gathering. We recall certain things about how our parents treated us but not other things. We recall a friend insulting us when it was actually a comment made on a television show. We clearly recall a pivotal experience in our life that was in fact only a recurring dream.

I noticed that when I gave lectures, I told an abbreviated story that was a composite of a number of other stories, just to illustrate a point. Before too long I could no longer recall the individual stories but only the abbreviated composite. Each time we retell a story, that replaces our old memories and our memories change and morph over time.

You can experiment on yourself. Just start telling some story about yourself—make it somewhat plausible. I guarantee that before too long you'll have trouble recalling that you made this up. Before much longer, and you'll become absolutely certain it is completely true. You remember it clearly after all, so it must be. That's how your neural network works. You cut, you bleed. You repeat experiences through stories or dreams or whatever, and they become memories. They become yourself.

> *Ever have a feeling of déjà vu? The sudden feeling that you have been in this very same situation before?*
>
> *I remember feeling it very strongly on a city bus. As I went to pay, the bus jerked forward, and I dropped a coin I was trying to drop in the basket. It rolled down the aisle and I had to crawl to retrieve it under people's legs.*
>
> *Suddenly it hit me so powerfully that I had done this exact thing before. It was such a strong recollection that it was disorienting.*
>
> *But what is more likely? That this was proof that we lived a previous life so recently that we still had city buses? Or that it was a minor mental glitch, an event that got stored away in my memory before I become completely conscious of it?*

Even more important than recalling events is the problem of remembering feelings. Our recollection of feelings is extremely malleable. We can quickly grow to hate a dear friend or partner largely because we retell stories over and over again that gradually deteriorate into a "powerful, unforgettable recollection" of how terribly we have been treated in the past. If we are disposed to think badly of someone, all our memories will be colored by that lens. Perhaps, a good indicator of the person we are now is the tone we impart upon the docudramas we recreate to recall events and how those events made us feel.

In fact, studies have suggested that having an amazing memory actually makes you less happy. People with exceptional memories tend to never let go of any slight or insult. They only get angrier and more unhappy as time goes on. I submit that their memories are not actually that great and that they likely tend to create a more unforgivably offensive version of their memory each time they recreate it.

In the 1968 cult film Barbarella, she asks the angel Paigar why he would save the evil queen after she had tortured him so cruelly. Paigar tells Barbarella:

"An angel has no memory."

While people with poor memories tend to be happier and more positive, they also tend to be poorer at socializing, networking, and maintaining long-term relationships.

In fact, neuroscience is increasingly providing evidence that forgetting isn't a failure of memory. It is an essential feature of memory. We have evolved nanomachines that work to disassemble our memories to help us to remain sane and mentally healthy.

In any case, Lucy Liu always reminds me that a little humility when it comes to the fallibility of our own memories is a good thing.

Booze in the Punch Bowl

🗣 *Given that facts, perceptions, and memories are so untrustworthy, thank heaven I have my beliefs to anchor me!*

Beliefs only make it worse.

We've discussed how susceptible our neural networks are to bogus facts and our amazing ability to rationalize away any inconsistencies.

We've discussed how incredibly unreliable our perceptions are, and how extensively our subconscious prefilter and even fabricates them. We really do just see what our unconscious wants us to see.

We've discussed our memories, how these can be so easily fooled, and how they morph over time in accordance with our biases. Each time we recall something, we are playing the telephone game inside our brains.

If all that isn't bad enough, it gets dramatically worse when we add belief to the mix.

In experiments where the researcher shows a subject quickly flashing images on a computer screen, the subject tends to preferentially perceive and remember images that reinforce their beliefs.

As they affect our cognition, beliefs are essentially a very powerful bias. And these biases tune how our subconscious filters what we see or do not see, hear or not hear, and how we remember it. We all wear blinders of our beliefs.

Those belief-filtered perceptions and memories feed back to further validate our beliefs. They make us certain that "everything we see and hear" confirms our beliefs.

Each time we recall our filtered memories, they get recreated to conform to our beliefs even more strongly. These belief-modified memories further reinforce our perception of the validity of our beliefs. Each iteration of these thought patterns further strengthens those neural network associations in our brains.

What we end up with is a great feedback loop that provides the evidence to support and strengthen our biases and to give us confidence that those biases are based on solid perceptions and experiences.

Is it any surprise that people can become absolutely certain of even the most irrational beliefs? That they can become convinced that every bit of objective evidence proves that their irrational belief is undeniably confirmed by evidence and logic?

What are beliefs but a form of bias, an assumption of sorts, by which we color all our perceptions, and memories, and neural network weightings that all prove that our beliefs are fact-based and self-evident, that they are proven by everything we see and recall?

Many of the challenges to objective thinking that we have discussed are innate. We cannot directly control perception or memory or our neural network training.

But we can take belief out of that intoxicating cocktail.

Studies Show That...

🎙 *Regardless of the problems, scientific studies have shown conclusively that religion and faith offer demonstrated benefits.*

We have acknowledged that beliefs may bring some benefits, but we disputed the notion that beliefs are necessary to achieving those benefits.

For example, it seems clear that church attendance is associated with a significantly lower suicide rate. The association is so strong that it is probably safe to assume causation. This correlation has been reaffirmed by over a hundred scientific studies in the literature.

Since these studies have adjusted for the demographic selection of churchgoers as well as the effect of social interaction, it appears that the most likely reason for this reduced suicide rate is the belief that suicide is a sin, perhaps punishable by eternal damnation.

If one is primarily and exclusively concerned with preventing suicide, then convincing people that they will be eternally damned if they do it is probably an effective approach.

However, this prescription only narrowly prioritizes suicide over all other concerns. It does not consider the negative effects of attending church regularly or of adopting clearly nonsensical beliefs.

Nor does this consider whether there are other, better ways to reduce suicide. It does not even consider whether fact-based approaches, even if they don't reduce suicide rates quite as effectively, are still not healthier overall.

And while suicide prevention is one benefit of religious belief, and while there are others, there are far more claims made about the benefits of religion and faith that are far less credible.

Studies supposedly show benefits of religion and faith that include better performance in school, lower divorce and crime rates, less racial prejudice, higher charitable giving, and even greater general happiness.

Reporters, advocates, and opinion writers are quick to promote any such studies because they get lots of clicks. There is no shortage of articles or op-eds touting the supposedly scientifically proven benefits of religion and faith.

But we do need to be smart consumers of these studies. Not all are sound science. Many of these are very questionable studies designed by advocates to find validation of their beliefs. Others are decent enough studies that are misrepresented and overextended by advocates to persuade.

Following are just a few of the ways that studies, or the reporting of those studies, can be compromised.

Researcher Bias

This is a very real problem that even the most unbiased of researchers have to wrestle with in each and every study they design and analyze. It's all too easy for any researcher, in thinking they know what the answer must be, to minimize contradictory results and emphasize confirmatory ones.

In the case of passionately religious researchers, it is particularly difficult to trust that their very strong bias does not bias their assumptions and conclusions.

Researcher Fraud

There are some cases in which the researcher quite intentionally commits scientific malpractice.

In the case of studies of religion, with immortal souls hanging in the balance, the motivation to commit fraud for the greater good is presumably at least sometimes too strong to resist.

In the case of religiously motivated anti-abortion research, for example, examples of outright fraudulent research have been conclusively exposed.

Suggesting Causation

Most clinical studies are observational, or association studies. That is, they simply show that two variables are both observed in or associated with a given population. This is valuable information. But proving that those two variables are directly related to each other is quite difficult. Proving causality between one and the other is even more difficult. Even if two things seem to be related, they may be indirectly associated through some third thing called a confounding factor.

For example, a study may show that churchgoers give more to charity. That is merely an association. But advocates use that observed association to suggest that church attendance promotes ethical behavior even though the researchers themselves never made that more general claim.

However, it may well be that church attendance and charitable giving are not directly related at all, let alone that church attendance promotes charitable giving in the way advocates suggest. The most we could say based on the research is that, for whatever reason, people who go to church are also more likely give to charity.

Maybe the reality is that older and wealthier people tend to go to church. Age and earning may be only two of many confounding factors.

Failing to Mention the Negatives

Often in promoting or reporting study results, the benefits are touted without mentioning the negatives. Advocates often tout selected admirable ethical qualities of religious people but fail to mention other studies that show, for example, that religious people are far more likely to support torture, guns, violence, and drone attacks. To be fair, opponents of religion often do the same thing in reverse.

Failing to Mention Better Alternatives

Another way advocates misuse studies is by failing to mention better alternatives. For example, religious advocates often tout the morality of religious people, implying that religion is the only way to achieve these values. But you don't need religion along with all its negative characteristics to be an ethical person.

Failing to Quantify the Benefits

Advocates will often claim a benefit without quantifying it, thereby giving a false impression of how important it is.

Misrepresenting Statistics

Advocates often misrepresent statistics. If they are trying to magnify a small difference, they report it as a percentage or ratio. If they are trying to exaggerate a tiny difference in a huge population, they cite the numerical difference.

Revising Analyses

One big thing that statisticians advise most strongly against, yet are asked to do all the time, is to revise their statistical analysis. The problem with this is bias. Researchers normally only think to revise the analysis if the results don't agree with what they expect and are likely to disregard a new analysis as "bad" if it doesn't provide better expected results.

Using Bad Indicators

In epidemiology, a surrogate marker, or indicator, is a specific metric that can be used to measure a more general condition. But a bad indicator tells one little or nothing about the general trait being evaluated.

Religious advocates often claim that believers are "happier" based upon highly questionable indicators such as divorce rate, which have little to do with happiness. As we all know, married people can be far more miserable than unmarried or divorced ones.

Choosing the Wrong Measurement

Even if we could measure happiness, it should not be assumed that happiness is the best or only goal. Believing that global warming is a hoax probably does make one sleep sounder. Allowing your kids to eat pizza at every meal will probably result in fewer observed food-related tantrums. But clearly these measures of happiness do not justify accepting those positions.

Too Much Confidence in Self-Reporting

Many of the narrow social studies used to make sweeping claims rely upon self-reporting, which is incredibly unreliable. People intentionally or unintentionally report all kinds of things in all kinds of ways for all kinds of reasons. For example, men are likely to brag about their infidelity while women are likely to conceal it. Self-reports are poor measures of the relative level of infidelity between the sexes.

Similarly, religious people are deeply invested in the belief that religion makes them happier and are very likely to report that they are happy even if they are totally miserable.

Non-Representative Populations

Selecting a representative population for any prospective study is probably the most common and difficult challenge in designing a study. You need to obtain a sampling of people that truly represents the population you intend to characterize.

In the case of studies that show the benefits of religion, we might see this, for example, when the researchers poll people who attend church and then suggest that this study reflects all religious people. People who attend church may swear less, but religious people overall may cuss even more than the general population.

Publication Bias

Finally, there is also a bias built into what studies get published and what articles get reported. Many publication vehicles are managed by advocates who only want studies that promote their message. Unsurprisingly we see lots of supportive articles published and few that run counter. There is even publication bias in objective media, which favors studies that generate clicks.

Researchers themselves are not immune to these forces. They want their work to be published, and it can be difficult to avoid massaging the message a bit to please your funders and your publishers.

Please, please, please don't conclude from this that you can never trust social science and that these studies never have any value at all.

Association studies are very valuable. We need to know when things are observed together in a given population. Heck, it was association studies that first linked smoking to lung cancer, far before causation could be conclusively demonstrated. Yet in retrospect it would have been wonderful if far more people had acted on the assumption that association was causation in that case. However, you should be a smart consumer of these studies and understand the ways that advocates misuse study results to contrive claims that advance their cause.

This is particularly important when we are predisposed to believe those claims and even more important when the people making and reporting those claims have strong religious or other biases.

When in doubt, look past the claims made by advocates or even by seemingly objective science reporters and read the typically more careful and restrained conclusions reported by the scientists who conducted the studies. With the internet at our fingertips, that is not usually very difficult to do.

Trust Science

🗣 *What I hear you saying is that we can never trust science.*

If that is the message you heard, I have failed in my mission.

This book is about facts and their importance in healthy decision-making. To ensure that the facts we rely upon for those decisions are the best possible, we need to be able to assess and compare the validity of the facts used to support the various arguments that advocate for competing decisions.

We discussed the importance of evidence cited to support those facts and went on to review some of the many ways that evidence can be misleading or incorrect. That doesn't mean we can or should ignore all evidence.

> *We have to rely on evidence, and we simply must get better at separating the good from the bad.*

We also discussed statistics and their essential role in describing and validating facts. There are a lot of ways that statistics can be misleading, but that doesn't mean we have the luxury of abandoning statistics.

> *Our only path to healthier decision-making is to become better consumers of statistics, recognizing misleading statistics when we see them.*

We even touched upon logic and the importance of recognizing specious logic when we hear it so that we can base our important decisions upon sound logic. We will dig into this even more later.

> *Despite all of the bogus logic that abounds, we again have no choice but to become better consumers of logic if we are to make better decisions.*

And finally, we discussed scientific studies and some of the ways that bias, poor scientific methods, or misrepresentations can reduce the reliability of information reported by some studies. But we have no choice but to rely upon studies to provide us with the factual evidence we require to make sound fact-based decisions.

We cannot allow those who misuse or abuse or are just bad at science to force us to throw up our hands in frustration and give up on scientific studies. To do so would be to abandon our strongest and best tool to find truth.

As complicated as it may seem, we must become better consumers of scientific studies and help to ensure that we demand the best possible information from researchers, funders, reporting media, and yes, even advocates.

Free Speech

I don't support spreading nonsense, but I do support people's right to do so!

I agree, up to a point.

I would be remiss to close this chapter without touching upon the role our First Amendment plays in confusing facts.

Freedom of speech is of course an important cornerstone of the democratic liberties we cherish. Some argue that any infringement of that right, anything beyond the proverbial fire in a crowded theater scenario, is too much.

But there is an optimum amount of everything, and it may be that our nearly absolute position is too extreme. In recent years, under the ceaseless assault of lies from the Trump administration and Fox News to name just two, it is becoming evident that we may be too extreme for our own good in our toleration of destructive lies in the public sphere.

It is not merely that particular facts are called into question. It's not simply a matter of head counts at an inauguration or whether Trump truly is "a very stable genius." It is about lies that cost lives by diminishing our faith in vaccines. It's about lies that undermine our free and fair elections. It's about lies that deny the existential threat of global climate change.

Even more insidiously, all of the routine, smaller lies and misrepresentations, as well as the systematic dismantling of reason itself, undermine the capacity of each one of us to judge facts fairly. I submit that we should not tolerate public officials and influential media personalities lying at will without repercussions.

Unfortunately, the media influencers, those people who make a living by speaking in the public sphere, almost invariably advocate for an extreme all-or-nothing view of free speech. Because they fear being held to account for something they might say, they argue that we must never ever curtail any "free speech" else we lose it.

But such an extremist position is a false choice. All rights must have reasonable limits. Who is to decide what is allowed? We all do. Just as we do with all societal norms. It is really not a hard choice on the extremes.

People like Donald Trump or Tucker Carlson would simply not be allowed to outright lie as they do in other free nations such as Canada. And certainly no one feels that freedom of speech is unduly repressed in Canada. They have managed not to fall down some imagined slippery slope into a propagandist state.

And neither would we. Open-mindedness and personal liberty do not require us to protect and perpetuate self-destructive nonsense in our public sphere.

Our American extremism with regards to free speech arguably enables and exacerbates our national pandemic of delusion.

Information Technology

Isn't it up to the media to present truthful and accurate information?

One would think so, even hope so, but that isn't going to happen anytime soon.

In fact, it is modern information technology and the monetization of echo chambers that has largely triggered and enabled our current pandemic of delusion. An echo chamber is an information silo in which beliefs are amplified and reinforced by continued repetition in a closed system that is insulated from rebuttal evidence.

It all sort of started when President Reagan eliminated the requirement that broadcasters provide news as a public service. By making news a for-profit venture, he opened the floodgates to the deluge of siloed news that we see today, much of it serving the bottom line rather than the public interest.

Then the internet and the appearance of "news" sources like Fox, Facebook, and Twitter dramatically increased the quantity of information while almost completely abandoning any regard for the quality of that information. Those sources are not vetted for accuracy and offer only the illusion of a legitimate discourse or peer review.

These dramatic changes in how we receive news, the huge quantity and uncertain quality of it, have become the vectors that spread and disseminate delusional beliefs around the world at broadband speeds.

For the coronavirus to spread across the globe requires natural mutations and air travel. For fake news and delusional beliefs to infect the planet, all that's required is a Wi-Fi connection.

Modern technology has succeeded in exposing us to vastly more information, much of it fake, than ever before. Unfortunately, every time our neural networks are exposed to fake information, it becomes less fake to us.

One can think of click algorithms as one more way, along with marketing and brainwashing and the rest, that our neural networks are gradually modified. Essentially, these algorithms say, "if you believe that, then check this out!"

Like our own brains, the current algorithms used by information sources like Facebook are agnostic to the truth or factuality of information. The algorithms don't care whether they are feeding us real information or fake news. That responsibility is totally passed along to the consumer.

These algorithms could do better than our own brains. They could attach an objective "trustworthiness quotient" to their content and they could gradually move people to more fact-based content. By incorporating a positive drift toward more factual information, they could gradually reprogram our brains to become more fact-based, rather than more gullible.

We can't just hope and wait for that to happen though. We can demand better news, we can exert economic pressure with our remote controls, we can cancel our Facebook account, because as part of the solution, it is each of us who must become a savvier consumer of information.

One way to do that is to appreciate the extent to which news algorithms may be influencing your perception of the facts. If you look into, say, "proof of Bigfoot," purely because you are skeptical, you will find some supportive articles and posts. The search engines will then feed you ever more supportive articles and posts, until finally you are convinced, based on all your objective extensive research and investigation that Bigfoot must be living among us. There is just so much information about it out there!

To try to avoid being nudged by this algorithm toward a false reality, make it a practice to explicitly search for the reverse. In this case, search for "debunking Bigfoot claims" and do that enough for the search engines to learn that you will quickly and reliably click on more of it. In that way, you might at least get exposed to the counterfactual position. Both may of course be nonsense, but at least you will not be left with an exaggerated perception of one side of it.

Lastly, appreciate that like-minded people gravitate to like-minded social environments. People self-segregate. Some socialize in the church basement, some hangout in a biker bar, and some meet in the library.

Likewise, different folks hang out in different social networking platforms. Choose yours carefully. Right now, Facebook and Twitter are notoriously bad places to feed your brain. They present a buffet all the junk food you can devour.

On the other hand, right now at least, more fact-based people tend to hang out on Reddit. This is amazing since at one low point Reddit almost became synonymous with toxic social media content. The company made an effort to purge that content, and more importantly, their community made a huge effort to self-police content, demanding citations and evidence of claims made there. That said, you still have to be cautious. There are less-traveled Reddit communities that are echo chambers of misinformation.

In the end, these various social communities are non-homogenous and quickly changing. What may be the best source for information on a given topic today may become a breeding ground of misinformation tomorrow. We all need to continuously assess whether our information sources are reliable.

Age and Experience

It's best to pay attention to people with the age and experience to offer sound perspectives and advice.

Age and experience can be valuable teachers. But there is no guarantee that one's experience has been good experience or that their age has resulted in sounder thinking.

I used to hire a lot of programmers. I'd look for talent first, then experience, then training, in that order of preference. When it came to experience, there were some candidates who had a lot of it, but their experience was almost completely doing things the wrong way and applying bad practices. Often it was the older ones who refused to abandon that "experience" and continued to apply old, obsolete tools and approaches to tasks far better served by newer methods.

Remember that our brains don't naturally just keep getting smarter. Their thinking mostly keeps becoming more engrained, more difficult to change. If that thinking was sound and scientific, their thinking may indeed keep getting more sound. But if their trajectory was to become more belief-based in their thinking, age can only likely bring even less sound and even delusional thinking.

So no, old folks are not inherently wiser. In fact, the bigger risk is that they become increasingly entrenched and intransigent after a long life steeped in beliefs and falsehoods.

I'm definitely not saying that age and experience cannot be immensely valuable. But we must appreciate that, like most other sources of information, there is no inherent reason that it is likely to be so.

We should view age and experience with the same level of skepticism we apply to other sources of information. Is it a sound, fact-based source, or a source that has been tainted by a long history of misinformation?

CHAPTER 4: DELUSION

As we have seen, distinguishing between facts and beliefs is fraught with pitfalls. Our ability to make good judgments is affected not only by planned confusion, but by our own compromised perceptions, memories, and judgment patterns.

Bad studies that attempt to claim the mantle of scientific credibility make the challenge even tougher.

Given all of that confusion, it is not surprising that beliefs sometimes slip into delusion. Beliefs at least are by definition subject to change. When beliefs become impervious to change, regardless of the amount of evidence to the contrary, they become delusions.

Yet regardless of how delusional they may actually be, it is extremely problematic to call out beliefs as delusions. There are many reasons for this, and in this chapter, we examine some of these delusional beliefs as well as the factors that make them so difficult to treat as such.

About Delusion

Wait a second! Are you claiming that anyone with a deep,
heartfelt belief is delusional?

I'm saying that people can hold on to delusions without crossing a line beyond which they would be diagnosed as "delusional."

Before the psychologists among you get all up in arms that I'm diagnosing my fellow human beings, let me assure you that I use the word "delusional" purely in a lay sense, not as any kind of clinical diagnosis.

Just because the word has particular meaning in clinical settings, that does not mean we are not allowed to use it in a more general sense. We don't need a judge to certify certain acts as criminal and we don't need a priest to proclaim certain behaviors as evil. We are perfectly free to apply those characterizations on our own.

For a fair and impartial definition of "delusion," we can start with the current Wikipedia entry, which defines it as follows:

> *"A delusion is a belief held with strong conviction despite superior evidence to the contrary. As a pathology, it is distinct from a belief based on false or incomplete information, confabulation, dogma, illusion, or other effects of perception."*

That definition establishes a very clear distinction between belief and delusion, one which is easily recognizable at least at the extremes. A belief is simply an unsupported conclusion based on insufficient information. A delusion is a belief that persists regardless of any amount of evidence to the contrary.

Or, simply put, a delusion is a particularly stubborn belief. Merely holding on to a delusion does not make one, practically or legally speaking, delusional.

Sophisticated Rationalizations

You may scoff at my belief, but my friend believes it too and he is really smart.

Really smart people can create really elaborate rationalizations.

The human mind is phenomenally good at rationalizing even our wildest beliefs to make them seem perfectly rational and logical to us. Therefore, the fact that something seems rational or can be rationalized should never be a test of validity.

This is even more true with ideas formulated by extremely smart and clever people. Smart people can create very complicated belief systems. These convoluted Rube Goldberg rationalizations can be very alluring.

I have a friend we'll call Pete who is a highly intelligent Ph.D. physicist. He also has a strong belief that God exists. Like all of us, he has an intrinsic need to rationalize his belief, to convince himself that his belief is not inconsistent with his self-image as a highly intelligent and rational scientist.

Pete is smart enough to realize that all of the typical arguments that people put forward to rationalize their belief are factually disproven or logically flawed. Therefore, he has created a more sophisticated rationale.

Pete essentially believes that the fact that we have morals proves that there is a God. His logic is a bit difficult to even repeat, but the abbreviated version begins with the assertion that we live in a predetermined universe, so therefore we have no free will, so therefore morals could only come from God, so therefore the existence of God is proven by inescapable logic grounded in fact.

Actually however, physics does not mandate a predetermined universe. As Stephen Hawking pointed out:

> *"I have noticed that even people who claim everything is predestined, and that we can do nothing to change it, look before they cross the road."*

Moreover, predeterminism in no way precludes morals, and if it did there is no basis to conclude that morals could only come from God. But look, if this sounds like metaphysical gobbledygook that's because it is metaphysical gobbledygook. But it is the kind of argument that an intelligent person will produce to rationalize their desire to believe in nonsense while still believing that they are perfectly rational and even quite clever.

Unfortunately, sophisticated arguments like his are very influential because their complexity creates a heightened illusion of credibility. If the rationale is complicated, then many people find it more credible. If it is so complicated as to be incomprehensible, a lot of people assume it must be genius.

But if we're being totally honest, it is not genius. It is really a bit delusional, is it not?

Everyone Else Is Crazy

🗣 *I agree that all those other religions are crazy. They didn't come to their faith through a careful analytical study of the Bible like I did!*

We can easily see delusion in others while remaining completely blind to the same delusions without ourselves.

Once I was chatting with a good friend with whom I never failed to have stimulating and interesting conversations. He is devoutly religious. He dedicates an enormous amount of time to Bible study and holds the belief that one can only come to know God through a direct and objective study of his written word, unfiltered by the interpretations of priests and ministers. We were having a frank discussion about faith, and I decided to run a question past him. Here's essentially what I asked:

> *"You know it seems to me that in the days of ancient Rome and Athens, people were every bit as smart as we are. They just didn't have all the facts we do. They didn't understand what the sun was, so they created myths of Apollo to explain it. Likewise, creating myths to fill in other gaps in their knowledge gave them a sense of understanding and security.*
>
> *Today we might not need gods to explain the sun or the stars anymore, but we are still frightened by the essential unknowns of the human condition. How did we get here, why are we here, what will happen to us? We still create myths to give us comfort, to give us the illusion of knowledge regarding those basic insecurities.*
>
> *We laugh at them for their silly gods, but don't we hold the same kind of beliefs for the very same kind of reasons?"*

To my momentary surprise, my friend's face lit up with total agreement:

> *"Yes, I agree completely. All the other religions today are just making up answers to explain things they don't understand. The only way to truly come to know God is by studying the Bible."*

This is illustrative of the amazing capacity of humans, particularly very smart humans, to rationalize their own beliefs. It reflects an almost infinite capacity to recognize the truth in others but fail completely to recognize it in ourselves.

We cannot often recognize the flaws in our own belief-based thinking and the rationalizations that convince us they are rational, even though we can easily see these flaws in others.

This is not surprising, since the rationalizations we create are based upon ideas we already accept and are the standard by which we judge their validity.

Belief and Insanity

🗣 *Are you really making the case that all belief-based thinking is crazy? That anyone who has strong beliefs is delusional?*

Well, yes and no.

Looking at it from a purely clinical perspective, what is the definition of insanity? If someone believes in things for which there is no evidence, or denies facts that contradict their beliefs, isn't that the most fundamental definition of delusional insanity?

I'll answer that rhetorical question—yes, it is.

A paranoid schizophrenic might believe that they really do hear voices. They would certainly deny any fact or reasoning that contradicts their conviction that someone is poisoning their food.

How is this fundamentally different from someone else's acceptable belief-based thinking?

Is it purely a question of numbers? If sufficient numbers of people share a mass delusion, then does that make it sane? Does that make their common delusion real?

Or is it more about how we view sanity and insanity?

We incorrectly think of sanity as a binary attribute. Either you are sane or insane. You are normal or you are crazy.

It's far more useful to think of insanity as a societal threshold limit on a spectrum of sanity. If you have a few irrational ideas, you are eccentric. If you have enough irrational ideas to exceed some threshold, then you are classified as insane.

But in reality, no one is completely sane or insane. Even the most clinically delusional people have moments of lucidity or have some behaviors that are perfectly normal. Conversely, even the sanest of us have our quirks, idiosyncrasies, and habits that are pretty crazy.

We can be perfectly normal in most situations but act irrationally in others. The ways that otherwise normal people do insane things, have insane ideas, are almost limitless.

We are all sane only part of the time. When an otherwise sane person reports seeing an angel or ghost, we give that eyewitness testimony very high credibility.

I would never have believed such a crazy story if it had not come from such a sane and rational person!

However, can it not be that a sane person is merely someone who has the same hallucinations as a schizophrenic, only far less frequently and less prolonged? Isn't the notion that we all have that possibility of an occasional mental glitch far more likely than the conclusion that angels and ghosts must actually exist?

Holding to a belief in the face of facts to the contrary, or in spite of a complete lack of any supporting facts meets the most basic definition of insanity. Does that mean that anyone who has beliefs is insane?

Doing wild things doesn't make you a wild person. Doing stupid things doesn't make you a stupid person. If so, one would have to conclude that all smokers are stupid people. Clearly, they are not.

Similarly, holding beliefs may be insane, but people who hold beliefs haven't necessarily crossed the societal threshold into insanity.

The Heaven's Gate cult member who believes that aliens hiding behind the Hale-Bopp comet are going to beam their souls aboard their spaceship after they commit suicide may have exceeded that threshold. Bible literalists who insist that the Earth is 6,000 years old have not. However, their beliefs are fundamentally no less insane. In another culture, the societal pronouncement of sanity might be reversed.

The knowledge that none of us is always sane or insane, and seldom completely sane or insane, helps us to understand our capacity for belief. It helps us to understand how even delusional belief can coexist with reason. It cautions us that our appraisal of the reasonableness of our own beliefs or those of others should not be colored by their sanity or their intelligence in other areas of their life.

Giant Windmills

Nothing wrong with a little delusion. Some of our greatest figures from history were great only because they were a little delusional.

Don Quixote gives us a cautionary tale of what havoc little delusion can create. Don Quixote was the titular character in a 1605 masterpiece written by author and playwright Miguel de Cervantes who lived in Spain during the turn of the seventeenth century. It tells the story of a country gentleman named Alonso Quijano who despairs of the world and comes to imagine himself to be a valorous knight named Don Quixote. Off he goes into the world like a missionary on a holy quest. Even though those around him see that his delusion is insane, they humor him out of respect.

Isn't this what we do today when we hold "respect" for others' beliefs as an almost unbreakable societal etiquette? What harm can it do? He is only doing good deeds, the family priest counsels. Isn't this the rationale that is almost universally expressed to advocate tolerance of belief-based thinking in our day?

But it turns out that his crazy antics aren't harmless. The very nature of his insanity is to reach out and impact those around him. Family and country folk must humor his delusions, pick up after the damage he causes, and are emotionally touched by his situation. Some, like Sancho Panza, are even drawn in to share in his fantasy.

In the end, Cervantes wrote a book that is both critical of and compassionate toward delusion and insanity. It proclaims that it is the noblest of causes to "dream the impossible dream," yet at the same time it mocks the belief-based thinking of his time as an insane delusion.

Don Quixote is a tragedy. Alonso Quijano is a noble character who only wants to do good deeds. However, he fails to find ways to do that in the real world, so the gives himself over to a fantasy world in which he can imagine he has succeeded. In the process, he creates havoc.

Cloud Angels

🗣 *Sure, you have to go back to 1600 to cite examples. People back in the days of Cervantes were not as sophisticated as we are today.*

I submit that we have not gotten appreciably wiser or less gullible than the people who lived and worked in Babylon in nineteenth century BCE.

A recent article in *People* magazine was entitled "Texas Driver Spots 'Spectacular' Cloud Shaped Like an Angel: 'How Awesome Is That?'"

Of course, people think cloud resemblances are fun. I do too.

But what is troubling is that the person who took the photo suggested that God had created the cloud formation specifically to lift his spirits. It was God speaking to him personally.

The reality is that at any given moment of any day from any point anywhere on Earth, there are clouds that we could imagine bear some resemblance to something other than a billowy mass of condensed water vapor floating in the atmosphere.

Some of these clouds might resemble heads, or alligators, or elephants, or pretty much anything really. The limit is our imagination.

It is fun, but not particularly newsworthy, to take note of the wacky shapes that clouds happen upon. That is, unless the image is religious, and in that case, it is apparently quite newsworthy.

The truth is that of all the clouds, or pieces of toast, or rotten peaches, or paint stains, that look like something, we don't get really excited about these random resemblances unless they resemble an angel, or Jesus, or Mother Mary, or some vague saint. All this random stuff is just random—unless it has a religious connotation. In that case, those random stains are inspiring, proof of God's hand in the world, miraculous, and fascinatingly newsworthy.

This all speaks to our powerful mental ability to detect false positives that conform to our particular confirmation biases.

Moreover, it also speaks to our intense desire and interest in any confirmation of our religious biases in particular. And I can see how a cloud pattern, or some lichen on a rock, can create powerful imagery. I had one such experience:

> I was on the beach in Costa Rica watching baby tortoises dauntlessly plunge into the ocean only to be thrown back onto the sand over and over again by the uncaring waves. It was late afternoon and I glanced up, only to stare in wonder at the sky. Directly in front of me were the very gates of heaven. A glowing pathway led up from just in front of me to a shimmering cloud platform. Upon it stood two gleaming pearly gates, connected by a vibrant golden archway, highlighted by dramatic halos of light. Within the great arch, in the distance, was a glowing point of light so divine that it could only have been the glow of God almighty.

The sight was so photo-realistically detailed and delineated with vibrant color and perfect proportions that it made the Texas cloud angel look like a child's watercolor splotch. I gaped in wonder for a moment before I thought to reach for my camera. But by the time I fumbled to work it, the lines had begun to blur, the light to diminish, and the effect to become far more abstract. That singular moment was past. Within seconds, the majestic gates of heaven that had revealed itself before me were once again just one more set of abstract cloud shapes.

Given that experience, I can understand how primitive people might be so inspired as to believe they had actually glimpsed a heavenly place revealed to them in the sky. I can understand how they might have taken this as proof of heaven and written about it.

Perhaps thousands of years ago someone glimpsed a sight very similar to my own and created our modern imagery of heaven based upon that one powerful awe-inspiring moment.

I can understand that. But what I cannot understand and cannot excuse is any modern person today believing that some vaguely angel-shaped cloud is particularly inspiring or reassuring, let alone believed to be a message from God.

And I find it doubly disappointing that a news outlet, even one that is merely reporting human-interest stories, would preferentially pick out this kind of "sighting" to report, thereby depositing yet another straw of religious delusion on the already straining back of reason and rationality of our culture.

Aliens

🗣️ *I don't believe in angels, but people who dismiss alien encounters
are either intentionally suppressing evidence or unaware of all the
evidence that exists.*

Let's address the topic of aliens then.

Scientific searches for evidence of extraterrestrial life are legitimate and important. But that does not legitimize a belief in alien encounters. Here is why I make that conclusion.

As we pointed out earlier, it is a probabilistic fact that extraterrestrial life exists. We know this because when we consider the number of galaxies, stars, and planets in our universe, there must be billions of planets capable of life. Even if only a fraction of those produces sentient life, there are still a huge number. It is simply a numbers game. Carl Sagan once commented "If we are the only beings to exist in the universe, it would be a terrible waste of space."

Further, since the same elements, the same building blocks of life, the same rules of chemistry and physics apply everywhere throughout the universe, the same sequence of reactions that produced us also occur elsewhere. Their fundamental biology, if not their physical form, would likely be quite familiar and easy for us to understand.

But even though there is a probabilistic certainty that cousins are out there, what is the likelihood that we could ever find them? That we might detect even as much as their electromagnetic footprints in space?

It is my opinion that the probability that we might detect signals from them is immensely slim. The likelihood that some message in a bottle might make it from one desert island to another is far greater than the chances of us noticing each other's signs and signals in space. And what are the chances that we could communicate?

Even in the astronomically unlikely event that we should pick up signals from another civilization, those signals would have been sent ages ago. The species that sent them would most likely be long extinct before those signals finally reached us. It would take an equal number of ages for any response from us to get back to them.

So, could they possibly visit us or we visit them?

Any transportation we could create to carry us into space would be fantastically slower than radio signals. Even allowing for the fastest travel permitted by physics, the idea that we could visit each other in any practical timeframe is not remotely possible. Barring direct evidence, the idea that aliens have or are visiting us has no legitimate basis for belief.

🔰 *But isn't that horse-and-buggy thinking? Science always finds a way to do things that no one could imagine earlier. Maybe alien scientists have technologies we do not.*

Barring any science fantasy wormhole generators, that is not going to happen. To claim that science will find a way to take us to other galaxies is analogous to claiming that science will one day find a way to allow us to walk on the surface of a neutron. It simply ignores physical limitations.

A blind faith that science can do anything is dangerous. It leads to a false belief in science that makes people rationalize reckless behavior and implausible explanations. After all, why bother to solve global warming? Surely science will find a way to save us from ourselves before the end!

But despite the vanishingly remote possibility of detecting signs of extraterrestrial life, the search continues. And that search is worth doing despite the odds of success. If we get really lucky, if we find evidence that extraterrestrial life once existed elsewhere, that discovery alone would transform human civilization. It would irreversibly change our fundamental perception of our place in the universe.

Could I be wrong on this? Might we host alien emissaries one day? I hope so!

But keep in mind that my assertion that it is impossible for aliens to visit us is the position supported by facts, the lack of facts, and by the more plausible logic. It is therefore not my responsibility to prove or defend this position, but rather it would be the responsibility of those on the other side to offer some compelling evidentiary or logical basis to reconsider whether aliens might be visiting us.

And to be clear, despite the popular myths and all the cable shows suggesting otherwise, there is no such evidence where we expect to find it.

Gullibility

Religious ideas have survived the test of time. If they were dangerous or harmful, that would have been exposed over the last two thousand years.

There's a sucker born every minute.

This phrase is generally attributed to the famous showman P.T. Barnum, although there are many conflicting stories as to its origin. Regardless of its source, Barnum apparently embraced it and subscribed to the view that "any publicity is good publicity" far more than he actually tried to sucker people.

It does seem true that there is no end of gullible people. The same cons and scams that bilked our grandparents out of their wages still work just as well today. The lies that our government used to get us into one war still work perfectly well to lie us into the next.

We don't seem to be getting any less gullible, and parents sure don't seem to do a very good job of training their kids to be skeptical thinkers. Maybe they figure it builds character for children to learn the hard way.

Anyone can be fooled, especially perhaps those who think themselves too smart to be conned.

We have to forgive a certain amount of gullibility. We all fall prey to a good sob story. Anyone can be excused for being tricked by a really well-executed con. We can even excuse people for falling victim to scams out of ignorance or the befuddlement of age. I actually have a lot of admiration for a well-executed scam.

But the type of gullibility that cannot be excused is the gullibility of belief-based decision making. When people are systematically bamboozled by belief peddlers and an irresponsible media to make decisions based on belief when they have full knowledge of facts to the contrary, then that is a societal problem that must be addressed.

Perhaps we have survived this long despite our beliefs, but as any financial firm will tell you, "Past performance is no guarantee of future results." And in a rapidly changing world, subject to the ravages of climate change, past performance is increasingly inadequate.

James Randi was a professional magician who worked under the stage name of The Great Randi until age sixty. Later, he became a professional scientific skeptic, investigating paranormal claims and exposing fraud. He exposed the fraud behind Uri Gellar's spoon-bending tricks and went on to expose faith and psychic healers and literally hundreds of other bogus claims.

Here is what James Randi said about the gullibility of belief:

> *"Why people are so drawn to the irrational is something that has always puzzled me. I want to be, if I can, as sure of the world, the real world around me, as is possible. Now you can only attain that to a certain degree, but I want the greatest degree of control. I don't, I'd never involve myself in narcotics of any kind, I don't smoke, I don't drink, because that can just easily fuzz the edges of my rationality, fuzz the edges of my reasoning powers and I want to be as aware as I possibly can. If*

that means giving up a lot of fantasies that might be comforting, I am
willing to give that up to live in an actual, real world."

His educational foundation offered a cash prize to anyone who could demonstrate any evidence of a paranormal event under controlled conditions. No one ever claimed the prize.

In addition, James Randi was infamous for his bold and controversial stunts to underscore the gullibility of the population and the media. He purposely perpetrated hoaxes to demonstrate how easily we can be fooled.

His Project Alpha Hoax exposed the shortcomings of many university-level paranormal research projects. His Carlos hoax exposed the gullibility of the media when he hired an actor to fool the Australian media into promoting a fake channeler of the 2,000-year-old spirit of "Carlos." He later revealed how it was all a hoax.

Following the advice of Randi, Uri Geller was exposed as a charlatan on Johnny Carson's *Tonight Show*. But that had little effect on the famous spoon-bender's popularity.

Unfortunately, exposing the trickery behind claims of psychic powers or paranormal events seldom has any effect on dampening belief in them.

Just as when the hucksters who produced crop circles came forward, or Houdini revealed his secrets to the Doyles, or when I admitted my own doll hoax, many people still insist upon continuing to believe in the hoax.

Even when clear, undisputable facts conclusively debunk beliefs, believers seldom reconsider their beliefs. They do not need to when they possess a powerful neural network that can easily rationalize away any evidence that contradicts them.

Rationalization

I cannot question everything.

You cannot. You have to decide at some point. But we should do so with the knowledge that we could be wrong and the willingness to revise our positions.

When Alonso Quijano sallied forth to right all wrongs as the wandering knight Don Quixote, he somehow managed to rationalize every perception or memory that might contradict his new identity. When Sancho failed to see that the windmill was in fact a monstrous four-armed giant sent by the Great Enchanter, it was only more evidence of his arch-enemy's great power.

Other people see angels in clouds.

It is easy to simply say, sure, they are crazy. However, again, we all have the capacity for self-delusion; none of us is completely sane or insane. Some of us just happen to apply our delusions more selectively than others.

In 1976, a Russian psychologist named A.R. Luria published a ground-breaking book called *The Working Brain: An Introduction to Neuropsychology*. It was the culmination of forty years of research, much of it involving the careful observation of the countless Russian soldiers who had suffered brain damage during the war.

Through careful observations, Luria was able to produce some of the first maps of brain function and to tie those regions and layers to incredibly specific perceptions and behaviors. One tiny layer of our auditory region might, for example, register sounds. The next tiny layer might assign pitch, and the next associate the sound with an instrument.

Damage to any on these discrete areas can impact only that particular, highly specific brain function. Luria described innumerable cases of highly specific brain lesions and their resulting effects.

He documented one now well-known type of lesion that causes dysfunction between the left and right hemispheres of the brain. When a patient suffers from this particular injury, they are unable to physically perceive an entire half of their own body.

These victims quickly come to accept their perception that they only possess half a body as a fact. Nothing the physicians can do or say to provide facts, evidence, or rational arguments will sway the patient from their belief. They will find ways to rationalize away every logical inconsistency.

It would be the entirely wrong conclusion to think of our capacity for delusional rationalizations as being a result of a brain dysfunction. Rather, these injuries simply highlight the tremendously strong ability we all have to create "rational" arguments to support our perceptions and beliefs, regardless of how outlandish and demonstrably false they may be.

Science clearly shows us that we cannot trust our own thought processes to bring us to the truth of a matter. Rationalization is only the process by which we arrive at an internally consistent and satisfying explanation for whatever it is we wish or need to believe or think we have observed. Rationalization that is not based on fact is the path to a false certainty in beliefs.

Lots of educational activities focus on exercising our ability to rationalize. But we are all naturally very good rationalizers. What we need to focus on more is our less natural ability to ensure that the rationalizations are based on solid facts and sound logic.

Only by developing and exercising those skills can we guarantee that we are not simply training our brains to better rationalize a giant where there is only a windmill.

Delusional Science

🎤 *A lot of very credible scientists research the legitimate underpinnings of faith and religion. To dismiss all of their work is to attack and censor science.*

Do you have one of those wacky friends? The one who is certain that the coronavirus is a hoax?

Your friend undoubtedly has an articulate rebuttal for every possible argument you can throw at him to prove that the virus is real. All the supposed evidence, he says, is faked. No one is dying of Covid. It's just a normal flu.

Your friend probably turns the tables on your skepticism quite cleverly. How can you be so arrogant to claim to know everything? Are you that close-minded? Surely you can't prove and therefore can't know for certain that you don't just have the flu. If you are as scientifically rigorous as you claim you must admit some possibility that it could be a hoax. Surely you can admit that reasonable people can disagree on this unless you believe purely as a matter of faith. The only intellectually honest position on this question must be agnosticism.

Your friend points to several well-regarded scientists who confirm that the coronavirus is a hoax. He recommends a plethora of scholarly books that supposedly debunk all those fallacious "scientific" arguments claiming that it is real.

But I do not actually need to read any of those books purporting to prove that Covid does not exist. No scientist should or must admit to this possibility merely in order to prove his or her scientific purity. We have all the evidence we need that the Covid pandemic is real. Any book that starts with the premise that it is a hoax is necessarily idiotic. There is no need for me to actually read it in order to legitimately dismiss the claim out of hand. Good scientists implicitly or explicitly dismiss an infinite number of implausible claims all the time every day by what we choose not to study. And that is rational science.

Similarly, as a good scientist and a rational, open-minded human, there is no reason to read yet more books with purportedly new theories about how the Holocaust did not happen or the moon landing was faked, or aliens built the pyramids or ghosts have been sighted in Oshkosh or a new perpetual motion machine has been developed by a kid in Hoboken.

I can dismiss all of these claims out of hand without reading past the tag line or glancing at the book jacket. Even reading them for entertainment value is dangerous, as are "ghost hunting" shows on television. The only reason to read them may be if your interest is in studying delusional thinking or the infection of magical thinking among otherwise healthy individuals.

I have read a great many supposedly scholarly books that purport to present a logical or scientific argument for the existence of God. As part of my research for this book, I took the time to slog through a three-foot stack of books that undoubtedly made Amazon the lucrative enterprise it is today. It was largely a waste of time and money on my part. Believers have had two millennia to come up with arguments and there are simply no new ones to be found.

But we do see new twists on occasion.

As a concrete example, I bought several books on **Neurotheology**. I did the world a service by throwing these out rather than reselling them. Written by Andrew B. Newberg and a host of his followers, these books typically spend 250 pages citing brain imaging and cognitive studies related to belief and God. Their real goal is to establish their science creds so that you will believe them when, in the last fifty pages, they leap to outlandish claims that go something like:

> *Since we have clearly evolved to believe in God, the only conclusion must be that God himself designed us to believe in him.*

The only sensible conclusion is that this is an idiotic conclusion. But then again, what can you hope to get from any author who starts from the implausible premise that God exists and works backward?

Religious books purporting to be scientifically legitimate examinations of the evidence for God pop up on Amazon every day like so many weeds. I can't read them all but I can still dismiss them all out of hand. There simply is no God, can be no God, and therefore every book claiming to argue this point is necessarily as idiotic as books arguing that Elvis is alive and well and living in a secret wing of Graceland.

And thus, dear reader, we finally reach the heart of my dilemma: Do I read these silly books and respond to them or do I simply ignore them?

We have had to deal with this same dilemma when it came to the lies perpetuated daily by Donald Trump. Does legitimate media address each one, or ignore everything he says?

Ignoring them is not easy. If no one pushes back on Donald Trump or the Neurotheologians, they seem to win the argument. And there are so many of them saying the same silly things that many readers interpret quantity as an indicator of legitimacy.

On the other hand, the time for engaging these silly debates is over. At this stage of human civilization, we must move past engaging in and thereby legitimizing these ridiculous debates. We should give no more consideration to religious ideas than we do to racist ideas or homophobic ideas or sexist ideas or the idea that vaccines contain tracking chips.

But that's not where we are, and it is hard to avoid getting sucked in. In 2015, a new book appeared on Amazon called *Can Science Explain Religion?* Written by a priest who is also a professor of religion, it purports to debunk the idea that belief could have evolved naturally. Do I buy this and read it so I can credibly criticize it, and thereby risk encouraging this nonsense? Or is it best not to even respond and hope that the rest of the country follows my sensible example?

After struggling with this dilemma for many years, I have come to believe that, after a question has been sufficiently considered and answered, refusing to engage further is the best strategy. This would be true of things like, say, evolution or the existence of God. Engaging in further debate on such things only feeds the beast. Like booing Donald Trump at a rally.

It's not an easy course of action, nor is it without risk or criticism. But in science we must first ask whether our basic assumptions are valid before we enter into discussions of the resulting questions. We must not let ourselves get caught up in grand debates over how Santa manages to deliver all those presents in one night when the very premise of Santa is pure fantasy.

And that is how we should respond to these books and these arguments—by dismissing them out of hand and with great prejudice and by refusing to entertain dependent arguments arising out of purely implausible assumptions.

Delusional Atheists

🗣 *You talk as if religious people are the only ones with crazy ideas.*
Lots of atheists have crazy ideas too.

Absolutely, I agree with you completely on that. Although I may push back a bit with regard to the pervasiveness and severity of those ideas, we do have our kooks.

A while back, I found myself on a mailing list from a man named Michael Roll. While he considers himself an atheist, Mr. Roll is also a self-professed spiritualist who has undertaken a personal mission to sell his particular fantasy as a non-religious, science-based idea. Since the 1960s, his "campaign for philosophical freedom" has tried to promote his spiritualist delusions.

Following are just a few of the ideas that he puts forth with great intellectual soberness and gravitas:

> *There is no God, but there is an afterlife that is part of the natural world. This spirit world exists on a "different frequency" and accounts for the unaccounted 95% of the energy in our universe.*

> *While the religious beliefs of others are nonsense, his essentially identical beliefs are based on "experiments and mathematical models."*

> *His evidence is largely based on the "research" conducted by Sir William Crooks between 1871 and 1874. Crooks observed the*

manifestations produced by several "materialism mediums," which he claimed proved the existence of a vast afterlife.

The media is in cahoots with the Vatican in a conspiracy to discredit legitimate science on the paranormal, including work linking sub-atomic physics with the afterlife.

According to Roll, "famous television scientist Professor Brian Cox [...] is let loose on the public because his false model of the universe is no danger to the Vatican and their powerful materialistic agents."

Roll also states, "2018 could just be the year that a few billion people will find out that the great philosopher Jesus started from the correct scientific base that we all have a soul that separates from the dead physical body. But most important of all, that Einstein started from the incorrect scientific base that the mind dies with the brain."

I am not going to waste any of your time refuting all of Roll's clearly delusional fantasies, any more than I would waste your time refuting the Narnia-really-exists theory. It particularly saddens me that Roll purports to be a student of Carl Sagan and quotes him extensively yet manages to do so in a way that is an affront to everything Dr. Sagan stood for.

What interests me more than debunking this one clearly delusional individual is the more general observation that atheists are not immune to magical thinking. While atheists may not believe in God, they may certainly believe in lots of other equally nonsensical ideas. Just calling oneself an atheist does not immunize one from delusions. Michael Roll's secular form of ratio-nalizing his magical thinking with "logic" is no different than the "logic" arrived at by Bible scholars.

Atheist delusions can be unique to an individual, but they are more often propagated by non-religious movements and fads. Spiritualism and New Age thinking are examples of non-religious structures of fantastical delusions about the world.

Even smart, logical, sophisticated thinkers are not insulated from spiritual delusion. Recall again our poster child, Sir Arthur Conan Doyle, the brilliant creator of the paragon of rational thought, Sherlock Holmes, who was also a passionate proponent of spiritualism. He clung to his beliefs in real magic even after Houdini proved to him that his magic tricks were merely tricks. Even after that irrefutable evidence, Doyle refused to be swayed from his insistence that Houdini's magic proved spiritualism was real.

That these kind of spiritual belief systems can so compromise the thinking of one such as Conan Doyle demonstrates that they are both highly seductive and tenacious. Many of my atheist friends do not share my concern about these non-religious movements because they do not have the institutional power of an organized church behind them. Fair enough. However, they still contribute significantly to a culture in which magical thinking is encouraged and rational thought diminished. They legitimize and normalize public debate on important matters in which "alternative facts" are even entertained.

I argue that while misguided atheists like Michael Roll claim not to believe in God, their belief in essentially the same kind of pseudoscientific thinking that actually supports faith-based thinking in all its forms. To attempt to use phony science fiction to rationalize a delusion does not make it less harmful than a purely religious belief. Indeed, the false invocation of the I of science may in fact make the delusion far more harmful and damaging.

From Belief to Delusion

There is still a legitimate debate to be had about religion by honest scientists.

Is there really?

Remember the formal debate between Bill Nye and Ken Ham on creationism? Ham challenged Nye to debate the topic and the notable exchange took place on February 4, 2014. Bill Nye became famous as the amiable "science guy" from his highly regarded show for kids that ran from 1993 through 1998. Mr. Nye continues to be a passionate advocate and popularist of science.

His opponent, Mr. Ham, was and is the president of the Answers in Genesis ministry and is a tireless evangelist preaching young Earth creationism, mainly targeting kids. Ham is a key founder behind the Creation Museum, a biblical-themed amusement park.

As I listened to the specious and frankly ludicrous arguments put forth with such conviction by Mr. Ham in that debate, I could not help but wonder whether belief is far too mealy-mouthed a word for what Ham and those like him suffer from. Is not delusion a far more accurate word to describe his kind of thinking? And if so, is it really helpful to be so very reluctant to call it what it is?

In the case of Ken Ham, his creationist views go far beyond a mistaken belief based on false or incomplete information. He maintains his unalterable convictions despite incomparably superior evidence to the contrary. No doubt, he would argue that the evidence for evolution is not actually superior. But any delusional person would similarly deny all evidence contrary to their delusion. Any objectively rational person could not help but conclude that the evidence for evolution goes far beyond merely superior to overwhelming and that the convoluted arguments that Ham puts forth to deny this evidence are utterly irrational.

Delusions can be subcategorized into four distinct subgroups. One of these, the **Bizarre Delusion**, is defined as follows:

> *"A delusion that is very strange and completely implausible; an example of a bizarre delusion would be that aliens have removed the reporting person's brain."*

I contend that the thinking of Ken Ham and other evolution deniers should be fairly and accurately categorized as a Bizarre Delusion. Their creationist views are certainly "completely implausible," and it would be considered "very strange" if they were not so commonplace. It is important to recognize that they have studied this a lot, and do not simply hold a completely uninformed and clueless belief in creationism. And they are evidently not just lying about their belief like at least some conservative politicians.

Ken Ham and his fellow creationists are truly delusional both in the layman's sense and according to the strict letter of the definition. Words matter, and they should be used accurately. In principle, if a more accurate word is available, it should be used. It seems undeniable that Bizarre Delusion is a far more appropriate word than "belief" to describe the thinking of Ham and those who share his delusions.

But words also have power, and we should avoid words that convey implications or elicit reactions we would like to avoid. So even if the bizarre thinking of Ham and others like him is in fact delusional by definition, what value is there in labeling it as such? Doesn't that just necessarily alienate those you would like to bring around to a less delusional way of thinking?

Even considering those possible undesirable side effects, the word "belief" is neither accurate nor helpful in describing these delusions. It is not merely polite and non-confrontational, but it actively helps enable these delusions. It suggests that such delusional thinking is harmless and even reasonable and acceptable when sheltered under the protective umbrella of other less bizarre beliefs.

But delusions are seldom harmless and never reasonable or acceptable. Calling this kind of delusional thinking "belief" gives it more legitimacy than it deserves. If we were to consistently refer to this kind of thinking as delusions rather than as beliefs, we would more accurately communicate the true nature and real-world implications of these tangibly harmful assertions.

Certainly, using the word "delusion" instead of "belief" would elicit a much more visceral response by opponents and allies alike, but I for one would welcome that reaction. I say call a delusion a delusion and stand by the implicit assertion that such delusional thinking goes way beyond mere belief and that it is irrational, unacceptable, and harmful.

Calling a delusion a delusion may be just the hit of reality that these deluded people need, or at least those influenced by them need, to honestly reconsider the soundness of their reasoning. At the very least, it may give some people, politicians in particular, some hesitation in associating themselves with these delusional ideas.

So, the next time someone espouses delusionary thinking, consider calling it out (nicely) as delusion. Instead of responding with the customary "I respect your beliefs but I don't share them," you might say something more provocative like "Sorry, but I can't give any credence to such delusions."

If the other party questions how you dare characterize their sincere, heartfelt belief as a delusion, you should be able to give them a very clear and compelling justification for your use of that word.

But do not overuse it. Although one could arguably call any belief in God delusional, to do so would only dilute its effectiveness. There is a wide gray spectrum between belief and delusion. Reserve the label of delusional for those like Ken Ham who are clearly at the delusional end of the spectrum.

Rebuttal to Ken Ham

But Ken Ham presents evidence and makes a great many strong arguments that you have not even bothered to refute!

I have already stated that rational people do not actually need to respond to every irrational argument. And further, being drawn into such inane arguments ad nauseam is counterproductive.

But in order to demonstrate the quality of "scholarly" debate that these believers engage in, I will summarize Ken Ham's thesis here along with my response to each:

Man is not the ultimate authority. God is.

Science agrees that man is not the ultimate authority. It simply acknowledges that verifiable and reproducible facts are.

Science has been hijacked by secularists.

This is the old "*I'm rubber, you're glue*" ninjutsu. But it's clearly the other way around, with creationists like Ken desperately trying to gain legitimacy by donning the mantle of science.

Some scientists are creationists.

Ken repeatedly attempts to argue by authority by trotting out testimonials from scientists who share his delusions. Yes, a very few scientists are creationists —and some priests are child molesters. What does that prove except that some priests can be pedophiles and some scientists can be crazy? By the way, I sincerely doubt that Ken would accept the literal belief of a few demented Hindu scientists as proof that the universe was created by Brahma.

Interpretations depend upon your presuppositions.

Absolutely, and the scientific method is the only method we have to prove or disprove those presuppositions. But science doesn't start by proudly proclaiming its presupposition that the Bible is the inerrant and irrefutable source of all truth and then work backward to prove it.

🗣 *The Bible predicts things, and we see them confirmed.*

This is no surprise when you proclaim anything you choose in the Bible to be symbolic and then take license to interpret those symbols however necessary to confirm your desired predictions. Nostradamus probably made many more correct predictions than the Bible.

🗣 *How could we have logic without God if we are just random?*

This is a centuries-old argument that is unworthy of a first-year philosophy class. The cosmos has no need for God. Your failure to appreciate that is not a proof.

🗣 *Observational science is legitimate but historical science is not.*

There is no such distinction except within Ken Ham's addled brain. He simply fabricated this artificial distinction to dismiss any science he does not like. Science is science. But when you try to understand what qualifies as "observational" science and what qualifies as "historical" science, you quickly see that the only criterion is whatever Ken Ham wants to believe. Anything he agrees with is by his definition the good "observational" science. Anything he wants to deny is by his definition illegitimate "historical" science.

🗣 *You must understand that parts of the bible are literal and other parts are poetic.*

Just as he dismisses any science, he finds inconvenient as "historical," he conveniently dismisses anything in the Bible he disagrees with as "poetic" while anything he chooses to believe is "literal." It must be very convenient when you can divide facts up based on whatever supports your beliefs. But that is also the unmistakable hallmark of delusion and even insanity.

❧ *The evolutionary tree should really be organized into "kinds."*

Mr. Ham again attempts to redefine reality to fit his insanity through in his concept of biological "kinds." This is a cornerstone fabrication by Ken Ham. By imposing his completely artificial notion of "kinds" of species as a starting point, he is then able to contrive completely ridiculous explanations for every undeniable flaw in creationism.

By starting with his construct of kinds, he is then able to argue that Noah could reasonably have carried every kind of animal in the ark, that the species diversity we see today could have plausibly arisen out of his kinds, and that there is no evidence of his kinds evolving into another kind, thus denying the evolution of species.

This is of course all utter nonsense, but if he can get people to accept his premise of kinds as a starting point, then he can get them to follow him down this rabbit hole into Alice in Wonderland-land. The Mad Hatter was also quite inventive and clever.

❧ *You can't know that what is true today was true in the past.*

Only if you are delusional. We actually do know that the laws of chemistry and physics apply everywhere in our universe without exception and always have.

❧ *You didn't observe the past directly so you can't know anything about it.*

So, Ken, then you can't know anything about your family history by leafing through a photo album—you didn't observe the events directly after all. The simple truth is that we can and do know a tremendous amount about the past. We can observe the past directly just by looking into space after all. Or we can simply study all the evidence just lying all around us like little fossilized photographs.

❧ *Dating methods don't agree.*

Technically true, but still a blatant technical lie. Any differences between various scientific dating methods are minuscule compared to their vast disagreement with the biblical claim of six thousand years.

❡ Can you name one piece of technology that could only have been developed starting with a belief in molecules-to-man evolution?

This is a red herring, an invalid diversionary question. But sure, we'll play this game. How about clones, genetically modified foods, transgenic plants and animals, hybrid species, designer bacteria, and an exploding number of patents for new life forms? The list goes on and on.

❡ You can't prove any instance of a new trait appearing that wasn't already there.

This is yet another red herring since most evolutionary changes are incredibly tiny and only accumulate into observable traits after exceedingly long periods of time. But even so, if Ken merely did a simple Google search of popular articles, he might find "10 Astounding Cases of Modern Evolution and Adaptation" reported by *Popular Science*. There are thousands of such examples including the sudden development of new survival traits among bedbugs here in New York City.

* * *

I hope this summary helps you to recognize and respond to these laughably fallacious sorts of arguments that some creationists put forth. Unfortunately, guys like Ken Ham and the "Neurotheology" club are practiced at making themselves appear to be scientifically literate, and they do appear to cite a plethora of legitimate arguments raising doubt in the science of evolution, but in reality they offer only smoke floating on air.

Stop Debating

❡ Sounds like you want to just shut down those who have legitimate opinions that you do not share. Isn't the only way to arrive at the truth through discussion, debate, and consensus?

That is a difficult and contentious question, and thoughtful people disagree on the right answer.

Although I have great respect for Bill Nye, and I recognize that the decision whether to legitimize someone like Ken Ham by engaging in a public debate is a difficult one. Can you achieve some benefit through frank, open debate? Or does giving his crazy beliefs a platform, making it seem like a legitimately debatable proposition, do vastly more harm than good?

The answer to this is subject to both principled and situational considerations. But I judged that Bill Nye should not have engaged at the time. And after the subsequent term of Donald Trump was so legitimized and emboldened by all of his media exposure, I am more convinced than ever that the time to engage, and in doing so to create a perception of factual equivalence, is past.

As has every successful movement before it, the atheist movement must now move past the debate stage. There are no new arguments to be made, no new evidence to be presented, and further debate only distracts us, legitimizes ridiculous claims, and introduces unfounded doubts about objective reality itself. As long as we continue to treat religious fantasy with undue respect, we are not fighting back but rather are complicit in perpetuating mass delusion.

Therefore, we must quit debating creationism as if it were a legitimate theory. We must stop quibbling over biblical interpretations and contradictions as if they matter. We must cease the sham of conducting research to disprove prayer. We must stop discussing faith healing as if it were merely a cultural difference.

Rather we must quietly assert, through our refusal to entertain religious claims and rationalizations, that the reality-based world has moved on.

It is not closed-minded or insensitive to simply discard out of hand any claims or opinions based upon religious authority or dogma. We don't feel conflicted about summarily dismissing assertions that are based upon a belief in white supremacy or a flat Earth, and those who espouse them are rightfully marginalized, although both of these ideas are making a troubling comeback.

Of course, we cannot eliminate delusional beliefs, but as with many other anachronistic ideas, we can marginalize them so that their influence is kept to a minimum. And make no mistake, many religious beliefs are dangerous, and even laudable religious beliefs inherently undermine our capacity for rational thought.

None of this suggests that secular society can or should relegate religious citizens to voiceless second-class status. On the contrary, we must engage in social justice debates with everyone. But like a judge who rules on the admissibility of arguments in court, we should reject out of hand any religiously based argument that is not consistent with objective facts and universal humanistic values. Practically speaking, a pluralistic society cannot function in any other way—unless it becomes a theocracy.

This stance is already standard for any number of groups who hold bizarre beliefs. Many people believe in ghosts, or discredited conspiracy theories, or Bigfoot. The difference is that those groups do not attempt, or are not powerful enough, to substantially influence public policy. We don't have a political Bigfoot wing fighting to introduce a Bigfoot curriculum in our schools, to build Bigfoot memorials on public property, and to push through legislation based on the teachings of Bigfoot. That makes it all the more important that we do not continue to indulge and normalize religious belief.

There was a time when we had to engage in public debate about white supremacy, slavery, racism, sexism, or any number of areas that we have since judged unworthy of the dignity of discussion. Similarly, there was a time when the "Four Horsemen of Atheism," namely Dawkins and Hitchens and Harris and Dennett, needed to debate about religion. But we have moved past that time. If we have not quite moved past it, doing so is the best way to move forward and avoid being mired in eternal debate.

The gap between our secular and religious worldviews is deep. At times it seems like a bottomless chasm. But that gap is not wide. Our common goals and needs as humans bring our two sides close enough together to form strong bridges on a wide range of social justice issues. But atheists must insist that where we disagree, those bridges must be built upon facts and reason and universal values. Religious beliefs cannot serve as the foundation to bring together those who do not share them. We must insist that our government limit itself to the real world in which we all live.

Although even atheists can get caught up in silly debates, the main reason we are activists is because we see powerful religious interests, perhaps unwittingly and with sincerely good intentions, pushing America toward delusional thinking and theocratic behaviors. And both, at any level, are anathema to our American ideals, including the free exercise of religion. Ironically, while we do not believe in religion, we atheists actively defend the separation of church and state that ultimately protects religious liberty.

So, in order to move forward, we must refuse to engage in arguments over fictions and get to work in the real world. We must listen to any reasonable, fact-based arguments. But we must insist that if religious believers wish to inform social policy in keeping with their religious beliefs, that they do so by sticking to objective facts and sound logic.

Intellectual Agnosticism

Shutting down debate doesn't sound very scientific to me. I thought scientists were supposed to be open to all possibilities, however unlikely.

That is a gotcha box in which believers have long attempted, with some success, to trap rational thinkers.

A good scientist must indeed be open to data, explanations, and theories that contradict their thinking. But that does not mean that they must remain agnostic with regard to any truth at all.

Intellectual agnosticism is when you remain "unconvinced" and "open" about things for which there is actually no legitimate debate or doubt. The term "agnosticism" is most often applied to a belief in God, but intellectual agnosticism can apply to anything.

News articles and opinion pieces touting the intellectual purity of agnosticism keep getting published everywhere you look. And these aren't written only by religious proponents but by scientific and academic intellectuals who claim that agnosticism is undervalued. According to them, being agnostic is not merely being undecided or ambivalent or apathetic, but rather it's a highly principled position that upholds sound scientific skepticism and empiricism.

Many authors gleefully note, as do many agnostics as their go-to-proof-by-authority, that even Richard Dawkins seemed to admit he is agnostic. His subsequent clarifications indicate that he actually used the term simply to allow for some purely philosophical distinction. Nevertheless, this well-intentioned but misguided and tactically disastrous declaration of philosophical agnosticism by Richard Dawkins, given his stature as a prominent atheist, has caused incredible harm to reason and rationality.

Don't follow Dawkins's lead on this one. Such statements of agnosticism only lead one into Pascal's trap, which we will discuss in the next section.

Skepticism is indeed a hallmark of the scientific method. But skepticism is not synonymous with gullibility, and science does not require you to abdicate logic and reason and common sense. Good scientists can and do reject an infinite number of ridiculous propositions out of hand every day. Healthy scientific skepticism does not require you to doubt everything. It merely requires that you withhold drawing conclusions regarding plausible assertions until sufficient evidence is obtained.

This is where the agnostics think they have an ironclad argument. Since science supposedly cannot prove a negative (e.g., God does not exist), then despite the lack of any plausibility, a good scientist must remain agnostic, refusing to completely rule out the possibility.

Gotcha!

First, scientific rigor does not require that scientists disprove every possible ridiculous statement. Imagine anything that is clearly untrue. Take for example, my claim that my banana is actually a sentient lifeform named Ned from planet Zorcon that just happens to exactly resemble a banana right down to the molecular level. Ned is in a coma right now and cannot respond or do anything un-banana-like, but he deserves the rights of personhood.

Healthy scientific skepticism simply does not require scientists to admit that my assertion might be true. It certainly does not require that they perform studies to try to prove or disprove this claim. Scientists have no burden whatsoever of disproving my absurd claim about Ned the comatose alien banana. It is entirely my burden to prove it, and until I do, good scientists can and should simply reject it out of hand.

And keep in mind, these agnostics do not claim God is a plausible belief, they rather claim that regardless of how implausible it may be, we must allow that it may be true nevertheless. These agnostics—cleverly they think—point out that science cannot prove a negative. This fallacy is often justified by quoting British astrophysicist Martin Rees who famously pointed out that:

"Absence of evidence is not evidence of absence."

What this correctly points out is that just because we see no evidence of something doesn't necessarily mean it does not exist. But in fact, this quotation would be far more accurate and less misused if stated as:

*"Absence of evidence is not **always** evidence of absence."*

Agnostics fail to recognize that a sufficiently conclusive lack of evidence—where we would expect to see it—absolutely can prove a negative.

This concept is quantified in statistics. In statistics there is a measurement called **power**. The power of a data set measures the statistical probability that if an expected result is *not* found in a data set in which one might reasonably expect to find it, that one can say that the expected result is actively disproven. Let's contrive an example for fun.

I do not need to even look in my bedroom to conclude with 100% certainty that there is no dragon in it. There is no such thing as dragons and no reason to even consider that possibility, so therefore I can dismiss any such assertion out of hand. Further, as a good scientist it is my obligation to dismiss such claims with prejudice.

But what if the claim is not a dragon but an elephant? Well, elephants do exist and while I cannot imagine how one would get into my house, I can easily prove or disprove this claim just by glancing around my bedroom. Having done so, I can legitimately conclude with 100% certainty that there is no elephant in my bedroom. If there were an elephant hiding under the bed or behind the curtains, I would reasonably expect to have seen at least some evidence of it.

Therefore, I do not need to remain agnostic with regard to the sincere heartfelt beliefs of the elephant-in-every-bedroom cult to prove I am a good scientist. I have sufficient proof to conclude with certainty that my bedroom is elephant-free and that all claims of an elephant in my bedroom are delusional.

God is like that elephant. He is *so* huge that if he existed, we would certainly have seen evidence.

There is none.

But let's argue that God is more elusive and secretive—like bedbugs. Let's say that the bedbug cult claims that I have bedbugs in my bedroom. Even though I don't see any bedbugs just by glancing around, it is still possible they may exist, and as a good scientist I take the advice of Martin Rees to heart and withhold conclusion pending further evidence, positive or negative.

So, I bring in trained dogs and bedbug residue detectors. I carefully examine all the places where they would be found if they were there. If, after that, I find no evidence of bedbugs I can conclude beyond any reasonable doubt that my bedroom is in fact bedbug free.

In all these simple cases it would be foolish to be scientifically agnostic. I do not have to claim to remain agnostic about whether dragons or elephants or even bedbugs are in my room to prove I am a good scientist. Such agnosticism would only prove that a fool exists my bedroom.

Similarly, no legitimate evidence of God, however secretive he may be, has ever been found, even though believers make extravagant claims about his tremendous influence over our world.

If God exists, it would be the most unimaginably colossal failure of science—a science that has measured infinitesimal gravity waves from distant black holes, a science that has proven capable of finding proof of even the neutrino, which has so little effect on anything that it can hardly be said to exist at all!

Yet that same science has somehow failed to detect any evidence whatsoever of the many wondrous miracles of God, let alone his direct daily influence in our world.

Irrational agnosticism is the exact opposite of good science. Science, unlike mysticism, relies upon the certainty that our cosmos is knowable, that it follows rules. Not just anything is possible. If it were, the cosmos would not be knowable at all, and science would be meaningless. In science, things are true, observable, and logical, or they simply do not exist and are untrue, period. To say that good scientists cannot know anything for certain is to turn science into mysticism.

To be frank, agnostics are not the champions of science and reason they imagine themselves to be. Ultimately their position renders science and reason invalid. If they insist that we cannot disprove things for which there is no proof, then they are necessarily saying we cannot positively assert anything at all. For anything you could assert as true, you could simply make up any story to cause all that evidence to be in doubt. Agnostics are required by their dogma to accept ridiculous nonsense.

You can have fun with agnostics. Make up some unprovable reason to claim something silly. Agnostics will be forced to admit you might be correct because they cannot disprove your un-disprovable fantasy. This exposes how bereft of any meaning their position really is. Truth and falsity, science and mysticism, evidence and belief all collapse upon themselves into a meaningless jumble of pseudo-intellectual nonsense if you accept the agnostic view of reality.

This creates a huge problem for agnostics. They think they are purists in being open-minded enough to admit that God might exist by making a philosophical claim that we cannot really disprove (or thereby even prove) anything whatsoever.

But they don't apply their intellectual purity to every possible ridiculous proposition. They only selectively apply it to this particular ridiculous God assertion. Though they might stubbornly claim to apply this thinking to everything universally, they clearly do not do so in practice.

In the end, either these are just smart people applying convoluted logic to rationalize a particular ridiculous proposition that they want to believe, or they are misguided atheists who mistakenly believe that agnosticism demonstrates their sophisticated and superior intellectual standing.

What harm does agnosticism cause? It undermines logic and reason and moves us toward a pseudoscientific kind of mystical thinking in which anything is possible. Moreover, if we fall into the agnosticism trap, if we give it any credibility whatsoever, then we accept that God might exist. And if we accept that God might exist, then we must accept **Pascal's wager**.

Pascal's Wager

🎙 *I don't see how you can argue with the logic of Pascal's wager.*

I cannot argue with it—if I first accept agnosticism.

Atheists who allow for agnosticism must accept Pascal's wager. And if they accept Pascal's wager then they must allow that a belief in God is reasonable, and therefore any religiously based public policy is also reasonable.

You're probably familiar with Pascal's wager. It says that even if there is only an infinitesimally small possibility that God exists, the consequences of eternal reward or punishment far outweighs any earthly cost. Therefore, a reasonable person should hedge their bets and believe in God. It is the kind of low-probability but high-impact cost-benefit analysis that we discussed earlier.

Despite its incredibly specious logic, Pascal's wager nevertheless holds powerful sway over a great many people. Lots of otherwise intelligent thinkers put it forth as a reasonable argument, even as an inescapable ironclad rationale. But there are many flaws in it, including the assumption that belief is a harmless hedge. In the end, it is no more than a silly trick of logic that can equally justify anything whatsoever.

By this logic, for example, you should send money to that Nigerian prince who emailed you. However small the chance that it's real, isn't it worth responding in case it is? In actual fact, the Nigerian prince is far more likely to be real than is God. Such a prince could plausibly exist.

But you might reject that argument with yet more pseudo-logic. You might argue that only heaven is sufficient reward to offer compelling enough stakes to accept Pascal's wager. And I then counter by suggesting right here and now that you will suffer damnation for infinity squared if you do not give up ice cream. Regardless of how small the ice cream threat, does not Pascal's wager demand you give it up? But I doubt you would accept that wager and actually swear off ice cream.

Of course, that sounds stupid to you. You reject it out of hand. But I have to ask, why does not Pascal's wager over the existence of God sound just as stupid?

And this brings us to the real problem with Pascal's wager. There is actually in fact no possibility, none, nada, nil, zero, absolute zero, that God actually exists. Someone will in fact actually win the $100 million Lotto, so, by Pascal's logic, that might be worth a $2 ticket. But no one can actually go to heaven because it does not exist. And you cannot claim "but it could" unless you really are equally willing to act on every other impossible proposition I might contrive.

This illustrates a fundamental problem with logic. As powerful and important as it is, logic has limitations. Thinking that abstract logic necessarily reflects reality can be like a Chinese finger trap, binding your thinking harder the more you pull against it.

In his very interesting book, *How Not to Be Wrong: The Power of Mathematical Thinking*, mathematician Jordan Ellenberg writes "reason cannot answer the question of God." If that is true, then it is our reason that is flawed. And it's easy to see how. Ellenberg is a mathematician. Even a mathematician can become too familiar and comfortable with mathematical concepts like irrational numbers which feel somewhat abstract. Our minds can conceive of symbols and rules of logic that cannot exist in reality. God is one of those. Pascal's Wager is one of those. It is a human conceptual model that leads to seemingly incontrovertible but nevertheless absurd conclusions.

To illustrate the problem of blindly accepting a logical argument without insisting upon testing that logic against reality, consider **Zeno's paradox**. In the fifth century, Zeno gave us his famous paradox that says that if we are to walk toward a destination, we must first get halfway there. Resuming, we must again reach half of the remaining distance, and so on in an endless mathematical series. Therefore, he concludes, we can never actually reach the destination.

The logic of this proposition has confounded thinkers ever since, as it is extremely difficult to refute by the rules of logic. But a guy called Diogenes the Cynic reportedly disproved it by simply standing up and walking across the room.

We humans have an amazing capacity to imagine things outside physical reality and to conceptualize logical systems of rationality that are imperfect in describing that reality or that extend beyond physical boundaries. But we have to be careful that our own cleverness does not make us stupid. Get up and walk across the room. God does not exist, and religion is not a harmless hedge.

Here's the bottom line. If your system of logic leads you to the conclusion that God might exist or that you cannot ever reach the other side of the room, it's because your system of logic is flawed or misinterpreted or because it has been extended beyond its applicable range or because you just want it to be true. If your logic cannot disprove flying pigs, you are not thereby proving that flying pigs might actually exist. You are merely encountering the limitations or failings of your logic.

And to my agnostic atheist friends who refuse to say with certainty that God does not exist, let me say this once again. If you allow any possibility that God might exist, any doubt however theoretical and infinitesimal, if you are afraid of being called an "absolute atheist," then you have lost the argument. By accepting Pascal's wager, you have fallen into what should more candidly be called Pascal's trap.

Because if there is any chance, no matter how small, you must accede to the logic of Pascal's wager and admit that it is reasonable to believe; that it is therefore reasonable to incorporate religious ideas into public policy.

You may think you can logic or qualify your way out of Pascal's trap but you cannot. You have been checkmated.

New Age Thinking

🖤 *I don't believe in religion. But I am highly spiritual, and I believe there is more to our universe than science can prove.*

It is very popular for many people to distance themselves from dogmatic religious thinking and organized religion. They consider themselves more spiritually sophisticated and open-minded than religious folk. Many subscribe to New Age or other similarly mystical thinking, which includes beliefs in reincarnation, spiritual energy, astrology, psychic powers, and a general belief that science cannot know everything.

According to *Influence* magazine, six in ten Americans hold New Age beliefs. New Age thinkers span all demographics but tend to most often be wealthier, middle-aged, Democratic, female, and most often Black or Hispanic. They tend to self-identify as "nones" and are less likely to have a college education.

New Age thinking is just more belief-based thinking, unrestrained by religious tradition and dictates. It is truly the "believe anything I want" school of thought. The New Age worldview offers freedom from both fact-based reality and religious mandates. It is seductive and alluring, and it has been one of our fastest growing demographic groups targeted by marketers.

In the 1995 book *How to Think About Weird Things: Critical Thinking for a New Age,* the authors summarize New Age beliefs as follows:

> *"There's no such thing as objective truth. We make our own truth. There's no such thing as objective reality. There are spiritual, mystical, or inner ways of knowing that are superior to our ordinary ways of knowing. If an experience seems real, it is real. If an idea feels right to you, it is right. We are incapable of acquiring knowledge of the true nature of reality. Science itself is irrational or mystical. It's just another faith or belief system or myth, with no more justification than any other. It doesn't matter whether beliefs are true or not, as long as they are meaningful to you."*

To find these people, you don't need to go to the New Age section of your local Wiccan bookstore. You can just browse the profiles on any online dating site. Many are startlingly up front about their New Age sentiments. They profess to be "not religious but very spiritual" and they use self-descriptions like "old soul" to describe themselves.

> *I once knew a woman who was a self-proclaimed witch. She cast spells over phone sessions with her coven and was convinced that their group was instrumental in shaping world events.*

> *I once had a dinner date with a Manhattanite who was convinced that she was highly psychic. She regaled me with tales of her psychic powers. She pointed to our waiter (who looked and moved like a dancer) and informed me that she sensed he was a dancer. When he confirmed that he was, she glowed with psychic radiance. Later she mentioned that it is well-known that most of the staff at that particular restaurant were dancers augmenting their Broadway wages.*

When their beliefs are questioned, New Age believers are highly adept at belittling and dismissing the very idea of factual thinking in modern sounding, quasi-intellectual terms. They point out that they are "supra-rational thinkers" and "intuitive." They point out that they are not limited by conventional thought and that there is far more to the universe than arrogant and unimaginative scientists can know.

These New Age thinkers are no less dangerous than religious zealots. In a 2020 article, Taisa Sganzerla wrote that "New Age communities are driving Qanon conspiracies in Brazil." The subtitle of the article read:

> *"These spiritual, pseudoscientific groups are domesticating Qanon narratives for non-American audiences."*

These are not religious delusions, but they are delusional and harmful, nevertheless. It is important to highlight the Qanon connection. It is an ongoing theme in this book that milder beliefs prime our neural networks to accept even more delusional beliefs.

Just Plain Crazy

🗣 *A lot of New Age stuff is just wacky fantasy.*

It is.

Most pseudoscientific and New Age beliefs can seem quaint and quirky. Some are outdated, even though most of them still come and go in surges of interest and popularity. Old Nessie is due for a reappearance on Loch Ness any day now.

Frankly, the term pseudoscience is really just a nice, polite, less offensive euphemism for "just plain crazy."

And these quirky, wacky beliefs can turn dark and dangerous very quickly.

Scientology, as just one example, is essentially a dangerous cult that is too big, too established, too rich to be brought down. It has an estimated 15 million members worldwide and there have been numerous allegations of egregious behavior including pursuing and detaining members who try to leave.

The founder of Scientology, L. Ron Hubbard, is a character you should read about. Perhaps no one individual in history has managed to popularize so many crazy ideas. His life story is a ludicrous litany of crazy.

As bad as Scientology is, it is even more disheartening to think about Qanon. They make the Scientologists look banal and mainstream, even quaint in their crazy beliefs and excesses.

Although not as entrenched in terms of infrastructure and organization, Qanon is by estimates as popular as many major religions. Facebook reports thousands of groups and pages and millions of members that support Qanon and its beliefs. As many as 15 percent to 20 percent of Americans are estimated to believe in some core Qanon theories. And let us just remind ourselves of just a few of these "theories":

- *Vaccines contain tracking chips.*
- *The coronavirus pandemic is a hoax.*
- *Prominent Democrats run a child trafficking ring out of a Washington, DC, pizza parlor.*
- *The world is run by a satanic cabal led by Hillary Clinton.*
- *Liberal celebrities drink the blood of children to worship Satan.*

- *World leaders have been replaced by reptilian shape-shifters.*
- *The Storm is coming, in which there will be mass arrests of high-level people.*
- *The Great Awakening is coming, in which everyone will realize that Qanon was right and this will start an age of utopia.*
- *Donald Trump is the hero of good in the upcoming Storm and Awakening.*

This is all fun and games until someone gets killed. And people are getting killed. In 2016, a North Carolina man shot up a pizza restaurant in Washington, DC, with an AR-15 because he was convinced by Qanon that it was the center of a satanic child sex abuse ring.

More recently, a California surf instructor killed his two children with a speargun because he had been convinced by Qanon that his wife was infected by lizard DNA. Naturally, the only responsible thing to do was to kill them. Not to mention the delusional beliefs underpinning the insurrection at the US Capitol on January 6, 2021.

These are not isolated incidents. The real-world repercussions of these fantasies are not limited to the realm of fantasy or church pews. They are symptoms of our global pandemic of delusion.

We perpetually ask how it can be. How can people get to the point at which they believe such utter lunacy? There are undoubtedly many pathways, but one has to consider that the descent into madness most often is a gradual slope. We start with Santa Claus, then Jesus, then ghosts, then demons, and so on until it seems like only a tiny logical little step forward to accept satanic child sex trafficking and reptilian shape-shifters.

Conspiracy Theories

🗣 *You may dismiss Qanon, but lots of conspiracy theories do prove to be true!*

You are right, many assertions that were initially dismissed as conspiracy theories have eventually proven to be true.

Conspiracy theories definitely deserve their own section in our analysis of fact, belief, and decision-making. What generates more contentious and passionate dispute between belief and fact than conspiracy theories?

A conspiracy theory is the belief that individuals or cabals are secretly manipulating information to conceal their activities from the public.

Suspicions of conspiracy can be leveled against any group, but most charges of cover-up are leveled against factions in the government who conspire to keep their misdeeds hidden from public scrutiny.

The phrase "conspiracy theory" has become synonymous with a crackpot accusation, something unworthy of serious consideration. There are certainly many conspiracy theories that are unworthy of serious consideration. Some conspiracy theorists have claimed that the government has long conspired to conceal evidence of alien spacecrafts and corpses in the Nevada military base known as Area 51. Other famous conspiracy theories include the supposed faking of the moon landing and the government-orchestrated assassination of JFK.

And of course, the most recent wave of utterly crackpot conspiracy theories has come from Qanon, Donald Trump, and the cyber destabilizers working for Vladimir Putin.

While most conspiracy theories range from unlikely to patently ridiculous, not many truly wacko theories have managed to gain widespread belief until recently.

On the other hand, there is a considerable list of conspiracy theories that have proven to be true despite a refusal of the mainstream media or public to give it serious consideration. These include Operation Northwoods, the Gulf of Tonkin incident, CIA mind control experiments, the Iran-Contra affair, and others.

Clearly, conspiracy theories can be true and sometimes are. Unfortunately, real conspiracies are easily discredited by associating them with the crazy ones. They are often ridiculed for so long that by the time they are finally exposed it is too late to do anything to remedy the issue or even hold any of the participants accountable.

One reason this is so common is that people are not particularly good at judging conspiracy theories on their merit. We tend to have a particular bias toward anything that gets labeled as a conspiracy theory, positive or negative, and we apply that bias to anything associated with or portrayed as a conspiracy theory.

Let's look at some of the typical positions that people take with respect to purported conspiracy theories:

The Scientific (Healthy) Skeptic

This is a Healthy Skeptic who withholds any conclusions without sufficient evidence. They dismiss as specious any claim of truth based only on authority. A Scientific Skeptic discards any previous conclusions when contradictory evidence is uncovered and accepts the new conclusions, however uncomfortable they might be.

The Stubborn Skeptic

This is a person who refuses to accept conclusions even when they are clearly supported by evidence. Examples of these include the ozone or global warming skeptic.

The Conspiracy Theorist

This refers to a person who frequently imagines causal relationships between unrelated events and fabricates facts to rationalize them. These folks are distinguished from Stubborn Skeptics by their illogical rationalization of laughably discredited conspiracy theories. For example, think of those who claim that reports of alien visitations must be true, and the fact that there is no evidence is proof of government suppression.

The Kool-Aid Drinker

This refers to a person who believes that their leaders are always truthful. They show no Healthy Skepticism with regard to the claims of their leaders and typically attempt to discredit any Healthy Skeptic by labeling them as a Conspiracy Theorist. Kool-Aid Drinkers often disingenuously attempt to paint Healthy Skeptics as being Kool-Aid Drinkers and themselves as Healthy Skeptics.

The Coincidence Theorist

This refers to a person who refuses to accept evidence that connected events are actual conspiracies. They rather insist that any evidence is coincidental. These people can be, but aren't necessarily, Kool-Aid Drinkers.

The Conspiracy Theorist always rationalizes ways to prove that their theory is correct while the Kool-Aid Drinker always finds ways to rationalize why the conspiracy theory is untrue. The Scientific Skeptic entertains conspiracy theories that have reasonable proof and dismisses conspiracy theories for which there is insufficient proof.

Normally, when something is labeled as a conspiracy theory, there are two possibilities:

1. *It is indeed a wacky proposition unsupported by any evidence.*

2. *Stubborn Skeptics and Kool-Aid Drinkers have applied that label to discourage inquiry and to discredit legitimate conclusions.*

Here's one example from recent history. Just one of the many demonstrated lies put out by the Bush administration in its effort to win support for their war in Iraq was the fiction of the aluminum tubes. The administration claimed that Saddam Hussein was purchasing aluminum tubes for use in centrifuges in order to advance Iraq's nuclear weapons program.

As soon as this assertion was floated out to the public, I did a quick internet search. It revealed many credible postings from engineering experts who pointed out that the tubes in question were entirely unsuitable for the purported purpose.

It is relatively easy to distinguish credible, scientific, well-researched, exhaustively referenced, unbiased technical articles from crackpot speculation. These online postings were highly credible and passed any reasonable sniff test. Nevertheless, anyone who questioned the official story was labeled a Conspiracy Theorist and their supporting material was dismissed as internet quackery.

Despite all the opposing information available, the mainstream press was silent. No one questioned administration representatives who appeared on news shows and repeated this claim incessantly. The crack reporters at these media outlets apparently were not able to use Google. President Bush made this same claim months later in his State of the Union address. Long after that, Secretary of State Colin Powell repeated the same lie once more before the United Nations. That lie, along with the timely urging of Tony Blair, was crucial in selling the case for war.

Only after that, after the truth of this claim could be contained no longer, did the mainstream media finally "break" the hot new revelation that this aluminum tube story was a fabrication. Unfortunately, it didn't matter by that time because the damage had all been done.

After finally being exposed, the truth of the aluminum tubes fiasco went directly from wacko conspiracy theory to water under the bridge. Sure, the administration lied, but that is in the past. We should all just get over it, move ahead, look to the future, and focus on what to do next.

The problem is that no matter how many times this happens, we don't learn from it. We are just told to forget it, to move on. Even though the Bush administration has been shown to have lied repeatedly and consistently, we still fail to call into question everything it put forth, as any courtroom judge would suggest. This is directly linked to our capacity to believe, to our compromised thinking. In this case, to our desire to believe that our government is honest and good. It's easy to understand why there are so many Kool-Aid Drinkers.

Thomas Jefferson worried that the public is too gullible, and people must be protected from themselves. From what I glean from his writing and his works, I don't believe he came to that conclusion based on a belief that we are stupid. Rather, he came to that belief based on an appreciation of the incredible persuasive and coercive power of authority.

Even though some of us are all too gullible in accepting any theory of government conspiracy, our natural patriotism contributes to making many others of us insufficiently skeptical of our government. What also contributes is our deep awareness of personal responsibility, of the reality that in a democracy we all hold some measure of personal responsibility for any misdeeds of our government.

The only way to arrive at the truth of conspiracy theories is to approach them as a scientific skeptic, to view all evidence without the bias of emotion or patriotism and without any persuasion by authority. As citizens, we all have a responsibility to follow the truth wherever it takes us, but as citizen scientists we bear special responsibility to uncover and advocate boldly for the truth.

Fact-based thinking is not possible without scientific skepticism. A skeptic rejects the validity of certain types of claims until they are subjected to scientific scrutiny. A skeptic demands reasonable proof before they accept a claim as true.

Belief-based thinking requires that skepticism be suspended. It requires that the truth of a proposition be accepted based on belief alone, without requiring any empirical tests to validate it.

Sometimes religious or New Age thinkers try to turn the tables on skepticism. They make the case that they are the skeptical thinkers, and therefore they are not going to dismiss a belief simply because there are no facts to support it. Alternatively, they invoke skepticism to justify ignoring facts that contradict their beliefs.

These are simply fallacious arguments without substance, but they can nevertheless be persuasive or at least confuse the argument sufficiently to cause a paralysis of judgment.

The Delusion Defense

If anyone who disagrees with you is delusional,
then most of humanity is delusional.

It is my view that all religious and New Age beliefs are delusions and that we should be willing to call them out as such. But that does not mean one must be compelled to do it all the time in every circumstance.

Certainly, I would not tell my aged grandmother that her belief in life after death is delusional, any more than I would tell my casual dinner date that her psychic powers are a delusion.

Even as strongly as my feelings are on this, I don't actually feel particularly compelled to call out all my religious friends and associates as delusional at every opportunity.

But I do still maintain that it is absolutely necessary to do so frankly, openly, and without compunction, when it comes to extremely delusional thinkers like Ken Ham who publicly propagate a large number of very bizarre delusions and influence a large number of people.

Calling out beliefs as delusions even in the most general manner creates tremendous practical complications. If believers were all thought to be delusional, that would produce profound ramifications in all manner of social and legal interactions.

It may be that the most pragmatic definition of belief would be "a delusion that we accept."

In his book *Bad Faith: When Religious Belief Undermines Modern Medicine*, Paul Offit looks at the faith healing beliefs of Amish, Christian Scientists, and Jehovah's Witnesses who feel compelled by their faith to commit murder by the withholding of medical care for their children and other loved ones. In a lecture I attended, Offit observed that our legal system essentially gives these families "one free murder" before the state is willing to characterize their beliefs as dangerous and harmful.

It seems that one free religiously motivated murder is the unfortunate consequence of a mistaken belief. But two are the result of a dangerous delusion.

In his book *Under the Banner of Heaven*, John Krakauer documents the history of Mormonism and the 40,000 Mormons who still believe much of it and practice polygamy. In particular, he documents the story of Ron and Dan Lafferty, Mormon brothers who felt compelled by their faith to commit multiple murders. The defense in that case argued for an insanity plea based largely upon the craziness of their religious beliefs.

Their defense argued that the delusional beliefs of the Lafferty brothers rose to the level of insanity and that their clients were therefore not fit to stand trial. However, psychiatrists for the state argued that their beliefs were essentially no different in any qualitative way from any other belief considered normal.

It could be argued that no person who believes in an afterlife truly understands the consequences of their actions.

In his book *Thinking About the Insanity Defense*, Ellsworth Fersch lays out the fundamental problem in the Lafferty case:

"Their strategy was to show that he was sane through comparison with other individuals. First, they pointed out all the similarities between his fundamentalist religious beliefs and the religious beliefs of people

with ordinary religious faiths. By doing so, they made his seemingly
outlandish claims and ideas seem much more normal. For example,
Dr. Gardner compared Ron Lafferty's belief in reflector shields to belief
in guardian angels. This strategy was effective because it forced anyone
who was willing to consider whether he was insane to also consider the
larger question of whether any religious person is insane."

Belief ties sanity and delusion into an almost inescapable Gordian knot. To uphold an insanity defense would be to imply that all religious believers are similarly insane. That would never be acceptable. But to exempt religious beliefs would make it extremely difficult to ever characterize anyone as insane or make any value judgment about any belief. It would make it difficult to interfere with any dangerous behavior such as faith healing when it is claimed to be based upon a "deeply held belief." That Gordian knot serves the narrow self-interest of believers.

These are extremely vexing conundrums even for psychologists. They have been completely muddled over this issue dating all the way back to Freud, who suggested that all religious beliefs are delusional and that religion is a mass-delusion.

On the more diplomatic side of the argument is the definition established by the American Psychiatric Association (codified in DSM-IV and V) which effectively says that a belief is a delusion—unless enough people believe that it is true. A cultural exception is granted to skirt the impracticality of concluding that the vast majority of the population is delusional.

Clearly if Freud is right, then that position leads necessarily to unacceptable clinical, social, and legal ramifications. However, if the APA is correct, then sanity is highly contextual. What might be sane in one society or in one group or at one time in history may be completely delusional and result in institutionalization in another setting. Precisely how many believers must I recruit in order for my insane delusions to be considered sane and immunized from ridicule? The APA view creates significant social problems for all aspects of society.

In his paper "Faith or Delusion? At the Crossroads of Religion and Psychosis," Joseph M. Pierre attempts to review the psychiatric literature in order to find a sensible middle ground. Pierre points out that:

"Neither Freud's stance that all religious belief is delusional nor DSM-IV's strategy of avoiding mention of religious thinking in discussions of psychosis is an acceptable way to resolve the ambiguity between normal religious belief and religious delusion."

One might think this question should be resolvable by simply looking at other criteria to evaluate sanity, not merely the presence of religious beliefs. But Pierre goes on in his paper to review the body of psychiatric works that attempt to distinguish faith from delusion using a wide range of possible criteria. None of these attempts prove to be satisfactory. Given sensitive social dynamics, it is difficult to make qualitative distinctions between "normal" beliefs and "delusional" beliefs. Attempts to distinguish these through indirect measures, such as excessive preoccupation, conviction, emotional valence, claims of universal validity, and level of contradiction all fail to provide a satisfactory distinction.

The situation we are left with is that we are precluded from ever admitting that religious beliefs are delusional, even though the APA indirectly defines beliefs as delusions held by a sufficiently large number of people. Instead, we are forced to make mostly arbitrary decisions about when to characterize a belief as a delusion.

But I have a suggestion to help with this problem. It seems to me that much of this Gordian knot is held together by a presumption, a prejudice, and a conceit that says that sanity and insanity are exclusive binary conditions.

I suggest that each of us has a myriad of ideas that could each be placed along a wide spectrum from sane to insane. If someone has a lot of delusional ideas a lot of the time, that person may cross the threshold of clinical insanity, but we all still do have some insane ideas some of the time.

If we would only stop applying to word "delusional" to people and instead start applying it with less reluctance to ideas, recognizing that we all have some delusional ideas some of the time, then I think we could go a long way toward reaching the balance we need to respond to mass-delusional thinking in a more reasonable and consistent manner.

Respect for Beliefs

In an enlightened society we should respect and cherish all beliefs.

Back during my time as a Peace Corps volunteer in South Africa, I was routinely shocked by the lack of understanding of the universe among even the most intelligent and educated people. Many people thought that the stars are tiny dot-like things just nearby that fall to the ground as shooting stars.

That ignorance is largely a problem with the poor education in rural South Africa, but it is clearly also a symptom of deeply saturated belief-based thinking. It continues because of a lack of fact-based reasoning, not merely a lack of formal education. Fact-based reasoning is pushed aside, allowed to atrophy by a dependence on beliefs.

During my first weeks in my village, relatively sophisticated and intelligent educators told me to be careful of witches.

> *"Don't go out at night," they cautioned me. "That is when they come out."*
>
> *"Have you seen them personally?" I asked.*
>
> *"No, but a friend of a friend saw them."*
>
> *"What do they look like?" I inquired, so that I might recognize one when I see one.*
>
> *"They look like shadowy little people with horns on their head," they told me with certainty.*
>
> *"So, they look like how a wandering goat might appear in the darkness," I suggested.*
>
> *"Yes exactly," they confirmed. "In fact, if you capture one, it will transform into a goat to escape."*

Belief, ignorance, superstition, and fear—these all walk hand in hand.

Lest the reader think to belittle or deride those rural South Africans for their irrational superstitions, realize that these are otherwise intelligent, warm, generous, and tolerant people.

And before you feel superior and more enlightened, appreciate that the United States is one of the most superstitious and belief-based nations on

Earth. The South Africans would laugh and shake their heads at many of our nonsensical beliefs and superstitions.

While 86 percent of Americans dismiss or doubt the scientific principle of evolution, well over 90 percent of Chinese accept it as simple fact. When challenged with this statistic, the response of many Americans is to claim that this acceptance is because the Chinese live in a mind-controlled society where they are told what to believe.

Who is capable of greater mental gymnastics to defend their beliefs, the South Africans who believe in witches that transform into goats when captured, or the Americans who rationalize everything from astrology to UFOs? Who is the victim of greater mind control, the Chinese who acknowledge incontrovertible fact as truth, or the Americans who deny it?

In many ways, South Africa has a newer and much more enlightened constitution than our own. Many countries do. Their constitutions have had to accommodate the reality that their people represent a wide range of religious belief systems.

To their credit, and despite an overwhelming Christian dominance, the very idealistic government of South Africa enshrined a respect for all religions into its constitution. In keeping with the spirit of the constitution, the school system charter mandates that schools must present all religious views equally to their learners.

When I helped teach in the rural schools there, I was pleased and very surprised to see that the science textbooks did present the big bang theory of universal creation. In one textbook, however, it was listed in a section entitled "Myths of Creation." The big bang and natural evolution were listed as the fourth myth, after the stories of how Bumba vomited up the sun, of how Amma molded the sun in pottery, and yes, the one of how it all started when the monkey stole the baby. The Christian myth was not presented in that section, presumably because that is not believed to be a myth.

Despite the very modern and progressive views of the South African government and its Department of Education, this is the outcome of a climate where belief-based thinking is allowed to flourish unchallenged. It is the result of a culture that is so concerned with being even-handed that truth becomes just another myth.

This was made even worse in practice. The teachers in the classroom were invariably the result of highly successful Christian missionary efforts. They had no knowledge of, or interest in, any religious views other than the Christian one. They simply used their freedom to talk about religion to proselytize for their faith and mock all the rest, including science.

This is the same thing that many would like to see happen in America. Despite any official policies and protections, this is what can happen when belief-based thinkers are allowed to exert their influence in the public sphere, and their beliefs are accepted with uncritical deference, without any respect for the truth as established by fact.

If teachers in any nation are given any opening whatsoever to bring their faith into the classroom, they will proselytize just as quickly as those teachers in rural South Africa.

I came away from that experience more dedicated than ever to our American principle of the separation of church and state. A well-intentioned policy of official respect for beliefs is so damaging that scrupulously keeping religion out of the public sphere, particularly out of education, is the very best alternative possible.

Religious zealots have no lack of opportunities to reach our children. There is no need to provide them with a platform in our schools.

CHAPTER 5: CLARITY

So far, we've talked about the importance of facts and about many of the things that complicate and obscure them. We've talked about beliefs and at least some of the factors that promote and perpetuate them. We then reviewed some of things that confuse facts with belief and followed that with a discussion of the progression from confusion into delusion.

If our perceptions are so very unreliable, as are our memories, and we can so easily fall prey to rationalizing any bogus belief, then what possible defense do we have?

We shouldn't take from all these obstacles that things are hopeless. Obviously, our species has done pretty well so far. But to overcome our immense modern challenges we must do better. Only through a clear-eyed appreciation of how vulnerable we are to beliefs and delusions and rationalizations can we hope to do better. After all, remember our first principle:

> *Decisions based on fact are inherently better than decisions based on belief.*

It is actually quite easy to remain fact-based by following a few simple practices. The first thing to do is to understand and recognize all the tricks and logical fallacies used to propagate beliefs. Become a smart consumer of purported facts and develop an innate baloney radar system.

The second is to understand and integrate the scientific method as much as possible into your life to ensure that your thinking remains grounded in facts. If you think in scientific terms, the scientific method will help you to come to the truth of a situation.

The third is to generally immerse yourself among fact-based thinkers and information sources. That is not to suggest walling yourself off from others with different views, or living in a bubble, or in an ivory tower. It doesn't mean you shouldn't engage with the world. But you can only stay mentally healthy by spending most of your time in a mentally healthy environment. Only in this way can you avoid infection and reinforce your resistance to infectious beliefs.

The fourth is to constantly go back to first principles. Look back not to your previous step out on that limb, but back to the solid tree trunk of basic assumptions. Only in this way can you be sure that you aren't fixatedly following the next crumb of logic out on an increasingly thin and dangerous branch of self-delusion.

This continuous reality check is something that scientists learn to do automatically. They constantly go back and reevaluate where they are with respect not to the last little logical step they made, but against the most fundamental starting point. If you always do that, then it is unlikely that you will go too far astray. At some point you will look back at the facts of the situation and realize that you have ended up way out on a limb.

In this chapter, we'll look at these and other ways to do better and offer some clarity that will help us to become better fact-based thinkers in a world mired in a thick fog of belief.

Good Karma

🗣 *Can't just a small dose of belief be a good thing?*

I admit to indulging in a wee dose of belief now and then. It's pretty clear that I argue passionately against most forms of belief-based thinking. But I do have to admit that sometimes a teeny tiny bit of false belief is helpful.

I rarely ever steal anything. In fact, if I realize that I was given too much change at the market, I'll invariably drive back to return it. I don't do the right thing because I'm such a noble upstanding person. I do it because of superstition.

You see, somewhere I picked up this deeply ingrained notion that if I keep that money, the universe will somehow take revenge on me. I'll stub my toe, or get a traffic citation, or spill coffee on my term paper. In some way I'll pay tenfold for my dishonesty.

Of course, that's silly. I know that's silly. Something bad will happen eventually, and when it does, I will falsely ascribe the cause to be my earlier bad behavior. But nevertheless, the feeling of wanting to avoid this bad karma is so powerful that it still can compel me to do the right thing.

Perhaps this belief in karma is just something learned from popular culture, but I rather suspect that our species carries the hardwired seed of this idea which gets reinforced by false associations acquired during one's lifetime. It makes evolutionary sense to me that such an assumption is a helpful genetic trait. Within social structures, what goes around does in fact often come back around. To enforce cooperation, societies tend to develop universal moral values, with moralizing religions that rise and fall.

These are developed as byproducts of general perceptual and cognitive mechanisms that can lead to the belief of causal connections with norm adherence.

Our innate fear of karmic payback is almost certainly a component of what we perceive as our nagging conscience. It's most likely a rudimentary example of our evolved moral behaviors.

Here's the danger in this. It leads many people down the rabbit hole into religion-land. If we believe in a little karma, why not an almighty god who personally ensures payback? If a little karmic fear is good, then the fear of eternal damnation is even better. If our sense of personal karma is hardwired, then in a very indirect sense, so is our belief in God.

But one essential principle you learn in toxicology class is that everything that is beneficial at low doses becomes toxic at higher doses. A little superstition may have some positive benefits. But a full-blown belief in God requires a level of superstition and a perversion of logical thinking that is so extreme as to be dangerously toxic. That level of belief is so debilitating to our logical faculties that it can compromise our ability to think rationally about critical issues like democracy and climate change.

And by the way, I know that my belief in karma is simply an artifact of my pattern matching algorithms. I know it is not real.

So, feel free to embrace a healthy sense of karma like as you would a magic show: with a full and complete understanding that it's not real. But don't let that indulgence lead you down the treacherously slippery slope into religion or New Age beliefs.

Santa Claus

🎙️ *If a bit of karma is a good thing, then what about a belief in Santa Claus? It makes my kids so happy to think Santa is real.*

Except you can give your kids all that fun without stunting their rational development.

Only an extremist would want to declare war on Christmas and ruin that wonderful holiday. But it does not detract one bit for our children to know that Santa Claus is fantasy. Kids have great fun at make-believe tea parties or battling imaginary aliens with toy guns. They know it is fantasy and it doesn't spoil their enjoyment one iota. On the other hand, let's examine the harm it does to perpetuate the myth of Santa Claus as true.

Once kids learn the truth, that they were fooled by adults they trusted, it does make many kids feel betrayed and made a fool of. But you'd think that, once fooled by a story about an all-powerful man who sees everything you do, rewarding you if you are nice and punishing you if you are naughty, they would be unlikely to be fooled by the very same story about God.

Except it doesn't appear to work that way. Instead of "Fool me once, shame on me; fool me twice, shame on you," learning about Santa Claus the hard way doesn't seem to inhibit most kids one bit from being fooled into believing what is essentially the very similar myth about God.

This is completely in keeping with everything we have been saying about the danger of belief.

It supports the view that our brains don't completely work in the way we might think, weighing new data against previous experience to form a conclusion, at least not without training in critical thinking.

Rather, this supports the neural network theory that our brains simply learn whatever thinking patterns they are exposed to, beneficial or not. Whether it is intentional or not, exposing our kids to the Santa myth, before they have learned critical thinking, programs their impressionable neural networks to accept similar assertions without critical analysis.

Exposure to belief makes it easier to believe the next unfounded proposition. Santa Claus, innocent as it seems, is the beginning of James Randi's slippery slope.

Therefore, have all the fun you like playing Santa Claus or any other fantasy role-playing with your kids. But their development is not served well by maintaining that these things are really real, and it does not reduce their enjoyment by one iota to let them in on the game.

This applies not only to Santa Claus but to all beliefs that we intentionally or inadvertently infect our kids with. Each one compromises their belief immune system and makes them more susceptible to less benign beliefs.

Our Amazing Brains

🗣 *I am more than just a bunch of neurons!*

Although, gotta say, being a bunch of neurons is pretty damn awesome… It is natural to think of our consciousness as something that is more tightly linked to a soul than to our physical bodies. But the hard truth is that we evolved from older species, we are only animals, and our minds, even our very consciousness, is really just a physical phenomenon.

This realization does not need to make us feel diminished whatsoever. On the contrary, appreciating that our psychology is merely a physical process is truly exciting to think about.

Our incredible neural networks should make us feel truly amazed and proud.

Back in the 1980s I worked as a research scientist, and one of my first successes was to apply early neural network technology to paint formulation chemistry. That experience gave me fascinating insights into how our brains operate. A computer neural network is a mathematically complex program that does a simple thing. It takes a set of training inputs and an associated set of outputs, and it learns how they connect by essentially computing lines of varying weights between them. Once the network has learned how to correctly connect these training inputs to their outputs, it can take any new set of inputs and predict the outcome. Or, reversing that, it can predict the best set of inputs to produce a desired outcome.

In the case of paint formulations, neural networks allowed me to "train" the neural network with paint formulations as inputs and the associated paint properties as outputs. Each known formulation is called a "training fact." The result is that, once trained, properties could be predicted for any new, novel formulation. Conversely, the formulation needed to achieve a particular set of properties could be predicted.

This provides an immensely powerful machine learning tool and also a very helpful model of brain function. We are exposed to "training facts" every moment of every day. As these new training facts arrive, the neural pathways they stimulate are reinforced and strengthened. The more often we observe a connection, the stronger that neural connection is weighted. Essentially, we are continually training and adjusting our pattern recognition system.

At some point, a connection grows so strong that it becomes undeniably obvious **common sense** to us. Unreinforced connections, as with our memories, decay and eventually become so weak that they are eventually forgotten.

Note that this happens whether we know it or not and whether we want it to happen or not. We cannot *not* learn facts. We learn language as children just by overhearing it. Whether we intend or want to learn is largely irrelevant. Our neural network training does not require conscious effort and cannot be ignored by us. If we hear a "fact" often enough, it keeps getting weighted more heavily until it eventually becomes intuitively obvious to us.

Pretty amazing right? It is. Like most things in nature, it's a stunningly complex system built from simple basic functionality, like an intricate fractal structure made from only triangles. Our consciousness is the ultimate emergent behavior of our individual neurons and their simple connection rules.

But here is one crucial limitation. Neither computer or biological neural networks have any intrinsic way of distinguishing whether a training input is valid or complete nonsense. Rather, they judge truthfulness based only upon their learned weighting.

If we tell a neural network that two plus two equals five enough times, it will eventually accept that as a fact and faithfully report five with complete certainty every time it is asked. It has no inherent way of judging the quality of data it receives. Likewise, if we associate the spilling of salt with something bad happening to us later, that becomes a fact to our neural network of which we feel absolutely certain.

To be precise, there are ways that computer-based neural networks can identify bad data, for example, if the analysis fails to find any satisfactory solution. These nuances are beyond the scope of this book, but they only extend the power of the model.

This inherent vulnerability of our neural networks, the fact that it cannot distinguish good facts from bad ones, wasn't too much of a problem during most of our evolution since we were almost exclusively exposed to real, true facts of nature and the environment. It only becomes a debilitating liability when we are overwhelmed by abstract symbolic facts that are not limited by reality and can represent utter fantasy.

Today, most of what is important to our survival are not "natural" facts that must be valid simply because they happened. They are conceptual ideas that can be repeated and reinforced in our neural networks without any physical validation. Take the idea of a God as one perfect example. We hear that God exists so often that our "proof of God" pathways strengthen to the point that we see proof of God everywhere and his existence becomes intuitively undeniable to us.

This situation is exacerbated by another related mental ability of ours: rationalization. Since a neural network can happily accommodate any "nonsense facts," regardless of how contradictory they may be, our brains have to be very good at rationalizing away any logical discrepancies between them. If two strong network connections logically contradict each other, our brains excel at fabricating some reason, some rationale to explain how that can be. When exposed to contradictory input, we feel disoriented until we rationalize it somehow. Without that ability, we would likely be paralyzed and unable to function.

Rationalization is a necessary adaptation. It allows us to continue to function, even when our neural networks have been trained with actual facts we cannot reconcile. For example, we see lightning, that is real, but we cannot relate it in any satisfying way in our minds. So, we rationalize an explanation, perhaps a story about gods, that makes it all fit together and feel sensible.

Our ability to rationalize is so powerful that we can rationalize ludicrously nonsensical facts. Even brain lesion patients who believe they only have half of a body will quickly rationalize away any reason you give them, any evidence you show them, that proves they are wrong.

Our neural networks are always being modified, regardless of how smart we are—whether we want them to or not, whether we know they are or not—and those symbolic training facts, unfettered to reality, can be absolutely crazy.

But our only measure of how crazy they are is our own neural network weighting, which tells us that the strongest connections must be the truest.

> *In mental health, anosognosia is a type of mental illness in which someone is unable to assess their own mental condition. But to some lesser extent, none of us can fully rely upon our mental faculties to self-assess.*

Our brains then, when modeled as a neural network, exhibit the following critical behaviors:

> *Our neural networks are trained by repeated exposure.*

> *Our brains assume repeated training facts are true, and the way we decide what is true is what our brains have been trained to believe.*

> *The concepts repeated most often eventually become the most obvious, common-sense concepts to us.*

> *Our neural networks have no mechanism to ensure internal consistency. The way we reconcile contradictory facts is by contriving some rationale to explain away or dismiss those contradictions.*

This model gives us insights into how we think that lead to very different attitudes and approaches than the more soul-based view of a non-physical, independent psyche. Our brains are not magical singularities that cannot be understood or manipulated. Rather, they are a part of our cosmos, our knowable universe, just like everything else.

Brain Cake

🔊 *All this stuff about neural networks is too confusing.*

Let's look at it a slightly different way.

Did you ever think about the amazing range of fantastic things you can cook up with essentially just flour, sugar, and water? It's dizzying.

With mostly just those simple ingredients and some heat, you can bake a mind-boggling range of breads, cakes, pastries, pastas, tortillas, crackers, pancakes, pretzels, biscuits, crusts, and even glue. Thinking about how to make all those things can take aspiring chefs a lifetime to fully master.

But in the end, they are all really just variations of a very simple set of ingredients and conditions. Understanding the commonality that underlies all that complexity is extremely enlightening.

When we look at complex, or at least little understood systems, they can seem to be beyond comprehension. It can seem impossible to ever understand them. In fact, the more you learn about them, the more complicated and inexplicable they become.

But you get to a point, after having grappled with all that complexity, that you start to see the big picture, the simple underlying ingredients and conditions that give rise to all of it. All of that apparent complexity becomes much simpler and more understandable. Appreciating the underlying elegance helps you to make far better sense of all the diverse ways it is expressed.

Genetics, and all of the variations we see expressed in life, largely boils down to different combinations of the four molecular bases of DNA: A, C, T, and G. Those are the flour, sugar, and water that get cooked up in the almost endless variety of life.

Likewise, evolution seems incomprehensibly complicated—until you understand a few very fundamental mechanisms of natural selection.

The same is true of our entire universe. The universe is composed of a cosmic range of phenomena from subatomic to galactic in scale, but in the end it can all likely be simplified down to one universal equation. It is all ultimately cooked up from the flour, sugar, and water of a handful of subatomic particles.

I submit that we should expect the same situation with our understanding of brain function. Our brains are highly complex but not incomprehensible. Eventually, when we have struggled sufficiently with all of the seemingly independent aspects of brain function, we will start to perceive the forest beyond those trees.

If we model the brain as a neural network that is tuned for pattern recognition, we can now envision one underlying system from which much of our observed behaviors can emerge.

In the neural network model envisioned in this book, the flour, sugar, and water of cognition essentially boil down to pattern recognition and pattern association. Let's try to put it all together into one model:

Our neural networks detect patterns of structure or behavior. When we retain a pattern, it becomes a symbol in our brain.

When we identify a structural pattern and associate it with the closest known symbol, we have identification and recognition.

When we identify a structural pattern and associate it with a behavioral pattern, we have a generalization.

As almost a side effect of pattern recognition, we can detect things that don't fit into known pattern—exception recognition as it were.

As with any other pattern recognition function, our pattern-recognition and matching system is highly subject to error, and in humans these errors are tuned to favor false positives.

When our pattern-recognition and matching system is fooled by sparse or misleading raw data or as a consequence of their tuning parameters, a large number of cognitive biases can occur.

Our pattern matching system has no inherent ability to judge the objective correctness of data. It can incorporate belief just as readily as it does fact.

When we identify patterns of data obtained through our senses, those become perceptions. Those perceptions are subject to all the same pattern-recognition flaws and biases.

Rationalization is essentially a path-finding algorithm. We look for the strongest pathway between two symbols that are not directly connected. That pathway becomes our rationale. It does not need to make sense but it becomes what makes sense to us.

The pathways produced can be extremely complex, with symbols recursively triggering other nested symbols and feeding back in unexpected ways to form a connection like a ray of light bouncing wildly in a house of prismatic mirrors.

Memory can be thought of as a rationalization process as well. Our neural network searches for a set of symbols that most closely fit what it is we are trying to recall.

Subjective reports, the reasons or rationale we give for why we do things, are another rationalization process. When asked why we did something, our neural network searches for the pathway that most closely connects what we did with how we see ourselves and wish to portray ourselves.

Perceptions, memories, and subjective reports are also subject to the same errors and biases. And as with any rationalization, there is no inherent mechanism to ensure that the paths found are true, logical, or even sane.

Our library of symbols is continually being updated with new patterns of structure and behavior. The strength of the associations between them are highly malleable and are continually being strengthened through repetition or weakened by atrophy. This gives rise to learning and all of the methods by which thinking can be changed.

This is not to suggest that this is a complete and universal view of cognition that accounts for every behavior. And while it can help us understand the underlying mechanisms, we cannot always see how those are manifest in any particular complex behavior. The same is true of genetics, or of physics. We cannot always trace how sequences of A, C, T, and G molecules translate into a particular complex trait, but it is incredibly informative to understand that they do.

While the model presented here cannot show us the particular cascade of cognition through our mental houses of mirrors that leads to a particular thought, it is extremely informative to understand the simple underlying mechanics at work. Further, when applied in the real world with real people, the model has real predictive value.

The Evolution of Belief

You say that we evolved our ability to believe. That proves that it must be a good thing.

If it exists in us, it evolved. Period.

Whether it be physical or intellectual traits, if it exists, it evolved. Whether we are talking about perceptions or logic or emotions, ethics, altruism, abstractions, pattern recognition, or even consciousness—it evolved.

So yes, our capacity to believe and to rationalize those beliefs is also an evolved trait. But people have a lot of misconceptions about evolution.

One of the most common misconceptions is that evolution optimizes the individual, making them as "fit" as can be. That is a fundamental misunderstanding of evolution. Actually, evolution does not care one whit about individuals. It only optimizes to ensure the survival of the species.

If that means that the species can succeed better if the female praying mantis eats her mate after insemination, so be it. If it means that older individuals fall prey to disease and die young, increasing the food available to child bearers, then that susceptibility becomes a beneficial genetic trait.

So not all evolved traits are good for individuals. And even those evolved traits are not actually the best possible; they are merely good enough, like our fragile spinal columns.

Another misconception is that all evolved traits are beneficial for the species as a whole. Some traits are simply inconsequential. They get a free ride since they don't really matter. Other successful traits are actually negative with respect to the entire species. The species survives despite them, not because of them.

The last misconception I'll mention is the idea that just because a trait evolved, and indeed has been helpful to our survival in the past, means it is a good thing. Past benefits are no guarantee that particular trait still serves us well any more or that it will continue to be a beneficial trait in the future.

Untold billions of species have gone extinct over the course of our evolutionary history, and many of those went extinct because of the very traits that served them well for a period of time before their environment changed, and then those same traits became fatal liabilities.

We are rapidly transforming our own environment. As our population increases, as technology exerts its pressures and influences, and as we pollute and consume, we essentially become aliens suddenly teleported onto another planet. It would be foolhardy to imagine that because a trait or behavior pattern succeeded on old Earth, it will continue to serve us well on the new Earth we are creating.

> *Lots of people like to claim that competitive capitalism promoting unbridled consumer growth has brought us all the things we enjoy today. But even if true, that does not mean that it is a viable system to provide a sustainable economy and a viable planet moving forward.*

When we accept that everything evolved, it is a fun exercise to think about why? Why are eggs egg-shaped? Did it have a benefit or was it merely an inconsequential random trait? If so, what evolutionary benefit did it offer?

I advise that the first assumption should be that all traits have, or at least had, an evolutionary benefit. That's a pretty good bet.

In fact, there is normally not just one benefit. Arguments about the "real" benefit of an adaptation are usually pretty silly. The answer is probably that all of the benefits were important.

But if you cannot show any evolutionary advantage, you should also consider that the trait could simply be inconsequential—at least until it isn't.

So, with that quick background, why did we evolve to be such superlative believers? Was it simply an artifact of other cognitive traits, or did it offer advantages?

I speculate that our capacity for belief may have been helpful during much of our evolution. Or at least it was not overly detrimental in sparse tribal societies.

Evolution doesn't care about facts. It is totally agnostic with regard to the truth of a proposition. All it cares about is that the species survive to reproduce. It is conceivable that an absolute belief in an untruth has had more survival benefit than recognition of the truth.

For one thing, beliefs compensate for the imperfections or gaps in our systems of perception and memory. As we have discussed earlier, each individual may see the same things but perceive them quite differently—literally differently, not just in the prosaic sense. But more than that, our memories of those events can diverge dramatically over time.

Now think about early man. How are they to have cohesion as a group, to avoid dispute, to connect intimately, unless they share common memories, common views of the world? The evolutionary solution is to make our memories and our very worldview malleable. Through a process of group suggestion, repetition, and rationalization, it is ensured that the group will increasingly share the same common experience, real or not. In a relatively sparse experiential environment, it is more important that shared experience be agreed upon than that it be true.

That is just one hypothesis to postulate how belief might have been an evolutionary advantage at one time. There are certainly many.

That was the past. What may have served us well in an early tribal environment no longer serves us well in a complex and abstracted modern world. If we aren't able to adapt, to develop the ability to distinguish clearly between true facts and belief, we may not survive.

Fortunately, now we can understand how our neural network systems work and we can understand their limitations. We can compensate for our innate evolutionary proclivity for belief.

We have technology to help us, if we use it correctly, and we have the scientific method. By using these wisely, we can achieve not only a shared worldview but a shared worldview based on fact. A shared, common worldview that is inarguably more conducive to our long-term survival as a species.

Healthy Brain Training

🗣 *If our neural networks are so vulnerable to adopting bad facts, filters, and thinking patterns, what hope do we have?*

All of our limitations can be overcome.

The fact that our neural networks are agnostic with regard to the validity or falsehood of a fact is a good news/bad news situation. The bad news is that we are terribly vulnerable to adopting the most insane views. The good news is that our brains learn valid information and sound thinking patterns just as easily, if we are preferentially exposed to them.

The reality is that we are constantly exposed to lots of "training facts," good and bad. There are two ways to handle this:

1 *Expose your brain mainly to good (true) facts.*
2 *Train your brain to distinguish good facts from bad.*

The first strategy is important. We should limit our exposure to bad facts and maximize our exposure to good ones by carefully selecting what we read, watch, and whom we personally interact with.

But we should not live in an information bubble. That is not good for Fox News viewers and it's not good for anyone. Unless we wish to live in an Amish village or in North Korea or in a cultist enclave, we need to engage with all sorts of people with all sorts of ideas.

That being the case, we need to train our brains to distinguish sound facts from bogus ones. Our ability to distinguish the quality of information is a pattern-recognition problem like anything else. Our networks are trained to apply perceptual filters and to recognize patterns of logic on the information we receive.

Are they tuned to accommodate beliefs and other nonsense and to produce crazy rationalizations to support them, or are they tuned to recognize patterns of scientific validity and prioritize those facts higher? How we interpret these facts is itself a learned neural network pattern.

If on the one hand, we are compromised by repeated rationalizations of beliefs to accept them readily, then that's bad. But we can also train our neural networks to recognize good facts. And we can do this by exposure to people who exhibit sound patterns of thinking and logic.

That should give us hope.

The scientific method is a proven way to help ensure that our conclusions align with reality, but science can only be applied to empirically falsifiable questions. Science can't help much with most of the important issues that threaten modern society, like should we own guns or should Donald Trump be president. Our flawed neural networks can make some of us feel certain about such questions, but how can we be certain that our certainty is not based on bad training facts and a failure to recognize them as such?

First, always try to surround yourself with validated training facts as much as possible. Religious beliefs, New Age ideas, fake news, and partisan rationalizations all fall under the category of "bad" training facts. Regardless of how much you know that they are nonsense, if you are exposed to them, you will get more and more comfortable with them. Eventually you will come around to believing them no matter how smart you think you are. It's a physical process, like the results of eating too much fat.

Second, contrary to what some might think, our brains are malleable, subject to change. We cannot prevent it. Indoctrination works, brainwashing works, marketing works. Repeated exposure to good facts and sound thinking makes us sound thinkers just as easily as chronic exposure to Fox News will make us angry and delusional. We *can* change minds, no matter how deeply impervious they may seem, for the better as easily as for the worse. Education helps. Good information helps.

There is a kind of exercise therapy called the Feldenkrais Method that was designed to help athletes in particular to become aware of their patterns of muscle movement, and to then strip out "bad" or "unnecessary" neural network programming to improve athletic efficiency and performance. I maintain that our brains work in essentially the same way as the neural networks that coordinate our complex muscle movements. As in Feldenkrais, we can slow down, examine each tiny mental step, become keenly aware of our thinking patterns, identify flaws, and correct them—if we try.

I'd love us to develop a Feldenkrais Method for the brain. Methods to help us become aware of our own "bad" programming and correct it.

Third, rely upon the scientific method wherever you can —or at least other sources that are science-based. Science, where applicable, gives us a proven method to bypass our flawed network programming and compromised perceptions to arrive at the truth of a question. Practicing good science is healthy exercise to clean up our neural networks and train to recognize sound patterns of logic.

Fourth, practice recognizing fallacies of logic to strengthen your pattern-recognition to detect baloney. This can help you to quickly and even unconsciously identify bad rationalizations in yourself as well as others. I provide a summary of many of these fallacies at the end of this book.

Finally, just be ever cognizant and self-aware of the fact that whatever seems obvious and intuitive to you may in fact be incorrect, inconsistent, or even simply crazy. Having humility and self-awareness of how our amazing yet deeply flawed neural networks function helps us to remain vigilant for our limitations and skeptical of our own compromised intuitions and rationalizations.

Your Three Misconceptions

You don't know me! Where do you get off claiming you know my mind?

I don't know you personally, but I guarantee that most of us suffer from three critical misconceptions about how people think. These mistaken assumptions confuse and frustrate much of our thinking about ourselves and others. I fall prey to them myself.

#1 Our Brains Ensure Consistency

Our first misconception is that our brains ensure consistency. Because we rationalize so well, we generally assume that human thinking must be internally consistent and consistent with external facts and basic logic. This false perception of our own internal consistency leads to all sorts of other mistaken assumptions.

This incorrect assumption causes us to look for consistency where there may be none, and to jump to unfounded conclusions about motivations and likely behaviors.

We assume that if someone believes A, then they certainly must not believe B, as that would be logically inconsistent. We assume that people do not act in logically inconsistent ways or with disregard for reality.

But our brains have little ability to ensure internal consistency. The reality is that our human neural networks can easily accommodate a staggering level of inconsistency. We learn whatever training facts, good or bad, that are presented to us often enough. Our brains have no inherent internal consistency checks beyond the approval and rejection patterns they are taught.

If we drop our assumption of consistency, if we fully appreciate that people can think wildly contradictory things simultaneously and reconcile them happily, we can avoid a lot of ineffective strategies in dealing with them.

#2 Rationalizations Are Rational

Our second misconception is that we are rational creatures. In actuality, we have an amazing ability to create completely irrational rationalizations in order to make our disconnected observations or unfounded patterns of belief seem totally logical and consistent to us.

Our virtually unlimited capacity to rationalize any contradictory or mutually exclusive ideas was a necessary evolutionary adaption to allow us to function despite the incoherence caused by flaw #1.

But again, this assumption of valid rationalization causes us a great deal of confusion and mistaken conclusions about people and their ideas. It leads us to look for or apply bogus secondary rationales to explain the irrational rationales of others.

#3 We're in Charge

The third misconception is that we generally make conscious decisions. We get fooled by our perception of, and need to attribute intent and volition to, our thoughts and actions. We imagine that we decide things consciously, when the truth is that most everything we think and do is largely the instantaneous, unconscious output of our uniquely individual neural network pathways. We don't so much arrive at a decision as we rationalize a post-facto explanation after we realize what we just thought or did.

Again, this misconception leads us to ascribe a lot of incorrect assumptions about people's motivations and the subjective explanations they provide.

When we ascribe post-facto rationalizations to explain our neural network conclusions, we mistakenly believe that the rationalizations came first. Believing otherwise conflicts unacceptably with our need to feel in control of our thoughts and actions.

Our consciousness is more like the general who follows the army wherever it goes and tells himself he is in charge. We feel drawn to a Tinder date. Afterward, when we are asked what attracted us to that person, we come up something like her eyes or his laugh. But the truth is that our attraction was so automatic and so complex and so deeply buried that we really have no idea. Still, we feel compelled to come with some explanation to reassure us that we made a reasoned conscious decision. I suspect that our illusion of conscious control is probably related strongly to our perception of consciousness.

Why are these flaws so important?
Understanding these flaws, and particularly how they interrelate, is incredibly important. Truly incorporating them into your analysis of new information shifts the paradigm dramatically. It opens up powerful new insights into understanding people better, promotes more constructive evaluation of their thoughts and actions, and reveals more effective options for working with or influencing them.

On the other hand, failure to consider these inherent flaws misdirects and undermines all of our interpersonal and social interactions. It causes tremendous frustration, misunderstanding, and counterproductive interactions.

I'll try to give you an appreciation of this through some typical expressions of bafflement we often voice or hear voiced. Each of these are caused by these mistaken assumptions:

🗣 *I don't understand how Bob can believe X. He is so smart!*

We often hear this sort of perplexed sentiment. How can so many smart people believe such stupid things? Well, remember #1. Our brains can be both smart and stupid at the same time, and usually are. There are no smart or stupid brains; there are only factually trained neural network patterns and speciously trained neural network patterns. Some folks have more quality programming, but that doesn't prevent bad programming from sneaking in.

It should not surprise us to find that otherwise smart people often believe some very stupid things. And we should not assume that because someone is smart in some areas, they cannot be crazy in others.

🗣 *Bob must be crazy if he believes X.*

Just as no one is completely smart, no one is completely crazy. Anyone can have some crazy ideas that exist perfectly well alongside a lot of mostly sane ideas. Everyone has some crazy programming, and we only consider them insane when the level of crazy passes some socially acceptable threshold.

🗣 *I believe Bob when he says X is true because he won a Nobel Prize.*

A common variant of the previous sentiments. Bob may have won a Nobel Prize, he may teach at Harvard, and may pen opinion pieces for *The New York Times*, so therefore we should give him the benefit of the doubt when we listen to his opinions. However, we should also be cognizant of the fact that he may still be totally bonkers on any particular idea. Conversely, just because someone is generally bonkers, we should be skeptical of anything they say but still be open to the possibility that they may be reasoning more clearly than most on any particular issue. This is why we consider "Argument by Authority" to be a form of specious argument.

🗣 *It makes me so mad that Bob claims that X is real!*

Don't get too mad. Bob can't fully help it. His neural network training has resulted in a network that clearly tells him that X must obviously be absolutely true. Too much Fox News, religious exposure, or relentless brainwashing will do that to anyone, even you and me.

🗣 *How can Bob actually claim that he supports X when he denies Y?*

First, recall flaw #1. Bob can believe any number of incompatible things without any problem at all. And further, flaw #2 allows him to rationalize a perfectly compelling reason to excuse any inconsistency.

Bob believes in X, so he'll never support Y.

Not true. Remember our flaws again. Bob's neural network can in fact accommodate one topic without changing the other one and still rationalize them perfectly well. All it takes is exposure to the appropriate training facts. In fact, consistent with flaw #3, after his network programming changes, Bob will maintain that he consciously arrived at that new conclusion through careful study and the application of rigorous logic.

Bob is conducting a survey to understand why voters support X.

Social scientists in particular should be far more cognizant of this one. How often do we go to great efforts to ask people why they believe something or why they did something? But remember flaw #3. Mostly what they will report to you is simply their post-facto rationalization based on flaw #2. It may not, and often does not, have anything to do with their extremely complex neural network programming. That's why subjective studies designed to learn how to satisfy people usually fail to produce results that actually influence them. Bob should look for more objective measures for insight and predictive value.

Bob should support X because it is factually supported and logically sound!

Appeals to evidence and logic often fail because people's neural networks have already been trained to accept other "evidence" and to rationalize away contrary logic. It should be no surprise that they reject your evidence and conclusions, and it doesn't accomplish anything to expect Bob to see it, let alone berate or belittle him when he does not.

I hope these observations have given you a new lens through which you can observe, interpret, and influence human behavior in uniquely new and more productive ways. If you keep these misconceptions in mind, you will be better able to put observations about people in perspective and, more importantly, arrive at more reasonable expectations.

The Binary Fallacy

I get it. Some people are smart and others are just dumb.

That is totally the wrong way to view people. Not only wrong but wholly inaccurate and counterproductive.

Very little in nature is binary. Most everything lies somewhere along a spectrum. That is certainly true for most of the attributes we ascribe to people. Here are some of the attributes that we generally view as binary:

Sane or insane
Smart or stupid
Good or bad
Criminal or law-abiding
Male or female
Gay or straight
Brave or cowardly
Healthy or sickly
Kind or unkind
Generous or miserly
With us or against us

There are certainly many more. Even though we think of these as discrete and mutually exclusive, none of them are really binary traits. Of these, I want to look at two in detail because they strongly impact how we view facts and beliefs.

The first is the spectrum of sanity. Rather than trying to force everyone into either a sane box or insane box, we would be far better served by appreciating that no one is fully sane or fully insane. Yes, some of us cross some societal threshold into clinical insanity, but all of us exhibit the same behaviors and quirks, only less often and less severely.

Appreciating that no one is fully sane dramatically expands our potential explanations for behaviors and phenomena that we otherwise might ascribe to paranormal or supernatural causes. For example, not only crazy people can have sporadic episodes of lucid dreams, or hearing voices, or seeing something imaginary. These things can, on occasion, happen to any of us. That explains a lot of otherwise inexplicable events.

Likewise, appreciating that smart and stupid are not binary traits helps us to explain and avoid a huge number of perplexing experiences with people.

If we recognize that everyone is smart about some things and stupid about other things, this allows us to, for example, exercise greater skepticism regarding dubious information reported by otherwise credible people. Conversely, it makes us appreciate that people who are not smart about some things, can be incredibly intelligent about others.

In fact, it isn't even sufficiently nuanced to think of sanity and intelligence as a simple continuum. It is more accurate and helpful to think of them as complex bar charts. Each of us has our own fingerprint-like bar chart of things we are smart or stupid about and things we are sane or deluded about.

For example, some of us may be strong in characteristics in the realm of, say, art. Others may have specific strengths in the realm of spatial reasoning, like the ability to recognize symmetry or reflections. At the same time, we are all weak in other specific traits or entire areas. We each have our own unique bar chart of mental strengths and weaknesses, but the overall bar chart adds up to roughly the same total area for everyone.

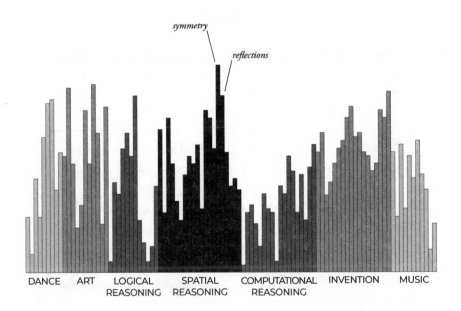

If we think of sanity and intelligence as bar charts unique to each individual, we can more effectively appreciate each person's unique strengths and not be surprised that they have some seemingly inconsistent weakness. We stop expecting them to be smart about all things or dismiss them as stupid about all things. We can appreciate that everyone can be perfectly sane in some things and totally irrational in others.

Instead of imposing one binary judgment on people, we must get good at recognizing when they are being smart and sane, and when they are being stupid and insane. Note that while we can all be sane in some ways and crazy in others, this does not imply that these are compartmentalized. Belief can still compromise and diminish our rational faculties.

Changing Minds

🗣 *In my experience, it is impossible to change anyone's mind about anything. I know because I've tried!*

That is a very commonly expressed frustration.

In fact, in this period of Covid vaccine hesitancy, it has become very popular to talk about the so-called **backfire effect,** which suggests that the more evidence you give someone that contradicts their beliefs, the more entrenched they become in those beliefs. It can indeed be hard to change minds. We don't always succeed, or at least we don't often see evidence of the effect we have made, but we certainly can change minds. We can change the very way people think. It can be pretty easy to do, in fact.

Consider that you most likely feel that your own mind could be changed. You feel that you are rational and open-minded and that you would respond to credible evidence or sound logic and change your opinions.

🗣 *So why are you so sure that no one else's mind can be changed?*

Another proof is that we actually see opinions beliefs change all around us all the time. Our beliefs have been and are being continually shaped, even transformed, by sales and marketing, education, culture, indoctrination, religion, propaganda, media, personal experiences, news, and a host of other influences. Beliefs in particular are some of our most fluid of ideas because they are not fettered by physical constraints.

> 🗣 *So why are you so convinced that all these things we*
> *routinely rely upon to change minds do not work?*

One additional proof is simply that we are here. We could not have survived the gauntlet of evolution without a tremendous ability to adjust our beliefs in response to new information. It is unreasonable to think that we could have adapted to a rapidly changing world without that innate capacity. And it is consistent and reasonable to assume that this malleability doesn't care what kind of belief we are talking about, deeply held or not.

> 🗣 *So how is it that so many people think our human brains*
> *are so set and intransigent that minds cannot be changed?*

No doubt it is quite difficult to change minds. But that doesn't make the effort futile. Consider dating. For many of us it's frustratingly difficult to find a date, let alone true love. We can't seem to convince anyone we're worth dating and so we conclude that dating itself is hopeless.

But people all around us do it all the time and we can too. And as with dating, there well-known techniques that have proven to work extremely well in the art of persuasion in general. These include establishing trust, reframing the debate, making it personal, making it their idea, systematically dismantling rationalizations, and moving the other party along in small incremental steps.

One huge reason we have so little apparent success in changing minds about beliefs and opinions is because we work under a false assumption. We imagine that people change their minds by a logical, rational recognition of superior reasoning. This is totally unrealistic. No matter how inescapable your argument may be, no matter how irrefutable your evidence, it probably won't make a lot of difference.

And that makes perfect sense if we understand how our neural networks actually work. Our brains cannot assess "superior logic." They can only recognize patterns and, if they get through our biases, adjust our neural network connections accordingly.

So, it's really just a matter of getting your message through, bumping up those particular pathways, over and over again, until they eventually become dominant. I know it sounds dismissive of human intelligence and will and reason, but it's just the way it is. As Nobel Prize winner Daniel Kahneman pointed out:

> *"A reliable way to make people believe in falsehoods is frequent repetition, because familiarity is not easily distinguished from truth. Authoritarian institutions and marketers have always known this fact."*

Science has suggested that our minds, the thinking part of our brain, where facts are stored and associations are made and patterns are recognized is not in our brain as much as it *is* our brain. It is probably wrong to think of our brains as being "programmed." Rather, our brains are the program. Our software is anatomical. It resides in the physical connection of our neurons, our neural network. When changes are made to our thinking, physical changes are made to our brains at the cellular connection level.

We couldn't really "copy" our mind to another brain the way we transfer software. To "mind transfer" we would have to physically alter all the neurons and all the connections in the second brain to match the first. We would have to make a physical copy of the brain down to every individual neuron and each connection. And by the way, there are an estimated 86 billion neurons in our brains.

Our neural networks are a three-dimensional web of actual physical connections. But we can imagine mapping them onto a two-dimensional plane like a projection onto a flat map. For discussion purposes then, our neural network associations can be envisioned like a hydrological map of rivers spanning the United States.

When we are born, we don't come with a flat, blank map. We have inherited connections, like a system of shallow rivers. These give us our innate, pre-packaged behaviors and personality. Some call this "hard wiring," but it's actually just as soft as any other programming.

Newborns have some innate neural connections. As they interact with their environments, their neurons are tuned, by becoming sensitized to specific stimuli, and their neuronal networks are pruned.

Once the infant mind starts to perceive things, it is like rain falling onto the landscape. It forms little rivulets that by repeated exposure can grow into rivers. Some of those, if repeated long and often enough can deepen into Grand Canyons in our neural network map.

For example, infants use organized visual search patterns to identify and explore cues like edges. Neural networks that process responses to control eye tracking movements depend on populations of neurons tuned to identify movement direction and speed. Sensory information is transmitted by connections to and between other areas of the brain to evoke thoughts and emotions, learn or form memories, and perform other high-level functions.

This landscape can be altered at any time. It is impossible to keep it from changing, except by subjecting it to only the same limited training facts over and over.

So, can thinking be altered? Can people be convinced? Absolutely. In fact, they cannot prevent it. But can it be very difficult? Even seemingly impossible? Absolutely.

The trick is to simply expose folks to alternate training facts. That is easier said than done, since you have to break through all the current filters that limit what they are willing to hear and how they interpret it.

But it can be done. We see it being done all the time. One way is through brainwashing, which we discussed earlier. Other, less rapid techniques include socialization, school, changing peer groups, indoctrination, advertising, marketing, and propaganda to name only a few. These things all do work, if not as quickly as we'd often like them too. It can take time to fill in the Grand Canyon and dig another canal.

So, don't lament that our minds cannot be changed. And don't despair if your efforts do not seem to have any effect. They do. Every new training fact you add fills that river up a bit more. Eventually, one more drop will cause it to become the primary thought pattern that is now the new deeply heartfelt conviction.

When I was in the Peace Corps in South Africa, I used to speak to groups of teachers. Each time I touched upon the subject of corporal punishment it would create a furor. The teachers would vehemently insist that their teachers punished them, and they are very happy with how they turned out!

Eventually I decided that I would not raise the topic again. Each time I did, it simply derailed discussion of other topics. Coincidentally, the next day, a colleague told me that a group of those same teachers approached him and shared their heartfelt passion for stopping corporal punishment.

This experience made me realize that when your audience engages with you, even angrily, it means you're reaching them. Your message is causing conflict that their neural networks are struggling to resolve. It's when they sit there passively that know you're not getting through.

So much for the "backfire effect." Instead of that term, I would call it the "immune response" effect. When a medical treatment produces a response, however swollen and red and painful, it may be a good sign. Those temporary reactions will likely recede, and the patient will eventually respond well to the treatment.

We rarely see the ultimate effect of our example or our arguments upon others, but our understanding of neural network learning assures us that we do contribute to a cumulative effect, regardless of how intransigent the other party may seem.

Don't try to tell me you cannot change anyone's mind.

And as my final proof, do you feel even a bit more optimistic about your chances of having a real impact on individuals and on society after reading this? If so, I have changed your mind at least a bit. If not, that only proves that I failed to make my case or perhaps that you simply cannot perceive how your thinking has been influenced.

Sudden Changes

You talk about changing minds as a long process. But I've seen people make dramatically sudden changes of perspective.

I'm glad you, my imaginary colleague, pointed that out! In the last section we discussed how changing minds requires a long process of repeated exposure to new ideas. Even brainwashing takes a great deal of time and considerable planned effort. But we have all seen cases where people suddenly have a profound change in their ideas or attitudes. How do we explain this?

First, we have to recognize that some of these apparently sudden changes might simply be the last straw, the final drop in a long process that finally makes the new neural network connection ever so slightly stronger than the old one. Our brains don't care if that new connection is radically different from the old one.

But there is certainly another way that minds can be changed. Rather than slowly and laboriously thickening the lines on our neural Etch-a-Sketch, you can just shake it up and quickly clear the patterns, suddenly wiping out the entire screen.

Electroconvulsive therapy can be thought of as one example of this kind of shake-up, or perhaps some other emotional shock to the old neural network might have a similar effect in leveling the landscape as it were.

But more commonly, our neural networks can exhibit dramatic changes as a result of the most seemingly random and unrelated stimulus. You inform someone that aardvarks walk on their toes and suddenly they change political parties. Go figure. But we do see seemingly inexplicable "attitude adjustments" or fundamental shifts in opinion or personality all the time.

In the context of our model, this is explained by the fact that our neural network is so complex, and so full of "bad programming," that any little change can have a profound and seemingly unrelated effect. Using our waterways model, an avalanche, some new idea, blocks a pass, and an entire river is diverted along a completely different pathway.

Voilà! A sudden dramatic and sweeping change in thinking.

Now, such unpredictable changes aren't much help in practice. We can rarely figure out exactly what string to pull in the parlor to cause the bell in the kitchen to ring, but we need to recognize that it happens. These seemingly random changes could result in the acceptance of beliefs as easily as real truths.

> *My eyes were suddenly opened! It could only have been divine revelation!*

Sudden changes can be made to happen. If you happen to be smart or lucky, you can accomplish this with just a tiny and seemingly unrelated change in the inputs. You pull on just the right string, and the blinds open up to expose a dramatically new vista.

For example, "language guru" Frank Luntz perhaps instinctively leveraged such changes. He didn't try to overcome or rewrite people's neural network programming. He merely changed estate tax to death tax, and that caused many folks' neural networks to completely switch tracks.

Sudden changes, subtle or dramatic, can and do often occur in our complex neural networks, resulting in profound changes in our perspectives, attitudes, perceptual filters, memories, beliefs, and personalities.

Attitude Adjustments

🗣 *Maybe you can influence people's minds about facts, but changing attitudes is a lot tougher.*

I'm not so sure. An attitude is really just a manifestation of neural network patterns like everything else. As such, attitudes are subject to all the same biases and influences.

Attitudes can drift and shift by all the mind-changing methods we discussed earlier, and they can change suddenly as well. When I was in college, I spent a couple years living, studying, and teaching in India. I didn't notice it at the time, but over many months my attitude gradually drifted quite negative. I started to perceive everything around me as dirty and disgusting. Everyone around me was stupid and obnoxious.

One day I was walking toward the university. The sun was hammering me. The hill was unforgiving. Cow dung dotted the road. On either side were the typical crowds of grinning idiots gaping at me as if I was some circus freak on parade. Everything stank and every sound was an assault upon my senses.

When I reached the university, it was empty. A groundskeeper noticed me and explained it all by simply saying "sympathy strike." Just great, I said to myself. This happens almost every week, another wasted hike up here. I sat down as much out of disgust as to rest up for the long trudge back to my house.

As I sat there, fuming, my attention was caught by a young girl playing in the grass. She was catching leaves as they fell from a grand old umbrella of a tree.

As I watched her, something snapped. Not snapped for the worse, but for the better. It was as if some dislocated mental shoulder had suddenly snapped back into its socket and only then did I realize how painfully out of joint it had been.

After that seemingly random adjustment, everything was different. There were birds chirping happily as they flitted about. There were people calmly going about their business. The breeze was sweet.

As I retraced my steps back to my house, all the same things were different. There were little wildflowers sprouting from the most unlikely cracks. People were regarding me with kindly, innocent interest. The street vendors were preparing all sorts of appealing snacks.

I didn't perceive a filthy, threatening place anymore but a safe and endearing community. There was beauty everywhere for anyone with eyes to see.

What had changed? The street had not suddenly transformed. The people had not been replaced. Only my attitude had changed, and my perceptions changed with it.

I had always thought of the phrase "attitude adjustment" as merely a figure of speech. I never thought of it as a real thing, a physical thing, a sudden change like a chiropractic adjustment. But it can be.

My brain had flipped just as surely as if I had taken off the vision-flipping goggles. It suddenly corrected and flipped my attitude right-side up again. And when my attitude changed, so did my perceptions. Now I noticed all sorts of things I hadn't noticed before. My bias-colored lenses had suddenly changed colors.

Attitudes are how we feel about our situation. They are controlled by our beliefs and reinforced by our filtered perceptions, and, like memory, attitudes are incredibly malleable.

Here's the really encouraging thing about this story: Attitudes can change, and sometimes they can change very quickly. And when enough attitudes change, entire cultures follow.

Generalizations

I think it's important not to stereotype but rather to evaluate every person by their own individual merits.

It is indeed important to recognize each individual according to their deeds, not solely based upon their associations. But let's not naively deny the practical utility of generalization. Generalization is one of our most fundamental and important cognitive pattern-matching functions. The capacity for cognitive control, using and maintaining abstract rule-like representations—generalization with flexibility—in the prefrontal cortex to guide processing is fundamentally human. The prefrontal cortex continues to develop until late adolescence and allows us to engage in new tasks by making use of information experiences acquired from other tasks.

But to discuss these fundamental brain processes requires that we dip our feet into the hot-button areas of generalization, stereotyping, and prejudice. This is a fraught discussion but a necessary one. Let's try to look at them from a pattern-recognition point of view, shall we?

Pattern matching applies to behaviors as well. We are able to match patterns of behaviors as quickly as we do patterns of shape. We quickly learn to identify not only a tiger in the brush but also the specific hunting patterns of different predators. Our ability to recognize and predict new behavioral patterns has meant the difference between survival end extinction.

The fact that we are still here proves that we are pretty good at it. At some point long ago, we learned to recognize the pattern of a tiger in the trees and the pattern of their movements. As nomads, we may have encountered unfamiliar animals, such as mountain lions. We noticed that they looked and moved somewhat like the tigers that had been allowed to approach too close and killed three of our tribesmen. Consequently, we made an essential generalization: Tigers are dangerous. Mountain lions probably are too. Run.

Once we predict a behavioral pattern, we generalize. Generalization is an essential survival trait. What is the risk of *not* generalizing and being wrong? You become cat chow.

In order to survive to this day, we had to become very good at generalizing behavior and acting on the assumption that all similar individuals behave like representative members of their group. Or to put it in more accurate evolutionary terms, those individuals who did not sufficiently generalize didn't survive to produce offspring.

Generalization is a critical cognitive function not only in recognizing predators but in everything we do. We simply could not function if we insisted on never assuming some consistency of traits and behaviors based on whatever limited experience we have with that group of people or things.

The universe would become essentially chaotic, and we could not function within a completely disordered universe, or more properly, an ordered universe in which we did not recognize any order.

But generalizations do have their unfortunate side effects, most notably stereotyping, profiling, and prejudice. From the cognitive perspective, generalizing is when we associate the pattern of an individual as being consistent with a generalized pattern. For example, this animal is a tiger.

Stereotyping is when we match an individual pattern with a general pattern based on some features but fail to detect other features that distinguish it. For example, we mistake a kitten for a tiger.

Profiling is a second-order generalization. We associate an individual with a group and associate that group with some other attributes. Profiling can be fair and correct. But profiling can become unhealthy when we unfairly stereotype an individual and then, maybe unfairly as well, associate their group with negative attributes. A fair profiling example may be, "That's a tiger so it is dangerous." A less fair profile may be, "That's a kitten so it is dangerous."

Lastly, prejudice can be seen as a more focused association problem than merely unfair profiling. When it progresses to prejudice, the generalization becomes more pervasive, tainting everything the target does with negative associations. This can become completely divorced from any reality.

For example, "Kittens have no redeeming characteristics whatsoever. The only good kitten is a dead kitten."

Although stereotyping, profiling, and prejudice can be unfair and even damaging, it does not mean we should deny the absolute necessity of generalizing.

Whenever we generalize, we should all understand that there can be exceptions. Exceptions do not disprove the legitimacy of, nor the need for, generalizations.

Generalization is an essential pattern-recognition adaptation, but so is recognizing exceptions. The ability to recognize exceptions to patterns is also a natural ability of ours. Recognizing exceptions is itself a form of pattern recognition and is an equally important survival trait. If we are not able to recognize exceptions to rules, then we lose out on the unique benefits that those opportunities can offer.

We can and must quickly retrain our generalizations to incorporate changing facts. When there are sufficient exceptions, when our generalizations are no longer generally true, we have evolved to adapt them, refine them. Without the ability to recognize exceptions, retraining would not be possible. This is an ongoing part of our continual neural network updating.

But we should not merely relegate this kind of reevaluation to a subconscious process. We should speed it up through intention and awareness and openness. We should train our neural networks to better allow in evidence that is contrary to our generalizations.

If we gain new evidence, say, that an individual deviates from the group norm, we should consciously reconsider our feelings about those individuals. When an entire group changes behavior, we should be open enough to allow our neural networks to revise our perception of and generalizations about that group. Easier said than done, I know. Especially when all of our biased perceptual filters get in the way.

The process of recognizing invalid generalizations is further exasperated by our mutually reinforcing interactions that create self-perpetuating feedback loops.

For example, Person A is frightened by people from Group B. Everything she has heard about people from Group B is that they are dangerous. She sees a person that she associates with Group B approaching her in a dark alley.

She becomes apprehensive and tenses up. Person B from Group B, being very good at pattern recognition as well, notices that Person A has tensed up in his presence. Person B knows he is a nice person and does not deserve to be feared. That stereotyping makes him feel angry, perhaps even prejudged, so he grimaces in disgust. Person A, also very good at pattern recognition, sees Person B scowl and tense. That makes her afraid and reinforces her stereotype about Group B.

We see these kinds of scenarios play out all the time all around us. Is it any wonder that social groups can be trapped in mutual distrust and animosity for so long? Is it any wonder that entire countries can continue to make war for generation after generation?

Our innate ability to generalize, recognize exceptions, and refine our generalizations fails when beliefs are substituted for facts, when old information is propagated by our group as a belief, not as a fact. When this happens, they cease to have rational justification or practical value. Worse, these generalized ideas can become immune to revision by exception recognition since they are not real to start with. They simply become unfair, damaging, and immutable stereotypes and prejudices.

To a great extent, we must recognize that fact-based generalizations are fair and necessary, that each individual must accept any legitimate generalizations they inherit by associating intentionally or unintentionally with a certain group. It would be simply unreasonable of me as an older white male to expect that I could approach a little girl on a playground without raising the suspicion that I may be one of a small minority of child molesters. It would be unreasonable of me to insist that I not be judged by my group. We have to accept the worst legitimate stereotypes of our group, whether we are a non-pedophilic priest, a sweetheart of a gangbanger, or a perfectly sane Trump voter.

Potential victims don't have the obligation to treat us as harmless pending any bad action on our part. Rather, it is our responsibility to prove we are different, to earn trust as an individual and ultimately for our group. But at the same time, it is also the responsibility of the other party to overcome their generalizations if warranted, to be open to evidence that individuals or even the entire group can now be trusted, and to revise their generalizations to be fairer and more fact-based.

But again, while fair generalizations are good. Generalizations based on beliefs are particularly problematic. Unfair stereotypes and prejudices based on false beliefs, beliefs with no basis in reality to allow for revision, are the festering pustules caused by our underlying pandemic of delusion.

Revising Stereotypes

🗣 *You can sometimes change people's minds, but changing their stereotypes is much more difficult.*

Theoretically, a stereotype is no different from any other neural network patterns. There is no reason that our stereotypes should not be created and altered in the exact same way as any other belief. If we are exposed to "training facts" that contradict the stereotype, eventually that stereotype will change.

As we discussed earlier, a prejudice is simply a type of stereotype, an incorrect generalization. Therefore, even prejudices can change.

I don't mean to make this kind of change sound easy, and again it is particularly difficult if those generalizations are based on beliefs that are resistant to falsification, but I do want to emphasize that change is possible. Further, as with learning other patterns, it happens whether we want it to or not.

My friend Mike and I greatly concerned the nuns at Saint Matthew's elementary school because our hair extended slightly over the tops of our ears. This made us radical hippies. The nuns took draconian measures to dissuade us from a life of ruin and immorality, up to and including revoking my status as lunchroom milk monitor!

I always held a measure of disdain for their foolish stereotyping. How narrow-minded and bigoted they were! But then later in life, I started to see a lot of young men in their late teens and early twenties with bald heads and tattoos.

Every time I saw young guys walking along on the street my emotions boiled over. Skinheads! Bigoted neo-Nazi right-wing white supremacists! Why else would anyone voluntarily shave their head except to make a statement that they supported those hateful ideologies?

Sigh… I had become the nuns at St. Matthew's elementary school.

For the first time, I really understood how they felt and why they reacted as they did. It was a humbling realization.

I saw that my stereotype regarding shaved heads was no longer true (if it ever really was), but I still had trouble shedding my emotional response. Emotion lags well behind reason.

But eventually that changed. I can now report that I can look at a bald-headed guy and not have a gut-level feeling of fear and outrage.

I realize that one anecdote doesn't say anything about how common something is, but it does prove that it is possible. We can reprogram our neural networks, even when it comes to strong prejudicial stereotypes. What helped me to change that stereotype was interaction with bald-headed, tattooed guys. They were just fine! They didn't spew neo-Nazi propaganda even once!

It makes evolutionary sense that our generalizations can change. We would not survive long if that were not the case. While our neural networks are great at recognizing patterns, they are also great at recognizing variations from those patterns. We have evolved to allow for exceptions to generalizations. Enough of those exceptions, and our generalizations eventually adjust.

But I cannot point out often enough, that generalizations can become immune to revision if they are based on ideas or beliefs that are not subject to falsification. And they can be particularly difficult to change if our pattern recognition systems are so compromised by belief rationalization, that any evidence of falsity is quickly and easily rationalized away.

Question Your Sanity

So how can I ever know if I'm thinking rationally?

Strictly speaking, you can't. You cannot always trust what you think. You cannot always trust what seems obvious and self-evident to you.

In fact, we are often the worst judges of our own thoughts and conclusions. By definition, whatever our neural network thinks is what seems inescapably logical and true to us. And our neural networks can think practically anything.

Given that we can't fully trust our perceptions, or memories, or rationales, we should have a deep humility for and skepticism toward our own thinking.

Our first thought must always be, Am I the one whose neural network is flawed here? Here's a personal anecdote to illustrate.

Up until fifth grade, I said all my R's like W's. That is, I would say "I wode on the twain." This is a fairly common speech impediment called rhotacism.

Everyone constantly tried to correct me. Some were gentle, some were mocking, but everyone would interrupt and tell me, "No, you rode on the train."

I was incredibly frustrated and upset every time someone corrected me. What is their problem? I would angrily respond by saying "Wight! I wode on the twain! That's what I said!!"

Nothing could make me hear the difference, and therefore nothing could make me entertain any explanation other than that everyone else must be crazy or malicious or both.

Then one morning I got called down to the lunchroom. There was a cute speech-therapy student visiting from nearby Marquette University. After a quick confirmation of my problem, she instructed me to watch her mouth as she said "rode" and "wode." Notice, she said, how my tongue curls when I say "rode" but lays flat when I say "wode."

Immediately after seeing the difference, I said "I rode on the train" as if it were the most natural and obvious thing in the world.

She just smiled and said, OK, you can go back to your class now. My seemingly intransigent rhotacism was completely cured in one simple ten-minute session.

All it took for my neural network to shift completely was a different type of input.

Sometimes we can recognize that our own thinking is suspect, and sometimes we might accept it when others point it out, but most of the time it is exceedingly difficult for us to recognize, let alone correct, our own network programming. Yet sometimes, as with my rhotacism, our neural networks can suddenly change either by accident or by careful, intentional exposure to alternate input. But usually, we are largely unaware of network changes within us. It usually happens through repeated exposure to different training facts. And when it does happen, it is often so gradual that we swear that we have not changed at all. Still, there are ways that we can self-assess.

We can develop legitimate confidence in our information sources, particularly those that rely upon scientific-caliber evidence and validation. We can become good enough at recognizing fallacious logic that we can have some confidence in our ability to detect bogus arguments. We can give honest consideration of opposing arguments and contradictory evidence before we draw a conclusion.

Also, we should pay attention to what we are saying. If we frequently start a rebuttal with "But this is different because," chances are good you are engaging in rationalization. Yes, often analogies can be incorrect, but if you persist in dismissing every argument with some special case why your belief is an exception to the rule you would otherwise accept, you should be skeptical of our own thinking.

Perhaps our most undervalued trait is our ability to accommodate ambiguity. That is, be OK with the fact that we don't know, that the jury is out, and that we do not yet have enough information to draw a conclusion or make a judgment. Prefer not to have an answer over simply making one up. Society values people who quickly form strong opinions. But we should place higher value on people who are willing to acknowledge that we simply do not know enough as of yet to form a strong opinion.

But keep in mind that just because we cannot fully trust our own thinking doesn't mean we should question everything we think. Nor does it mean that we should be paralyzed and too uncertain to ever formulate a firm conclusion about anything.

We simply cannot and should not question every idea we have learned or allow ourselves to be razzle-dazzled into indecision by the Merchants of Doubt. We have learned the Earth is spherical. We shouldn't feel so insecure as to question that, or be intellectually bullied into entertaining new flat-Earth theories to prove our open-mindedness or scientific integrity.

Global climate change is real. It's a thing. It's happening. Act on it.

God is a purely made-up fantasy. Get off your agnostic fence and discard modern mythologies along with the ancient ones. Doubt everything until it's clear that you should be absolutely certain—then still be willing to change your mind based on new evidence.

Evaluating Rationality

*If it is so difficult to assess our own rationality,
how do we assess the rationality of others?*

You may have read articles that reference the often-cited Linda the Bank Teller case conducted by researchers Daniel Kahneman and Amos Tversky back in 1983. In it, the researchers describe an outspoken person named Linda who is smart and politically active and who has participated in anti-nuclear demonstrations. They then ask the participant to indicate whether Linda is more likely to be a) a bank teller or b) a bank teller who is also an active feminist.

No direct evidence is given to indicate that Linda is either a bank teller or a feminist. She is smart so she might be a bank teller, and since she has been socially active, she might be a feminist. But logically it is far more likely that Linda is only one of these things than that she is both. Yet most people, given the choices presented and regardless of education, answer that Linda is probably both a bank teller and a feminist. This is an example of the conjunction fallacy, in which a person mistakenly believes that multiple conditions are more likely than a single one.

Although this study is frequently cited in popular science articles, the conclusions drawn from it have been strongly criticized or at least given more nuanced analysis. An example of one such popular science article describes research by Keith Stanovich. In his work he used the Linda case methodology along with other tests to measure rationality. This study has been used to suggest that the Linda case is a strong indicator of rationality.

I find that assertion very troubling.

First off, while the Linda case does expose the conjunction fallacy, we are all are susceptible to a huge number of logical fallacies as I document later in this book. While everyone should be taught to do better at recognizing and avoiding logical fallacies, failing to do so probably does not adequately correlate to irrational thinking.

If subjects were made aware that this was intended as an SAT-style logic gotcha, many would answer it in a more literal context. But we normally assume a broader scope of inference when answering this sort of question, and the pattern-recognition machines we call our brains are capable of all sorts of fuzzy logic that is completely independent of, and much broader than, strict mathematical logic. In the real world, it might well turn out that women like Linda are in fact more likely to be both bankers and feminists. Moreover "both" is a far richer answer in the context of most real-world interactions. The more logically correct answer is less insightful and interesting.

This is not to suggest that we should become lax about adhering to principles of logic, but only to suggest that a simple brainteaser is not a very powerful indicator of overall rationality. Furthermore, evaluating rationality based upon a single fallacy-recognition test diminishes the profound complexity of rationality.

I suggest that there are far stronger indicators of rationality. Does the subject believe in God? Do they deny climate change? Evolution? Do they hold pseudoscientific beliefs? Is their thinking muddled by irrational New Age rationalizations? Do they insist the world is only six million years old and that humans coexisted with dinosaurs, as does Ken Ham?

Any of these simple, objective measures would be a far better measurement of rationality. One could simply tally up the number of these objectively irrational beliefs and assign a fair and representative rationality quotient. Except we cannot do that. All of these direct indicators are too entrenched and widespread to be overtly linked to irrationality. Doing so would put the vast majority of our population on the low end of any absolute scale. So, instead, we use safe, bland, non-confrontational indicators like the Linda case that are at best weak indicators and at worst undermine important and frank questions about rationality.

The Dragon in the Garage

I can't prove what I believe, no one can, but I know it's true.

In their great 1995 book, *The Demon-Haunted World: Science as a Candle in the Dark*, Carl Sagan and Ann Druyan tell a story that brilliantly illustrates the typical dialogue of rationalization between the believer and the scientist. Here's my own adaptation of his story:

> *"I have a fire-breathing dragon living in my garage," the believer announces.*

"That's amazing!" says the scientist. "Can you show me?"

"It's right there," the believer points toward an empty space in the cluttered garage. "Oh, I didn't mention it is an invisible dragon."

"I see," says the scientist, considering. "Well then let's spread flour across the floor to see its footprints."

"That would work," the believer agrees, "except for the fact that it's a floating dragon."

"Hmm," the scientist considers. "Well then I happen to have some infrared goggles in my car, I'll get them at take a look at the dragon's breath."

"Won't work," says the believer. "His fire is magical so it's heatless."

"Then let's spray-paint the dragon," suggests the scientist, unwilling to give up.

"Good idea!" says the believer, "except for the fact that it's incorporeal so the paint won't stick."

It goes on and on like that, and each test that the scientist suggests is countered by some special reason why it won't work.

This story illustrates the practical problem of trying to disprove a proposition that cannot be proved. Still, my inability to prove that the dragon does not exist does not prove that it does. But the larger philosophical and practical question that Dr. Sagan asked is this:

> *"Now, what's the difference between an invisible, incorporeal, floating dragon who spits heatless fire and no dragon at all? If there's no way to disprove my contention, no conceivable experiment that would count against it, what does it mean to say that my dragon exists? Your inability to invalidate my hypothesis is not at all the same thing as proving it true."*

In fact, the only interesting thing about the dragon is the fact that you believe that it exists. What does that say?

Now let's carry Sagan's invisible dragon story even further.

Reporters get wind of the story, and the invisible dragon makes the headlines. Accounts start to trickle in from other people who report that they too have invisible dragons living in their garages. People swear that they can sense the presence of the invisible dragon in their garages. They can psychically feel the heatless fire of their breath. They have no doubt that their fortune has changed for the better since a dragon moved into their garage.

Before long, reports start to flood in to the new Disciples of the Invisible Dragon website. People everywhere are reporting invisible dragons. Surely so many people could not be simply deluded. Their sheer numbers proves that invisible dragons really must exist.

There has to be something to this!

Despite their skepticism, scientists continue to investigate reports of invisible dragon evidence. Dragon footprints appear on garage floors, but they never seem to get created while scientists are present. Obviously, they are told, the dragons remain perfectly still when they are being watched. One person comes forward with a burnt finger, claiming that it was caused by the heatless fire of a garage dragon. He becomes a celebrity among believers for having been touched by a dragon.

And so it goes. Believers continue to put forth supposed proof of invisible dragons. The scientists remain skeptical but become silent, reluctant to take a firm stance for fear of insulting the heartfelt belief of so many obviously sane and sincere dragon worshipers.

Before too long, there appears a growing cult of people with gryphons in their attics. They ridicule and dismiss the idea of garage dragons as inherently silly and sacrilegious. Let's hope that they don't bomb each other's houses and start a dragon vs. gryphon holy war.

There are indeed some things that we know to be true but cannot prove with a scientific degree of certainty. Yet, at times, it is critical that we insist upon it. Maybe we need our own version of the Serenity Prayer. Perhaps we can call it the Science Prayer:

> *Grant me the knowledge to determine what is true,*
> *The courage to reject what is false,*
> *And the passion to care about the difference.*

Competing Arguments

I understand all this, but I'm not sure it helps me to decide between two competing arguments.

I get that. There are no silver bullets here. There are no paint-by-numbers methods to get to the truth of a claim, let alone judge between competing claims.

Most often what we deal with in the real world are two individuals or two groups, each advocating for their side of an argument. Each side presents some strong arguments but also some very dubious ones. Each advocate emphasizes the benefits of their own position and the negatives of their opponent. At the same time, each minimizes the negatives associated with their own position and the benefits of the opposing side.

This calculus can simply be too difficult to calculate. It is not surprising that many people abandon the effort and simply find some element of faith or doctrine in the debate to lay their money down upon.

Oh, their side supports abortion? OK, then I support the other side. I don't need to hear any further details.

Sometimes this is a rational thing to do. If a new regulation, for instance, will dramatically decrease CO_2 emissions, I would likely support it. I would not need to consider arguments about how much it might harm coal jobs in Pennsylvania. But usually we don't have any overriding principle or consideration to resolve competing arguments. Both make good points.

This is when it is so critical that we all have neural networks that have been well-trained to reject bogus evidence, logic, and statistics: to sense flawed scientific studies. I for one have justifiable faith in our very powerful pattern-recognition systems. If they are trained with facts and tuned to eliminate biases, they can recognize patterns of truth, of superior cost-benefit, even when it isn't instantly consciously rationalizable.

Additionally, we should factor in the instincts, the neural network pattern recognition, of others who we know to have sound reasoning in this particular subject matter area. Listen to trusted, proven experts.

Whom Do We Listen To?

I want to become more fact-based, but everyone has strong arguments. Who do I listen to?

My rhetorical friend, this is probably the most important question that you have raised. Even if we appreciate how important facts are, how dangerous beliefs are, how unreliable our perceptions and memories are, how agnostic and malleable our neural networks are, and how susceptible we are to creating and accepting bogus rationalizations, how in the world do we find anyone we should trust? I'm not going to offer any simple answers or easy formulas, because there are none. It's a constant struggle.

First, we must acknowledge as a given that there is simply too much information in the world to digest on our own. However smart we may be, our scope of personal knowledge is far too inadequate to allow us to fully understand, let alone analyze, much of what we must make decisions about. Therefore, we have no choice but to rely upon experts.

The question then becomes, which experts can we trust? What colleagues, what teachers, what relatives, what clergy, what news sources, what experts, what pundits, what political party should we put our trust in? The first conclusion we should reach is: not any single one of them. We should trust no one person or group exclusively.

I mentioned earlier that I had spent time in the Peace Corps stationed in South African schools. As part of my work, I gave science presentations to classes of students. These were so much fun. The students were invariably engaged, inquisitive, and eager to ask questions.

Several times teachers suggested that I come and present to the entire school. I would always answer that I would love to and asked what topic they would like me to present. They always wanted me to decide, and I would suggest evolution, and the conversation would end there.

But to my amazement, one day an educator walked up and asked if I would like to give a presentation to the school. I said certainly, what would you like me to present? To my amazement, he said evolution.

So, I gave a presentation to the entire grade school body on evolution as most of the teachers stood stoically in the back, arms folded, mutely communicating their hostility toward this topic. The students, however, were fully engaged. Afterward, I took questions. One student raised his hands and asked the toughest question:

> *Sir, he said, you are telling me I should believe in evolution. But my parents and my teachers and my priest all tell me this is dangerous nonsense. Who am I to believe?*

Yup, that was a grade-schooler. Talk about putting me on the spot! I thought about it a moment and gave the only answer I could come up with under those circumstances:

> *Well, you should not take my word for it. You should never take anything on authority. Not mine and not anyone else's. Anyone, no matter how smart, can be wrong about some things. So, what you should trust in is what seems to be supported by the most evidence and by what you yourself see around you in the real world.*

I hope that was a good answer, and I hope that at least some of those learners, and maybe even some teachers, were brought around a bit on that day. I have to trust they were. Often when you work in a helping profession, you have to take it on faith that your efforts do matter. So, I offer you, dear reader, the same meager advice that I offered those students.

> *Trust the claim that is supported by the best evidence.*

I have a lot of liberal friends who think that as long as they read *The New York Times* they are well-served. Usually, they are. But on the other hand, there are lots of op-eds on the *Times* that are absolutely terrible. Even highly respected columnists write a lot of crap. And it must be pointed out that the *Times* was a key propaganda vehicle exploited by Seitz and the other Merchants of Doubt to discredit important science.

On the other hand, while *The New York Times* is generally good, Fox News is generally horrible. The evening commentators, at least, offer mainly clearly demonstrable lies and specious arguments intended to manipulate and incite. That does not mean, however, that they might not occasionally get something right.

Given that we must rely upon secondary sources, and further given that we cannot trust any one source, where does that leave us? I can only give general advice on how to train your neural networks to filter for solid facts and sound logic:

- *Don't trust any one source all the time. Retain a healthy skepticism even toward sources you generally trust.*
- *Give preferential credibility to sources that have a proven track record of veracity.*
- *Give a higher weighting to sources that have no personal stake in the matter at hand.*
- *Give a higher weighting to sources that base their conclusions upon legitimate science.*
- *Give a lower weighting to sources that ask you to accept anything on faith or trust.*
- *Don't accept premature conclusions reached before sufficient facts have been considered.*
- *Beware of conclusions that are based on a lot of assumptions.*
- *Have increased skepticism toward sources that urge you to only listen to them.*
- *Don't be influenced by personality or forcefulness of presentation or appeals to emotion.*
- *Always try to poke holes and consider the matter from different perspectives.*
- *Give a higher weighting to sources that do not employ logical fallacies to support their arguments.*

Take the time to really study the examples of fallacious argument types presented at the end of this book. Any time such arguments are used, you should distrust and perhaps discount that particular argument.

If you review the most common types of fallacious arguments, you will start to recognize them. The more you recognize them, the better you will be able to tune your neural networks to automatically detect and reject them.

And one final bit of practical advice is this:

- *When in doubt, trust in Wikipedia.*

Wikipedia is a vast treasure that is shared freely with everyone. It contains much of the accumulated knowledge of mankind, far eclipsing the ancient Library of Alexandria. The English version alone has over 6.3 million articles. At last count, it houses over 55 million articles in 309 languages.

Contrary to the ill-informed snobbery of some, the accuracy and reliability of Wikipedia is outstanding. It is totally untrue that "anyone can put anything" on Wikipedia. Articles are carefully vetted by a crowdsourced spectrum of experts following very careful and specific requirements of verification.

Any unfounded doubts about Wikipedia are objectively disproven by the many studies have been conducted to evaluate the quality of the material presented there. Wikipedia has consistently proven to be on a par or better than those authoritative gold-standards like encyclopedias, textbooks, and journals. Where there are criticisms noted, these are typically omissions, not inaccuracies.

No small part of the reason that Wikipedia has such a high quality of information is that it follows many good scientific practices in peer-reviewing information and requiring trusted citations for all information provided. Most scientific is the fact that it is self-correcting. When errors are detected, they are caught and corrected very quickly.

In fact, I will toss in my view that the single best thing that mainstream science could do to improve the quality of its science would be to dump a largely for-profit, privatized publication industry and replace it with a far more nimble, open-source publication platform built like Wikipedia. I won't say that the current peer review system that private journals follow makes me laugh, because it really makes me want to cry.

CHAPTER 6: INSPIRATION

We've talked a lot about facts and beliefs. We have stressed how important it is to look at the world through unbiased lenses and to objectively assess ideas based upon validated evidence and sound logic. We have talked about how our complex thought patterns, even our very consciousness, emotions, and social behaviors arise from very simple neural network mechanics.

But that reductionism does not mean that we need to abandon the joy, the wonder, the magic, the inspiration of the human experience.

Some people think that a world without gods and magic would be too boring and mundane to imagine. They would rather live in a fanciful delusion than a bleak and dreary reality. But this is so not true. On the contrary, once you "reduce" the human experience to a natural phenomenon, it can become even more wondrous and more amazing.

Knowledge of our real origins, our real evolution, and our real place in the universe can offer a profound "spiritual" sense even stronger and more solid than that built upon the shifting sands of belief.

In the next chapter, we engage with our inspiring cosmos as revealed through science.

Our Cosmos

🗣 *But how can you just reduce humans to physics*
and everything we think to mere electronic impulses and
dismiss all the spiritual wonder of the universe?

I have New Age friends whom I love dearly and talk to regularly. These are very intelligent people in other areas, but unfortunately they don't know how much they don't know about the universe as revealed by science. Their ignorance of scientific knowledge is partly what allows them to rationalize their New Age belief that scientific inquiry is inadequate to arrive at real truth.

Here's the essence of actual conversations I've had with otherwise smart, professional, educated people with a New Age sensibility:

> *"But science can't tell us how big the universe is,"* one friend points out.
>
> *"Actually, that has been measured exactly,"* I answer.
>
> *"Well, science can't really know that there aren't worlds out there where our laws don't apply,"* she counters.
>
> *"But in fact, we can know that,"* I answer. *"We have looked out at the universe and verified that the laws of chemistry and physics apply everywhere."*
>
> *"Maybe, but there could be spirit worlds that lie beyond the reach of science."*

And on and on it goes. This is typical of the discussion one has with a New Age thinker. It has a different character than discussions with religious thinkers, but it is fundamentally no different.

What belief-based thinkers assert as an implicit part of their worldview is that the universe is mysterious, unknowable. That gives the religious believer the basis on which to claim that only God is the source of true knowledge. An unknowable universe allows New Age thinkers to dismiss rationality as a path to knowledge so that anything can be equally true for them.

The scientific worldview is fundamentally different. The worldview of science is distilled into the very title of the PBS series *Cosmos*, which aired in 1980:

> Cosmos: A Personal Voyage *was written and narrated by Carl Sagan and was one of the most widely watched PBS series in the world, broadcast in over sixty countries and seen by over 600 million people. The* Cosmos *series inspired a generation. It was remarkable not only for the science that it made intellectually accessible to a mass audience, but also for the sense of wonder and optimism that it conveyed.*

The word "cosmos" comes from the Greek term meaning *order*, an *orderly arrangement*.

To call our universe a cosmos makes a bold statement of worldview. It says that the universe is ordered, sensible. If it is ordered, we can observe it, understand it, and make sense of that order. Therefore, the universe is **knowable**.

That is a profound statement. It asserts that we, humans, can come to understand the universe. It isn't the province of the gods, unknowable to us. It isn't a realm of chaos, a place with no rules and no predictability. We can not only know the universe, we can also predict it. If we can understand it and predict it, then we have power over it. We are not helpless. We are empowered.

Belief-based cultures have typically not viewed the universe as knowable. That is a distinctly scientific worldview. If the universe were a watch, some might have said the watch is magical so therefore we cannot understand it, or sacred so therefore we must not try to understand it, or chaotic so therefore there is nothing to understand, or too complicated for us to possibly comprehend. But scientists said that we can open the watch, that we can carefully observe its mechanisms, and that we can learn how it works. It is knowable.

And in fact, in 400 years of scientific advancement, the universe has proven to be a cosmos. Through observation, hypothesis, and experimentation, scientists have come to learn the order of the universe so that we can predict almost every detail of its clockwork mechanism. We can look back in time to the beginning of the universe and predict ahead with clock-like certainty. We can look out across the great expanse of the universe and deep into its very atoms.

Do scientists claim to know everything then? Are they omniscient? Not at all, but that doesn't mean that they don't have confidence in the body of scientific knowledge they have acquired. You presumably accept that gravity exists. You have observed gravity in action enough to give you confidence that it is real and it is predictable. If you drop something, it will fall.

Now say that someone challenges you about gravity. How can you be so certain about gravity? How do you know that if you drop a rock on the moon that it will fall there too? Do you think you know everything? Can you completely explain gravity? Are you all-knowing?

You would probably consider that a silly conversation. Similarly, scientists have observed enough about the basic physics and chemistry of the universe to know exactly how it works everywhere and to make predictions that apply everywhere. With their instruments, they have actually looked out across the universe and deep inside it and figured out exactly how its clockwork mechanism operates.

More importantly, our scientific understanding of the universe has the very satisfying benefit of being reproducible and verifiable. It has the very satisfying quality of being fact-based and having been proven to be true. Can any priest, rabbi, swami, or imam legitimately make comparable claims?

Secular Morality

I grant you that science has revealed our natural universe, but religion guides our morality.

Humanism is the secular alternative to religious values. In fact, the US Constitution is one of the most profoundly ethical documents ever conceived by man. And it is a secular humanist document.

In the days when Thomas Jefferson and his small group of colleagues drafted the Constitution, letters were their blogs. People shared and discussed their views through handwritten correspondence. We are fortunate enough to have a large number of letters through which we have firsthand insight into the thinking of our founding fathers.

Jefferson was a religious man. He was a Unitarian who believed in God and in creation. In fact, his expressed views on creation were essentially similar to modern-day intelligent design theories.

Nevertheless, he viewed the Bible with great skepticism. He dismissed the miracles while still greatly respecting the morality of Jesus. In that way, he revealed the fact-based core of his thinking and the humanist basis of his values within the religious milieu of his culture. Thomas Jefferson and his tight group that created our democracy were foremost men of science and reason. James Madison used scientific metaphors in The Federalist Papers, and Benjamin Franklin was revered as the founder of electrical physics. John Adams wrote:

> *"All mankind are chemists from their cradles to their graves. The material universe is a chemical experiment."*

They were deeply conversant in much of the current scientific knowledge of their time. One needs only visit Monticello to see the wide array of scientific books and equipment that Jefferson treasured. He had fully mastered Newtonian physics and had stated that nature destined him to be a scientist. However, there were few opportunities for scientists in pre-revolutionary Virginia and so he threw himself into the pressing social problems of his time.

The fact that Jefferson coexisted in both worlds causes both religious and secular thinkers to continually try to claim him as one of their own.

But the essential thing to understand is how his views of religious belief influenced his view of government as expressed in the Constitution. Clearly, the Constitution reflects a morality that was inspired by the examples of Jesus, but not by the divinity of Jesus.

Jefferson viewed religion as an intensely personal thing that had no place in government. Writing to a group of Connecticut Baptists in 1802, Jefferson said. "Religion is a matter which lies solely between a man and his God." And then, in a letter to his good friend John Adams, he wrote, "Say nothing of my religion. It is known to God and myself alone."

Clearly, despite being a religious man, Jefferson believed strongly that religion should never be a matter that is either regulated or endorsed by the government. His concern was twofold. He wanted to ensure that government would never limit or interfere with the practice of religion. But in order to ensure that, it was essential that government never endorse nor favor any particular religion.

This deeply held view was expressed in the First Amendment to the Constitution and is commonly known today as the separation of church and state.

Unfortunately, many religious believers today do not appreciate the wisdom of Jefferson and his colleagues like James Madison. They actively seek to destroy the separation of church and state in order to enforce their religious views through public policy. Sadly, they do not appreciate that in doing so they would destroy the very wall put in place to protect their right to worship.

First and foremost, Jefferson worried that the people were gullible; that they could be easily fooled. So, by the way, did most of the prominent European thinkers of the time. Jefferson sought to create a system of government that could protect the people from abuses of power and at the same time protect the government from the corporate "wolves at the door." One must wonder how he would rate our current stewardship of that legacy under Trump and those following in his footsteps.

In any event, the United States Constitution is a secular document written by wise religious thinkers with a strong fact-based foundation. It is proof that a secular document can be every bit as influential and powerful as a religious document like the Bible.

There is one church that refutes the assumption that moral responsibility and ethical action can only occur through belief-based organizations. The New York Society for Ethical Culture is a church with a congregation that holds weekly services without prayer and preaches ethical principles without any reference to any god. It does good works without any fear of damnation or promise of heavenly rewards.

It was founded in 1876 by Felix Adler, whose goal was to organize a movement for social justice based on personal conscience, not on external influences. This unique church and a thousand other secular organizations debunk the myth that a belief in God is a requirement for ethical institutions.

Different but Equal

You say that some are more fact-based than others in their thinking. It seems very disrespectful to think of my fellow human beings in such a judgmental fashion.

Thomas Jefferson prominently enshrined the phrase "all men are created equal" in our Declaration of Independence. This phrase has ever since embodied perhaps the single most important and enduring foundation of the American experiment.

Certainly, all people of goodwill respect and value this "immortal declaration." And certainly no one limits their interpretation to the literal meaning of the word "created." For if children quickly and demonstrably became unequal, the idea of equality at creation would lose any practical or useful meaning whatsoever. So, we generally accept that "created equal" also implies that we remain equal throughout our lives, independent of what we do or do not accomplish in life.

But this must be much more than a mere rhetorical or theoretical equality. It must extend far beyond a begrudging recognition that all people have the right to basic human rights and dignity. It must be a practical working belief, one that operates at the real functional interpersonal level, allowing us to work together in this human project as equal partners.

Indeed, without a sincere and unqualified recognition of the equality of all individuals, our social fabric cannot endure. It is not possible to have a fair and just society if we feel, even deep down, that some are deserving and others are not, that some are superior merely by virtue of their social status or race or gender or even by their level of accomplishment in life. To allow for such fundamental bases of inequality is to travel down the road toward slavery and subjugation and exploitation and ultimately into the abyss of social dysfunction.

Yet, moving beyond a mere allowance of certain inalienable rights to a true respect for each individual's capabilities and worth is not easy. In fact, that is a huge understatement. For in our everyday life, in every social interaction we see that people are simply not equal. It is laughably obvious that in fact we are not equal by wide margins.

Some folks are brilliant, others stupid. Some sane, others insane. Some gifted, others inept. Some strong, others puny. Some have lived honorable lives, others, lives of ignobility. The truth is, we cannot help but observe glaringly wide disparities on any measure of worth you care to assess.

So how can we truly hold the ideal of equality alongside the reality of inequality harmoniously in our minds? How can we sincerely believe in equality without lying to ourselves about the reality? And how can we acknowledge the reality without lying to ourselves about our belief in the ideal?

This requires some rationalization. Rationalization is not always a bad thing. We all have to find some coherent model for reconciling contradictory ideas. Therefore, we all must find some kind of understanding that allows a recognition of equality to thrive, fully and harmoniously, in our individual brains and in our collective psyche, alongside the reality of inequality.

You may already have your own rationalization that works well for you. But here's how I rationalize it. It's not perfect, but no model can be. Still, it has long worked pretty well for me.

Excluding physical or chemical debilitation, a human's total capacity to think is neurologically dependent upon their physical brain size.

All human brains are the same size, or close enough so the differences do not matter, and nature does not go to all the effort to evolve unused brain matter. Therefore, our total brain "power" is essentially the same and all of it is used in some manner.

Brains exhibit a wide spectrum of capabilities. Think of it as an impracticably wide bar chart. Each bar is a narrow trait, like perhaps "math," or "kindness," or "neuromuscular control," but much finer grained than even those.

Everyone's bar chart is unique. It is a signature of who they are. Everyone has some high bars and some low bars. But the total area under the bars adds up to the same total power.

Some bars are particularly valued by society at any given time, some are measured on an SAT exam, and some are not. Some make you a business tycoon, some a starving artist. But although some signatures may be seen as more important to society, or lead to greater success, all are equal in total capability, and all are potentially valuable.

So, in my rationalization, all people are truly equal. True, some may be less appreciated or less helpful in a given situation, but all are nevertheless worthy of true respect in my mind for their unique strengths. There is no contradiction whatsoever with the observed differences between individuals. Aspiration and reality are fully reconciled.

This model has helped me to reconcile a sincere, fact-based, recognition of equality with undeniable, observable differences. It has in fact helped me appreciate equality by virtue of our differences. It has helped me to feel proud of my own personal strengths while simultaneously humble about my weaknesses and while still being as worthy and as flawed as anyone overall. It has helped me recognize that being smart or skilled in one area does not make anyone particularly smart or skilled in another. That has helped me apply a healthy level of skepticism to opinions put forth by "smart" people in areas outside their proven expertise and to allow that otherwise uninformed people can offer valuable insights in others. It has helped me understand that traits like "smart" or "sane" are not simple binaries but complex and nuanced and somewhat arbitrary. We are all smart in some things and delusional others. It has also helped me to value undervalued traits and to recognize that disrespecting people for one very low bar of their chart does not mean you disrespect them in totality and that respect overall does not require you to respect every trait.

And further, we should value the undervalued signatures in our society more than we do. It is our failure and our loss if we do not identify and utilize whatever unique strengths each individual has. There are no useless skill sets, only underutilized and underappreciated skill sets.

I think these rationalizations have led me in a healthy direction. Maybe this model will help you come to a more healthy and helpful view of equality that reconciles what we observe with what we aspire to and value.

The Oldest Ethical Culture

🗣 *Man has always been religious. Secularism is a modern experiment, and we should be cautious of putting too much faith in it.*

Actually, secularism is nothing new. As much as Jesus has dominated Western culture for the last two thousand years, Asian cultures have been largely shaped by a very different figure for even longer.

Confucius lived five hundred years before the time of Christ. He put forth a secular philosophy that has been equally influential. Confucianism focuses on human morality, proper behavior, and ethical action.

Even though the existence of gods was widely accepted at the time of Confucius, he taught that the intentions of the gods could not be known by man. If man cannot comprehend the mind of the gods, and certainly cannot influence them, then there is no need to consider them in one's actions. Essentially, his teaching suggested that it would make no ethical difference whatsoever if the gods did not exist at all. One could imagine that Carl Sagan might have plagiarized his Dragon in the Garage parable from Confucius.

Western religion is based on the presumption that the basic nature of man is sinful and corrupt and that we can only be motivated to do good through the threat of eternal damnation. Confucius based his philosophy on the belief that the essential nature of man is good or can be effectively good through the adoption of proper behavior.

While Western religion relies on dogma and doctrine to achieve social order, Confucius believed that social improvement was attained through reason and discussion. Confucianism is not a belief-based doctrine. It is a very secular humanist philosophy.

One cannot reasonably argue that the vast majority of Asian cultures are immoral or incapable of moral behavior because they do not have religious beliefs to guide them. Likewise, one simply cannot assert that humanistic philosophies cannot achieve the same goals that religions claim is their sole domain.

The amazing thing about Confucianism is that it is still so ahead of its time, and yet it is the oldest complete philosophy and guide to human behavior known to man. We may know more now but are essentially no wiser than the people of Confucius's time.

It's crucially important to understand and deeply integrate the difference between Western religion and Eastern philosophy. In the West, we're trained, inadvertently brainwashed from the earliest age to accept the basic principle that we are incapable of morality without assistance from God.

We are taught that we possess original sin and that our inherent imperfection caused us to sin in the first place. We are convinced before we even realize that we are being convinced of something that we are sinful, immoral, flawed, and incapable of goodness on our own. We come to accept the belief that goodness, ethical action, and moral thoughts all must come only from and through God. We believe that unless we accept him into our hearts we cannot be saved from our sinful ways. We are made to accept this ethical dependence as a given, a fact.

Given the power of that essential idea, it's not surprising that Western minds have great difficulty accepting that Asian societies are capable of goodness without the grace of a savior. It's easy to see why they find it nearly impossible to imagine how a secular humanist could ever truly be as moral as a believer who has accepted the help of God. It's understandable why missionaries to Mongolia cannot imagine how their secular Buddhist philosophies have anything to teach anyone.

Although religious believers may admit that nonbelievers are capable of goodness too, they inherently hold the position that only God can show us the true way. Given their worldview that man is inherently evil, it is a rational acknowledgement of reality for them to grant that nonbelievers can be good people too. Many of them grant that concession even if they believe themselves to be incapable of good without the divine intervention of the Lord.

But the second myth that their worldview propagates is the idea that one can be saved only by accepting their Lord and Savior. Even if the very existence of a good and ethical nonbeliever challenges their inculcation that man is inherently evil, they fall back on the illusion that the nonbeliever will unfortunately not be saved. Only the believers will be saved.

In the 1800s, German philosopher Friedrich Nietzsche put forth an inflammatory idea. He characterized human attitudes with a master-slave paradigm. For the masters, good is measured by strength, power, and success. For the slaves, their thinking is driven by their helpless and hopeless state. They seek to turn the strengths of the masters into flaws and the hopelessness of their own situation into true virtue.

This argues that Western religion is an expression of a slave mentality. It is an attempt to rationalize a hopeless existence by viewing the money lenders as corrupt and by glorifying the humble sufferers. The concept of an afterlife is a slave's rationalization to convince them that although they may be subjugated in this life, they will be the ones to enjoy eternal reward in the hereafter. As George Carlin used to say, religion is "the all-time champion of false promises and exaggerated claims."

To whatever extent this characterization by Nietzsche and Carlin is valid, it is easy to see why Christian ethics would be popular among the masses of humanity and encouraged by the elite. It is easy to see why their sense of superiority is so strong and their belief that they are saved is so powerful.

For Christian thinkers, indoctrinated into believing that man is inherently evil, it's difficult to imagine how nonbelievers can be moral. If their morality does not come from God, how can it be real morality? Is their morality false, merely an expression of Ayn Rand's selfish selflessness? In reality, morals come from the place that many Christians are least willing to accept: evolution.

When I give talks on science to grade-schoolers, I frequently get questions about why things are like they are. Why are eggs egg-shaped? Why does a praying mantis devour her mate? Why is my skin black while yours is white?

There are a zillion such questions. And every one of that zillion has the same basic answer: evolution. Each of those traits was favored in the particular niche that species occupied, allowing the species to survive better. Now, given that general answer, it is never-ending fun to speculate about or even experiment to prove how each trait gave that species an advantage.

Back to the original question: If morals do not come from God, how can we possibly have morals? The answer once again is evolution. As our frail animal ancestors struggled to survive in a hostile environment, "selfless" behaviors helped to increase the chances that the species as a whole could continue on. The very fact that morality exists in humans is strong evidence that it has provided an evolutionary advantage.

We like to think that self-sacrifice and noble actions are uniquely human traits, bestowed even by God alone, but the fact is that we are merely expressing inherited behaviors passed down to us from our animal ancestors, refined at each step along the evolutionary tree.

Animal altruism is a well-documented behavior, extending far back along the evolutionary chain. We can observe the roots of human altruism reaching as far back as the slime molds in which individuals will sacrifice themselves for the good of the community.

The point of this circuitous discussion is not to point out that Christians are wrong on so many facts, but to underscore the essential problem with belief-based thinking. Subscribing to a belief in made-up miracles profoundly impairs a full appreciation of the wondrous miracles of reality.

The Wonder of God's Universe

How can you dismiss all the wonder of God's creation?

I must have been about twenty-four years old, because I was engaged at the time. I was cornered by a future relation who asked me with great concern if I was saved.

After about an hour of valiant efforts to try to determine the cause of my blindness, she finally gave in to the realization that I was not going to be converted. Deeply saddened, she looked at me with the pity one feels for a truly lost soul and said that "I feel really sad that you will never know the wonder and joy of living in a universe created by God." I nodded sympathetically and told her, "That's OK, I feel equally sad that you will never know the wonder and joy of living in a universe created by random chance."

Belief traps the believer inside a box of ignorance, superstition, and fear. It is a box that they could easily escape if they chose, but they are too afraid of the unknown world outside. So instead, they prefer to remain inside the safe confines of their dark and tiny box.

Outside, an incredible universe awaits them, but they prefer to stay inside. Come join me, they urge, come inside and know the wonder and joy of living in my little box. Is it arrogant to claim that belief systems are little boxes of ignorance, superstition, and fear? Following are two accounts of the origin of our universe. Read them and decide which one inspires more wonder and awe, which one reveals the greater and grander universe all around us.

Genesis as Revealed by God

(Unabridged version)

1: In the beginning God created the heaven and the earth.

2: And the earth was without form, and void; and darkness was upon the face of the deep. And the Spirit of God moved upon the face of the waters.

3: And God said, Let there be light: and there was light.

4: And God saw the light, that it was good: and God divided the light from the darkness.

5: And God called the light Day, and the darkness he called Night. And the evening and the morning were the first day.

6: And God said, Let there be a firmament in the midst of the waters, and let it divide the waters from the waters.

7: And God made the firmament, and divided the waters which were under the firmament from the waters which were above the firmament: and it was so.

8: And God called the firmament Heaven. And the evening and the morning were the second day.

9: And God said, Let the waters under the heaven be gathered together unto one place, and let the dry land appear: and it was so.

10: And God called the dry land Earth; and the gathering together of the waters called he Seas: and God saw that it was good.

11: And God said, Let the earth bring forth grass, the herb yielding seed, and the fruit tree yielding fruit after his kind, whose seed is in itself, upon the earth: and it was so.

12: And the earth brought forth grass, and herb yielding seed after his kind, and the tree yielding fruit, whose seed was in itself, after his kind: and God saw that it was good.

13: And the evening and the morning were the third day.

14: And God said, Let there be lights in the firmament of the heaven to divide the day from the night; and let them be for signs, and for seasons, and for days, and years:

15: And let them be for lights in the firmament of the heaven to give light upon the earth: and it was so.

16: And God made two great lights; the greater light to rule the day, and the lesser light to rule the night: he made the stars also.

17: And God set them in the firmament of the heaven to give light upon the earth,

18: And to rule over the day and over the night, and to divide the light from the darkness: and God saw that it was good.

19: And the evening and the morning were the fourth day.

20: And God said, Let the waters bring forth abundantly the moving creature that hath life, and fowl that may fly above the earth in the open firmament of heaven.

21: And God created great whales, and every living creature that moveth, which the waters brought forth abundantly, after their kind, and every winged fowl after his kind: and God saw that it was good.

22: And God blessed them, saying, Be fruitful, and multiply, and fill the waters in the seas, and let fowl multiply in the earth.

23: And the evening and the morning were the fifth day.

24: And God said, Let the earth bring forth the living creature after his kind, cattle, and creeping thing, and beast of the earth after his kind: and it was so.

25: And God made the beast of the earth after his kind, and cattle after their kind, and every thing that creepeth upon the earth after his kind: and God saw that it was good.

26: And God said, Let us make man in our image, after our likeness: and let them have dominion over the fish of the sea, and over the fowl of the air, and over the cattle, and over all the earth, and over every creeping thing that creepeth upon the earth.

27: So God created man in his own image, in the image of God created he him; male and female created he them.

28: And God blessed them, and God said unto them, Be fruitful, and multiply, and replenish the earth, and subdue it: and have dominion over the fish of the sea, and over the fowl of the air, and over every living thing that moveth upon the earth.

29: And God said, Behold, I have given you every herb bearing seed, which is upon the face of all the earth, and every tree, in the which is the fruit of a tree yielding seed; to you it shall be for meat.

30: And to every beast of the earth, and to every fowl of the air, and to every thing that creepeth upon the earth, wherein there is life, I have given every green herb for meat: and it was so.

31: And God saw every thing that he had made, and, behold, it was very good. And the evening and the morning were the sixth day.

Genesis as Revealed by Science

(Brief synopsis)

There may be infinite universes, but the only one we know about for sure is our own. Evidence proves that about 13.7 billion years ago our entire universe was squished into a tiny super-compressed ball. By the red shift of galaxies, we know that the ball exploded and it is still expanding and accelerating today. That explosion released a tremendous burst of energy that we still see today as lingering cosmic microwave background radiation.

The big bang released tremendous amounts of hydrogen, helium, and lithium, but few larger elements. After a billion years of expanding and cooling, gravity pulled this matter into clouds called nebulae. When pockets of these clouds got dense enough, gravity started fusing hydrogen atoms together, causing them to release energy and light up into stars. Soon stars lit up all throughout these nebulae, and they aggregated into galaxies.

Because of gravity, galaxies tend to group into galactic clusters. Galaxies pull on each other and can even collide, causing their billions of stars to form into spectacular galactic shapes and local groups.

Within those stars, and as a result of stellar collisions, fusion continues. Smaller atoms are fused into larger ones and gradually the fraction of larger elements in the universe increases. Our sun is at least a third-generation star. We know this by the distribution of elements that make it up.

When stars run out of hydrogen to fuse, they die. Depending on how large they are, they can simply become a cold white dwarf star, they can blow up in a supernova and leave a neutron star behind, or the very largest can turn into black holes.

In any case, their matter is eventually recycled back into new stars, the cycle of stellar life and death in our universe continues. Stars live and die, giving birth to new stars. But galaxies die as well, becoming giant clouds of dust once again called nebulae, only to be reborn by gravity into a new galaxy.

When we look at our universe through the lenses of science, we see not a static painting, but an exquisite dance of matter and gravity, swirling and living and dying on a cosmic scale.

And we are part of that universe, indivisible from it. Our bodies are the continuation of the evolution of the universe. We can show—we can even reproduce—the processes by which atoms formed molecules that eventually became us. At some point, a chemical reaction took place that produced more of the reactants. That was the first chemical reproduction on our planet. Their number increased in the chemical soup of our primordial world and gradually gained complexity to become simple virus like organisms that continued to evolve into us and all other creatures.

Our consciousness evolved over 40,000 generations of human beings as did our complex behaviors of morality and ethics. As Carl Sagan loved to point out, we are made of star stuff. We are the universe become self-aware.

The Multiverse Is Bigger than God

But God's creation is far grander than science can know.

It's hard to imagine, but there are certainly many belief-based thinkers who, after reading both of those accounts, would argue (and in fact legitimately feel) that the story of Genesis is more satisfying. Believing that a higher power was involved is so essential for them that they prefer a simplistic myth to the wondrous reality of the universe as revealed by science.

Our gods used to be gods of specific things: the sky, the sea, war, love. Then God took over and became the god of everything. But our understanding of "everything" keeps expanding, and as it does, our fanciful notion of God has to expand along with it to remain ever beyond the limits of mere science.

The visible horizon of our observable universe is 46.5 billion light years away in any direction. That is an immense distance, and this visible space around us contains about 100 billion galaxies, each with perhaps 100 billion stars. Our God of everything created all that too, presumably just for us to gaze at from afar.

But wait, there's more—much more. Today we understand that our universe is almost certainly unimaginably larger than that which we can observe. It is perhaps 100 billion trillion times larger than our observable universe. That makes what we can see just the tiniest mote of dust in our greater universe. In our observable universe, we can look into the sky and at least see what happened in the distant past. We cannot even see out into the darkness beyond that. But since it apparently exists, believers have no choice except to inflate God once more. God presumably created all that inaccessible space beyond the horizon as well, and just for us.

It gets better. Now we're beginning to understand that God apparently created an infinite multiverse just for us as well. I first recall being fascinated by the idea of multiple universes in 1966, when Mr. Spock met Captain Kirk's evil counterpart from an alternate universe. But just as Star Trek communicators became everyday reality, the science fiction of multiple universes has become legitimate science.

The multiverse may take many forms, but for now let it suffice to think of an infinite number of universes just like ours, maybe isolated in pockets of space, maybe superimposed upon each other, maybe both. Their infinity extends through both time and space. This infinite multiverse is not static. In it (if the word "in" even applies to an infinite space) universes appear, grow old, and die. Each is born with a particular set of fundamental parameters. Only a relatively tiny (but still infinite) fraction have parameters in the "Goldilocks" range, which allow organized structures. In a tiny fraction of those, life is possible. The rest are stillborn, or they survive for a short while as unsustainable regions of chaos.

How can it get more mind-blowing? It is a logical conclusion that in an infinite multiverse everything that could possibly happen must happen. For example, there must be a universe in which every possible variation of our own exists; in fact, there must be an infinite number of each possible variation—infinite numbers of each of us.

Whatever form it takes, we become even more insignificant within the time-space grandeur of the multiverse. So, our notion of God must once again expand dramatically to exceed even the non-existent bounds of an already infinite multiverse in order to remain the unbounded God of all things. And God created that infinite multiverse, so far beyond our ability to grasp let alone interact with, just for we infinitesimal humans.

I talk about God here knowing full well that it is of course completely silly to do so. I might as well talk about how our notion of Santa Claus must expand to encompass the belief that he has to deliver Christmas presents to all children in the multiverse on one night. Yet, unfortunately, we do focus our attention on our fantasy of God whenever these cosmological discussions take place.

Some "religious scholars" try desperately to keep God relevant in the face of our expanding awareness by arguing that in a multiverse in which all things are possible, God must exist somewhere. In an otherwise decent article, author Mark Vernon perpetuates this fallacy by repeating that since everything is possible somewhere, one must conclude that God exists in some universes. If God can exist somewhere, why not here?

This will certainly keep getting repeated, but it is simply not a correct interpretation of the science to say that in a multiverse "everything is possible." This is a perversion of the totalitarian principle in quantum physics, which states that "Everything not forbidden is compulsory." Any particular universe is still governed by its own physics, and there is a limit to the possible physics of any given universe. Impossible things, like gods and ghosts, cannot happen in any universe.

And even if some universe had some being approaching a god, it would still not be an omnipotent god of everything, and it would certainly not be our god. Therefore, I'm not sure how claiming that a God exists in some other universe does anything but admit that one doesn't exist in our own.

So, what is the most rational of the possible irrational responses for someone clinging to their belief in God in the face of a multiverse? The best would be simply to claim that God created the multiverse and not even try to invoke any pseudoscientific arguments. As you always have, just keep expanding your definition of God to supersede whatever new boundaries science reveals.

But really, adding God to the multiverse is simply adding fake infinity on top of real infinity. Like infinity plus infinity, the extra infinity is entirely superfluous and unnecessary. And what does it add to place God beyond infinity? It only replaces the insistence that something had to create the multiverse with an acceptance that nothing had to create God. It's silly, especially given the fact that our limited concept of "before" has little relevance in an infinite multiverse.

Better yet would be to finally give in and acknowledge that the multiverse has rendered your god small and insignificant and kind of pathetic. God is like a quaint old vaudeville act that can no longer compete with huge 3-D superhero blockbusters and looks silly trying. Back in the day, it might have been an understandable conceit to believe that God created the Earth just for us—or even maybe the solar system. But the level of conceit required to believe that some God created the entire multiverse just for us is wildly absurd. The idea that such a God would be focused exclusively on us is insanely narcissistic. The multiverse forces God to grow so large that it swells him far beyond any relevance to us or us to him.

So, abandon your increasingly simplistic idea of God and find comfort, wonder, and inspiration in our incredible multiverse. You do not need to feel increasingly insignificant and worthless in this expanding multiverse. You don't need God to give you a phony feeling of significance and meaning within it. All it takes is the flip of a mental switch and you can find comfort and wonder and meaning in our amazing multiverse. It's all just in your head after all.

I do not share the pessimism of some that we can never "see" or understand the multiverse. My working assumption is that even the greater multiverse is our cosmos, that it is knowable. If we survive climate change, we may eventually understand it more fully through indirect observations or through the magical lens of mathematics.

The Tao of Science

But religion gives me a feeling of profound connection to something greater. That's something science can never offer.

Lao Tse was a contemporary of Confucius who established the philosophy and psychology that is Taoism. It was adopted as the state religion of China four centuries before Christ.

The goal of Taoism is to help people to reach a state of complete harmony: oneness with the universe. It stresses the interrelatedness of all things, of all life. It encourages a deep recognition of the real biological connections in nature, the cycle of life.

Taoism teaches that reason is the barrier to reaching oneness with creation. To achieve awareness, one must suspend rational thinking. Science takes the opposite path to reach the same goal. The goal of scientists is not to reach oneness with the universe, but this can be the real result of the scientific journey. Through rational thought, one can achieve a profound sense of oneness with the universe, a feeling that is grounded in fact. Carl Sagan once made the observation that:

> *"To make an apple pie from scratch, you first have to create the universe."*

This is a powerful expression of scientific Tao, a simple statement that recognizes the unbroken chain of events that led from the big bang through 13.7 billion years of universal evolution to produce an apple pie. It reminds us that we too are the current culmination of a 13.7-billion-year-old chain of natural creation. Science shows us that the universe has evolved, is evolving, and growing in size and complexity as time goes on. It has a life; it is a kind of living thing that will eventually grow old and die.

The evolution of humanity is not a separate thing. It is a contiguous part of the evolution of the universe. We humans are made of atoms that were produced in the internal organs of the universe, the stars. We are literally a part of the universe, made of it and indivisible from it. We are a conscious part of the universe, a self-aware bit of the universe awakened into consciousness to regard itself.

We are part of the universe, our atoms were created in the universe, and they will be returned to it. But we cannot return, for we never left it. We cannot leave it; we are it and it is us. Further, we are all part of one another. We all share the same essential DNA that defines us. We have evolved as a community, multicelled organisms that together form a greater multicelled community.

We are not physically distinct. We breathe, we shed, we ingest, we eliminate—and in doing so we share our atoms. Chances are that each of us is made of some atoms that were once in almost anyone in history we can name. We are literally made of those who preceded us and of all animals.

We are intimately linked to all life through our shared ancestry. If we look back far enough, we can find a common ancestor between us and any other species on the planet. We share mostly the same DNA with all life on Earth, and even a tree could easily understand most of our unique human DNA. All living things are our relatives. We are intimately linked to them through physical processes and through our common ancestry. Even our behaviors and thoughts are part of a common evolutionary heritage, the multigenerational project of all ancestors that came before us. Our consciousness is a miracle, but it is not a miracle of divine creation, rather a miracle of nature. It is the unique biochemistry of thought that we experience as ourselves.

We are here by random chance, but also by the nonrandom processes that have led to us over 13.7 billion years on a universal scale of creation. What a wondrous thing that of all the infinite number of things that might have been, we happen to be.

How amazing, how wondrous that our awareness can so fully break out of the constraints of our fragile bodies! Through science we can see out across the universe, look into the very chemical reactions taking place on a distant star, look back across the entire 13.7-billion-year history of our universe and forward toward its death. We can look into the very depths of atoms at the subatomic particles that behave according to quantum mechanics. We can see incredible universes of invisible waves swirling around us like a million overlapping oceans.

How can a simple myth of creation compete with the real story as revealed by science? How can the possibility of astral travel seem more liberating than the intellectual journeys of science? How can stories of invisible ghosts compare to the invisible wonders of the universe that science can show us?

How can Taoism hope to instill a feeling of oneness by denying reason that can compare to the giddy wonder of the oneness attained by deeply attuning to the reality of our universe and our place in it?

Scientific Beliefs

🎙 *But in the end, we need something to guide us.*

Surely one cannot build a meaningful way of life based on a rejection of some other perspective. It may seem that throughout much of this book we have talked about what we don't believe in—about what you shouldn't believe in, about the inherent problems with adopting beliefs and belief-based decision making. What do we believe in? What can we truly believe in?

Fact-based thinking is not merely a denial of beliefs. It offers a powerful set of affirmative values and perspectives that enrich our personal lives as well as our collective emergent behaviors. Following is a short summary of some of these, scattered explicitly or implicitly throughout this book:

We live in a knowable cosmos, and we have the capacity to understand it.

There are such things as facts; reality is not some subjective construct.

Some facts are symbolic, probabilities, statistical, or logical facts.

A fact must be verified to be accepted as true.

The scientific method is our most reliable method for verifying facts and for arriving at truth.

A belief is not a personal and harmless delusion.

Belief-based thinking compromises our ability to judge the reality of a situation.

Decisions based on fact are inherently better than decisions based on belief.

Risk analysis is an important factor in assessing competing propositions.

The universe doesn't require a god.

Humans do not require a god.

Science doesn't dictate how we ethically choose to respond to the facts of a situation.

Thinking, morals, and ethics are evolved traits.

Humanist principles are our true moral and ethical compass.

We are random creations and that makes us no less special. In fact, it makes us even more amazing.

When we die, we just die, but that does not make our lives any less worth living. Rather, it drives us to do good works.

Those who seek to oppress seek to control rational inquiry.

New knowledge can and must be applied in rational, ethical ways.

Beliefs are not deserving of respect, people are.

We must learn to recognize and rebuke logical fallacies.

We are not assured that another dark age cannot descend upon us.

Humans have evolved highly malleable perceptions, memories, and beliefs that cannot always be trusted. Humans have the ability to rationalize almost anything as logical and obvious.

We must prevent the media, government, and special interests from misrepresenting scientific research.

All great progress has grown out of basic research. We must ensure that rational inquiry into the cosmos continues.

The truth of reality is not always intuitive, but we have the capability to grasp it.

The world is a far better place thanks to the heroic efforts of our scientists throughout time to know truth.

Good scientists don't make up answers to questions for which they don't have sufficient data.

Scientists have a passion for the unknown.

Mathematics can often reveal truths about our universe.

Good scientists have the ability to question their assumptions, abandon their biases, and defer to evidence.

Even the greatest scientists have blinders in some areas. It is only the consensus that matters.

Science is self-correcting. Mistakes may happen but verifiable truth is always discovered.

A scientific theory is not a guess. It is as close to certainty as we can come as humans.

Our country was crafted by people with a deep love of science who sought to protect the public from corruption and coercive thinking.

Scientists have a special responsibility to expose factual and logical errors and fallacies.

More scientific thinkers need to be involved in education and politics to ensure rational and factually based decision making.

The universe as revealed by science is far grander and more glorious than any myth.

Science can take one to a highly spiritual awareness of the universe.

A New Dark Age

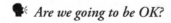 *Are we going to be OK?*

Right now, as things are going, especially during our current pandemic of delusion, one cannot honestly say yes.

Cultures have fallen throughout history, even in relatively recent history, and none of them believed it could happen to them. Sometimes it feels that humanity is just unequipped to survive its own success.

In *The Demon-Haunted World: Science as a Candle in the Dark*, coauthors Carl Sagan and Ann Druyan expressed prescient concerns about the growing trend away from fact-based thinking and toward an increasingly belief-based culture. All the trends, they pointed out, are trending away from fact and reason. Since their dire 1995 warning, our rapidly growing pandemic of delusion has only confirmed their worst fears.

During the Classical Period, prior to 400 CE, scholars gave considerable thought to the world around them. With the exception of the Ionian Greeks, they didn't apply scientific principles but rather arrived at their ideas through imagination and speculation. They were enthusiastic and prolific in their search for knowledge, and they were, for the most part, wrong. Nevertheless, the Greeks had a lust for knowledge, and they amassed information from around the world and consolidated it in their Great Library in Alexandria, Egypt. The library flourished for over 600 years, until roughly 300 CE.

With the Church back in Rome gaining power, Bishop Cyril in Alexandria saw the library as a threat to the belief-based dominance of church theology. The last Chief Librarian of the library was a rare and gifted woman named Hypatia. Hypatia was an astronomer, mathematician, and philosopher. She had the audacity to suggest that it is wrong to teach superstition as truth. In response, Bishop Cyril incited a mob into a killing frenzy. They dragged Hypatia through the streets and flayed the skin from her body.

Within a year the library was destroyed, all it of its priceless treasures lost to mankind forever. Cyril was sainted by the Church. This plunged Europe into the Dark Ages, a period synonymous with barbarism and intellectual repression. The very word invokes images of torture and misery. Essentially, no progress took place for over a thousand years.

It has only been the last 400 years or so since mankind broke free of the tyranny of belief-based thinking and has made any progress in the advancement of human knowledge—and that progress has been world-changing, to say the least.

These dramatic transformations illustrate how human society can and has changed in profound and fundamental ways. The Greeks surely believed that their time of reverence and passion for knowledge was only the beginning, that mankind could never go back to the days of relative ignorance.

Yet, with the rise of the church, the murder of Hypatia, and the ransacking of the great library, all that changed. Europe was plunged into 1,300 years of what could be called stagnation only in the very kindest interpretation. Where might mankind be today had we not wasted 1,300 of the last 1,700 years of civilization to the tyranny of belief?

But we have no basis on which to feel secure today. Religious zealots make progress every day to push religious beliefs further into the government and into the classroom. New Age thinkers propagate a worldview in which reason is something that is somehow narrow-minded and outdated. We elect presidents who consult astrologists, look forward to the rapture, deny evolution and even basic observable facts. Ever increasing numbers of people believe in an undying multitude of pseudoscientific scams. We have a media that creates an illusion of factual equivalency and abdicates its professional responsibility to verify the facts. Our news media and scientific community often forsakes its role in advocating for truth.

Carl and Ann saw all these emerging trends and feared for the future. They feared that, like the Classical Greeks, we could wake up one day to find that our New Age is here, and it is a New Dark Age.

With the rise of Trumpism, which degrades truth and reason to depths unseen in the modern era, Sagan's New Dark Age looms dangerously close. So, what do we do? Is there even hope?

I was at a town hall-type discussion with Naomi Klein, author of the influential book *The Shock Doctrine: The Rise of Disaster Capitalism*. An audience member pointed out that climate change has almost certainly advanced past the tipping point and asked whether it was even worth continuing to try to save the planet. Naomi did not miss a beat. She looked at the obviously despairing gentleman and said something close to:

> *Of course, what choice do we have? Do we just die? We are humans and we never give up. We have no choice but to continue to fight to survive.*

CHAPTER 7: SCIENCE

We've looked at facts and beliefs and perceptions and neural networks and even at the lunacy of Ken Ham. We've covered a sweeping range of topics related to our capacity to think rationally in this deeply irrational world that we have created. We've put forth the scientific method as one critical tool to keep us grounded in fact, particularly during our current pandemic of delusion.

We may understand the scientific method in theory, but we can develop a much more satisfying appreciation if we take a slightly deeper dive into some of the tools and methods of science that reveal our universe to us so clearly.

Further, by looking back a bit at our history of science, and of the journey we as a species have made in refining our scientific method, we can better emulate that same journey in our own thinking.

In fact, after reading this book, I highly encourage you to pick up a good book or two on the history of science. The story of science is fascinating and dramatic and inspiring. One inspiring and engaging book that I highly recommend is *The Scientists: A History of Science Told Through the Lives of Its Greatest Inventors*, by John Gribbin.

If you have the ability to attend or audit college, try to sign up for a good History of Science course. It will probably be one of the most interesting and positively influential activities you can participate in.

Science Super-Vision

How can science claim to know so much about things we cannot see or touch?

Because we can see, we can essentially touch things we cannot otherwise see or touch using instruments and indirect observations. Although we may never explore far from Earth physically, we can still observe the universe intimately through our various spectrographic instruments.

Think of spectrographic instruments as essentially like a pair of binoculars that allows us to watch people on the other side of impassible rivers. Or like a microscope that lets us see very tiny things that are invisible to the naked eye.

Except the range of spectrographic instruments available to science is astoundingly detailed and encompassing. They allow scientists to "see" not only what is in the visible part of the electromagnetic spectrum, but across the entire range from radio waves, to microwaves, infrared, visible, ultraviolet, x-rays, and beyond to gamma rays. There are specialized instruments dedicated to each region of the electromagnetic spectrum.

Altogether, the science of using and reading these various instruments is called spectroscopy.

By combining what spectroscopy reveals to us, almost everything we need to know about even the most distant or tiny objects in the universe can be learned. So, yes, although we are Earthbound, we can actually, literally see the universe and we can validate and expand our understanding of it.

We hear a lot about electromagnetism, electromagnetic radiation, and electromagnetic waves. Electromagnetic waves are alternating electrical and magnetic fields that self-propagate through space at the speed of light. Heat, for example, is simply electromagnetic radiation in the infrared range.

These waves are all around us and incredibly revealing. We can tell, for example, what elements are present in what proportions in a distant star, simply by looking at what parts of the electromagnetic spectrum its atoms absorb or emit.

Electrons orbiting atoms are held in their quantized (specifically spaced) orbitals by wave behavior and uncertainty. When electrons absorb a photon of energy of just the right amount, they can jump up to a higher energy orbital. Later, they reemit the energy in one burst or in multiple jumps to return to their most stable energy state. This forms the basis of chemical reactions, of properties, molecular shapes, color, scattering, and virtually every other chemical property and behavior. Each wavelength of energy we observe forms a distinctive fingerprint identifying the particular source and conditions that generated it. The cool thing is that this can all be seen through spectroscopy.

Likewise, molecules can absorb and emit quantized bursts of longer wave radiation, and nuclei can do the same with short wavelengths (or higher frequency) radiation. By looking at the full electromagnetic spectrum, we can tell almost everything there is to know about distant worlds as well as very tiny ones within our own world.

Another tool that enables us to see the unseen is mathematics. Through mathematics we can see what is happening even where spectroscopy cannot reach.

Experimentation is yet another tool we use to see and touch. By conducting experiments, we can indirectly observe subatomic particles or dark matter. The evidence those experiments provide is just as crisp and clear as a photograph.

In all these ways, science can see and has revealed immense hidden knowledge. It was like we had opened the box and scattered the million pieces of the cosmos puzzle atop the table of science. And gradually, that knowledge started to get pieced together. We painstakingly organized the pieces, putting them together to form distinct sections.

Maxwell joined the sections of magnetism and electricity to discover electromagnetism. Einstein discovered that space and time form one larger section of the puzzle called space-time. Matter and energy go together to form another section called matter-energy. Waves and particles fit together. All of the distinct types of electromagnetic energy are merely different wavelengths along the electromagnetic spectrum.

The more science we learned, the simpler and clearer the cosmos became. Eventually, there is every expectation that all those pieces will come together into one complete picture puzzle. When that happens, we won't have a cosmos that consists of many different phenomena, but a single phenomenon that is the universe which can be described through many different models.

That is the universal equation that scientists seek. At this point, the puzzle is almost complete. We're still checking under the chairs and behind the table to fit that last stubborn piece labelled gravity into the picture.

The Scientific Method

🎙< *You've been referring to this scientific method constantly, but I must admit that I am still not really sure what it is.*

Science isn't a body of knowledge—it's a process. It's a systematic procedure for arriving at verifiable truth, and for answering questions.

The process typically starts with the identification of some question for which the answer is unknown. This is typically a question that asks why something is the way it is.

The next step is to collect information through observation. This is when scientists use their spectrographic eyes to gather clues and evidence.

At some point the scientist must formulate a hypothesis, an educated guess to explain the observations. To be a valid hypothesis, it must be provable or disprovable through experimentation.

Once the scientist has a working hypothesis, they then devise an experiment to prove or disprove that hypothesis. A good experiment must carefully control any variables that could affect the outcome.

The scientist then gathers data from the experiment in a systematic manner and performs analyses on the data. Any experiments must be repeated to ensure that the results are reliable. They must usually apply statistical measures to assure that any results are actually valid.

Based on the results of their analysis, they determine whether their hypothesis has been confirmed. If disproven, they must go back to the drawing board and come up with a new hypothesis.

Whether confirmed or disproven, they publish their results for critical review by the scientific community. Once the results are published, peer scientists review the findings for logical consistency. They replicate the experiments to verify that the reported results are correct.

If it survives those validations, the hypothesis is accepted by the scientific community as a scientifically validated fact. If the results represent a significant body of knowledge and are supported by a wide range of scientific fields, then it may finally be promoted to a scientific theory. In very few cases, when the scientific theory represents a fundamental characteristic of the universe, it may become a scientific law.

Scientific research can be basic or applied. Theoretical (or basic) research seeks to discover basic knowledge for its own sake. Applied research has the goal of producing useful applications from basic research.

Don't confuse science with technology. Science is the process of discovering truths about the cosmos. Technology is the result of applied research and engineering.

Only a Theory

*Science proclaims knowledge as if it is fact,
but they really only have theories.*

One common expression used to belittle and diminish a scientific fact is to refer to it as "only a theory." Tucker Carlson and other commentators who are ignorant of science, disingenuous, or both, use this tactic religiously to discredit scientific fact.

This tactic relies upon a lack of appreciation by the listener of just what the word "theory" really means in the language of science.

In everyday parlance, the word "theory" is used in many ways. It is used in a casual sense to suggest any idea, hunch, conjecture, opinion, hypothesis, or speculation regardless of merit. For example, one might say in joking, "My theory is that the cow made off with the outhouse."

Indeed, a dictionary entry might have six distinctly different definitions of the word "theory." But for a scientist, only one of those definitions matters. A scientific theory is an experimentally validated model that explains all known evidence and is capable of making successful predictions of as yet unverified facts. According to the National Academy of Sciences:

> *"Some scientific explanations are so well established that no new evidence is likely to alter them. The explanation becomes a scientific theory. In everyday language a theory means a hunch or speculation. Not so in science. In science, the word theory refers to a comprehensive explanation of an important feature of nature that is supported by many facts gathered over time. Theories also allow scientists to make predictions about as yet unobserved phenomena."*

A theory is a prestigious title awarded in science after a detailed explanation has progressed successfully through the gauntlet of the scientific method from hypothesis, through experimental validation, and through critical peer review and replication to yield an elegant yet comprehensive model of some aspect of the cosmos. For conservative blowhards to deride evolution as "only a theory" is like saying that the Nobel Peace Prize is "only a prize."

Look at some of the other concepts that are "only a theory" besides evolution. The "theory of gravity" is only a theory. The "wave theory of light" is only a mere theory. Let's not forget "germ theory."

Who can say that gravity really exists—or that germs are real? These are only theories after all.

Evolution is not the only inconvenient truth that is attacked as "only a theory." In cosmology, the big bang is no longer a hypothesis. It is now a scientific theory. That's as close to absolute certainty as science comes, short of it becoming a scientific law. And then, in climatology, there is the "theory of global warming." Only a theory after all, no need to get all concerned about it.

Another red herring that the Merchants of Doubt throw into the debate in order to confuse and discredit inconvenient scientific truths is to claim that "even scientists disagree" about them. This is generally nonsense, intended only to confuse any argument and create the illusion of legitimate debate. For any assertion to become a scientific theory, it will have passed meticulous independent verification by thousands of scientists and the careful scrutiny of the entire worldwide scientific community.

In issues as important to special interests as evolution and global warming, there will always be those who benefit by finding so-called scientists who will muddy the waters. After some point of widespread acceptance, it must be concluded that these scientists are unqualified, biased, belief-compromised, or simply paid off.

Many scientists do have competing views regarding the details of the big bang, of wave behavior, of evolution, of global warming, and even of gravity. But they don't disagree about the existence of these things, only in certain mechanical details.

No one disputes the theory of gravity. No one disputes the fact that gravity exists. There is incredible debate and disagreement over exactly how gravity works. In fact, far less is known about gravity than about evolution or global warming. However, manipulators take any healthy and productive scientific debate over details of the mechanisms of evolution and point at these to claim that "even scientists disagree about evolution." That is simply a misrepresentation intended to confuse and mislead.

Certainly, you might argue, how can scientists be so sure? Everyone thought Copernicus was crazy, but he turned out to be right. How do we know that the one scientist who disputes global warming isn't the one who is correct?

The reason we can be confident to any reasonable degree of doubt is that this is no longer the fifteenth century. Today, any important scientific proposition is almost instantly peer-reviewed by hundreds or even thousands of scientists. If that dissenting scientist had valid, demonstrable evidence or even reasonable conjecture to call the theory into question, it would have been tested. Chances are high that the dissenting scientist is simply compromised by self-interest or belief.

Scientific Models

Scientists don't really know anything for sure. Some say light is a wave, some say it is a particle. They can't agree on anything!

A while back I attended a book club discussion on *The Meme Machine* by Susan Blackmore. In it, Blackmore puts forth a thesis of "memetic evolution" to describe how our minds work. In fact, her assertion is that our minds can only be understood in terms of memetic selection. Although that seems to be a wildly exaggerated claim, the scientific model she proposes is both stimulating and promising.

I don't intend to discuss memetic evolution here. I only cite it as one example of the kind of topic that many non-scientists and even some scientists have great difficulty discussing fairly. Often in discussing such topics, a great many unfounded criticisms are lodged, and these quite often flow from an inadequate understanding and appreciation of scientific models.

This is understandable. Unless you're a trained, experienced, and particularly thoughtful scientist, you probably have had inadequate background to fully appreciate the concept of a scientific model. In fact, if you look up the word "model" in most dictionaries, the scientific usage of the term is typically not even mentioned. No wonder many people have a very limited, if not completely mistaken appreciation of what a scientific model is.

A scientific model is not analogous to a plastic model kit intended to look just like the real race car in every detail. It is not at all like a fashion model, intended to present something in an attractive manner. Nor is it an aspirational model to be put forth as a goal to emulate and strive toward.

No, a scientific model is a working system that does not need to actually "look like" the real system it describes in any conventional way. The important characteristic of a scientific model is that it behaves like the real system it describes. How accurately a scientific model reflects the real system it models is measured by how well it explains observed behaviors of the real system and is able to predict future behaviors of the real system.

For example, in 1913 Ernest Rutherford and Niels Bohr put forth the atomic model of matter that we are all familiar with: a nucleus of protons and neutrons orbited by electrons. This was a highly successful model because it described a huge number of observed characteristics and behaviors of matter, allowed us to gain great understanding of matter, and most importantly allowed us to predict as yet unobserved traits of matter.

But in truth the Bohr model is a laughably simplistic stick-figure representation of matter. It describes certain behaviors adequately but completely fails to describe others. It was quickly extended by De Broglie, by Schrödinger, and innumerable others to include wave and then quantum characteristics.

Despite its almost laughable simplicity and innumerable refinements and extensions made over the last century, the Bohr model remains one of the most important and consequential scientific models of all time. Certainly, we can and should recognize and discuss the limitations of models. But we must not dismiss them out of a mistaken lack of appreciation of the limitations of scientific models. Often these misguided criticisms have the more widespread effect of unfairly discrediting all science.

We should better understand what a model is and recognize that when we are talking about a new idea like memetic evolution, or if we are looking at the brain as a neural network, that we are talking about a scientific model.

Next, we should recognize that a scientific model does not need to answer everything. We must recognize the limitations of every model, but the more important focus is on how useful it is within its applicable limits. Newton's laws do not describe relativistic motion, but in our everyday world Newtonian physics is still fantastically useful. Critics of science should not claim that a model—or science in general—is fundamentally flawed or unreliable because a particular model is not universal and does not encompass everything.

Many critics of science think they have scored points by pointing out that "you can't trust science because their models are always being replaced!" But models are hardly ever replaced, rather they are extended. The Bohr model was greatly extended, but the basic model is still perfectly valid within its range of applicability.

The fact that there are many different models of the same thing is not proof that "science contradicts itself and cannot make up its mind." We have the two major models of light: the wave model and the particle model. The wave model correctly predicts some behaviors, and the particle model correctly predicts others. Though they appear irreconcilably different, both are absolutely valid. Real light is not exactly like either model but is exactly like both models.

Think of your mother. She has a mother-model that describes her behavior as a mother. But she also has a wife-model, a career-model, a daughter-model, a skeletal-model, and many others. None of these in themselves completely describes your mother, and many may seem irreconcilably different, but all of them correctly represent a different set of behaviors in different situations and only collectively do they all communicate a more complete picture of your mother.

So, when discussing something like memetic evolution or brain function, it's proper and correct to ascertain its boundaries and to critique how well it describes and predicts observed behaviors within those boundaries. But it's wrong and counterproductive to dismiss it either because there exist other models or because it does not—yet—describe everything. Worst is to dismiss all of science as flawed because it puts forth multiple models of reality and extends them over time.

To describe and predict human thinking, B.F. Skinner put forth a stimulus-response model, Blackmore put forth a meme model, and I often focus on a pattern-recognition model. These are not in competition. One is not right and the others all necessarily wrong.

The fact that there are these three and many other models of human thinking does not reflect any fundamental weakness of science, but rather its strength.

It's unfortunate that far too few people have a sufficiently deep appreciation for and level of comfort with scientific models. We must do much better to understand and communicate these subtleties that are so fundamental and critical to science.

Science Is Alive

If science is so perfect, why is it always changing its mind? First, they tell us to believe Newton. Then Einstein comes along and we should believe him instead. How do we know he was not wrong too?

Despite all the built-in validations of the scientific method, it is fallible. It can make mistakes. But those mistakes cannot persist for long before they are exposed and corrected. Mistakes don't persist very long in science.

In 1989, the world got all excited about reports by scientists Fleischmann and Pons who claimed to have demonstrated cold fusion. Cold fusion refers to any hypothetical process to achieve fusion at low temperatures. If this could be done, it would mean cheap and virtually infinite energy for the planet. It turned out that they had not really achieved cold fusion. The important point is that this was discovered very quickly, and the claims of cold fusion were thoroughly debunked that very same year.

Science may be fallible, but it has one key attribute that belief lacks. It's self-correcting. It has built-in mechanisms to ensure that any mistake is discovered and corrected very quickly. All findings, all evidence must be fully shared and public. It's the responsibility of scientists to reproduce and validate all assumptions and results.

On the other hand, beliefs have no mechanism by which they can be validated by others, let alone any mechanism by which the believers themselves can come to learn and correct errors in their own thinking. Mistakes become tenets of the belief. They become truth simply because they are part of the belief. Self-correction is not needed because the belief is assumed to be true. Any evidence to the contrary is by definition a falsehood.

In science, any bias introduced by belief is quickly exposed and eliminated. Even one of our most famous scientists, Sir Isaac Newton, was not totally immune to the effects of the beliefs of his time. He put forth some brilliant theories that explained, among other things, the orbits of the planets. However, actual data of the orbit of Jupiter doesn't fit his predictions exactly.

Newton didn't dismiss the data, which was good. But he was known as a person who, with some justification, held his own intelligence in very high esteem. Rather than admit that his theory might be lacking, he instead insisted that the only explanation had to be that God periodically intervened to correct the orbit of Jupiter. Certainly, it was far more likely that God existed and took a personal interest in keeping Jupiter from falling into the sun than it was that Newton could have been only partially right.

This is a great example of how personal bias and belief can compromise the reasoning of even the most rare and accomplished thinkers in human history. But it's also a great example of how science self-corrects itself. Despite the great credibility and reverence that Newton engendered, it did not take long for Pierre-Simon Laplace to correct Newton's calculations. Science is self-correcting regardless of the stature of the person who made the mistake. There are no gods in science. Nothing is taken on faith.

Even Albert Einstein made mistakes. In retrospect, we can chronicle twenty-three scientific mistakes that Einstein made between the years of 1905 and 1946. However, all these mistakes were quickly identified and corrected. One could argue that had he not made those mistakes, the corrected answers would have been slower in coming. Science learns from its mistakes.

In belief systems, a mistake is permanent. Nothing is learned from it. It's never corrected. But in science, mistakes are good things. Mistakes are learning experiences and stepping-stones to truth. Mistakes show scientists what can be eliminated from consideration, and that helps point to the truth.

Likewise, scams don't survive scientific scrutiny for long. Perpetual motion machines and cars that run on water are proven quickly to be frauds. Scientists attempt to reproduce any claimed "breakthrough" in order to validate it. These tests always fail, and that knowledge is made public.

Beliefs don't need to be reproduced or verified. They are simply true. When one believes that a master of transcendental meditation can levitate, there is no need to demonstrate that in a controlled situation. If one believes that a Mother Mary blessed a believer with a visitation, there is no need to reproduce that event or even anything like it.

And the other important thing to understand is that science doesn't need to experimentally disprove every proposition that comes along. If someone proposes another perpetual motion machine that "really works," scientists don't need to waste their time disproving that claim. The claim is disproven by established theory, by the very laws of the universe.

If someone puts forth a proposition, they cannot claim it is correct because science has not proven it wrong. Firstly, some assertions can be rejected out of hand as having no reasonable basis in reality. Secondly, the burden must be on the claimant to provide some reasonable proof that their assertion is correct. If the claim has no basis in reality and has not been demonstrated to be true, then no reasonable person needs to regard it as worthy of serious consideration. Lastly, many detractors put forth the fallacious argument that science cannot be trusted because it's always "changing its mind."

That is hardly ever the case. In each of these cases it was a matter of science expanding to encompass more scope. Newton was not disproven by Einstein or even replaced by Einstein. Einstein simply added additional models to cover phenomena outside of Newton's range of applicability. For normal macro-level physics, Newton's laws of motion are still just as valid as ever.

Expansion is not replacement. Extension is not correction.

Basic Research

Science does a lot of good, but too much of it is a wasteful make-work scam for scientists.

A common perception is that basic research is a waste of money. Mocking and bashing selected scientific research projects is a typical political game played by senators and members of Congress looking to show their great common-sense fiscal responsibility. By bashing research that costs pennies, they distract you from the real scams that cost you billions.

But basic research is essential to the advancement of human knowledge and our ability to discover the technical breakthroughs that can ensure our quality of life and our very survival.

Late in the 2008 presidential election, vice-presidential candidate Sarah Palin scored cheap points by ridiculing "fruit fly" research as an obvious waste of public funds. What she didn't know or didn't bother to mention was that fruit fly research is critical to legitimate scientific research, including the research into autism that she was calling for as part of the same speech.

Certainly, we must be intelligent about spending our limited resources. But in the first place, the total amount put into science research is a drop in the ocean of money wasted on frivolous and ill-conceived wars and weapons systems. But more importantly, these grants are highly competitive. Grant money is hard to come by. In order for a study to have been approved, chances are that there is a lot more potential benefit to it than is reflected in the congressional fund-raising letter.

But beyond that, political leaders like Palin have no appreciation of the historical role of basic research. Back when James Clerk Maxwell worked on wave theory, no one had any idea how that work could possibly be of any value. If he had been receiving public funding, some legislator would undoubtedly have scored points by ridiculing that wasted expenditure on some "magical invisible waves."

If Maxwell's basic research had not been supported, then Hertz could not have confirmed the existence of electromagnetic waves and Marconi would never have produced the radio.

To look at it another way, assume that the Queen of England was desperate for some way to communicate with her widely dispersed fleet and her far-flung colonies. The very survival of her empire hinged on her ability to quickly coordinate responses to crises.

The queen offers her entire treasury to anyone who can find a way to communicate that is faster than a sailing ship carrying missives and reports. No matter how much she offered as a prize, no matter how many great scientists she commissioned and no matter how much resource she provided, they could never have conceived, let alone invented, radio. The best improvement they might have come up with may have been some faster breed of homing pigeon.

Without basic science, no true advancement can be made. No one can predict when basic science will produce breakthroughs, what totally unrelated research might produce those breakthroughs, or where those breakthroughs might lead.

If we become a society that mocks basic research, we become a society that ceases to make dramatic innovations. All we would be able to do is refine old technologies, to make better horse-and-buggies or breed faster carrier pigeons.

One of the most important spheres of basic research is space exploration. Although many leaders like to pander to their constituents by bashing the space program, the demonstrated cost-benefit of the program has been higher than any other human endeavor. Further, the potential for dramatically important breakthroughs through space research is overwhelming.

But moreover, space exploration is a uniquely human endeavor. We are explorers as a species. If we give up our desire to explore physically, we give up our desire to explore intellectually. Space exploration is a bold and tangible statement of our character as a species.

The moon landing was perhaps the apex of our achievement as a species. It was a triumph of humanity. Every step we take into space should give us a profound sense of pride and accomplishment.

Scientific Arrogance

Scientists claim to have the corner on truth. Isn't that the height of arrogance?

Conclusions put forth by science fundamentally differ from non-scientific assertions. Science is not so much a body of knowledge as it is a method for arriving at truth. This very formal process for validating facts is called the scientific method. A scientist is not merely someone who knows facts but is someone who is dedicated to the process of validating ideas by means of the scientific method. Scientists are people who have a passion to know the truth of all things and the training in the scientific method to discover and confirm it.

A good scientist must be willing to tolerate not knowing any answers for which there is insufficient evidence and willing to discard even their most deeply held beliefs when they are contradicted by facts.

So no, science is not arrogant. It does not claim to know everything, but it can objectively demonstrate the validity of any claim made by science to anyone who wishes to challenge it. No such guarantee of accuracy can be made by anyone who espouses truth based upon belief.

Science Isn't Perfect

Are you trying to hold science up as perfect? Is it capable of no wrong?

Certainly, there have been scientists who have been imperfect individuals, and there have been many cases where science as a whole has failed. Some scientists have worked on immoral or dangerous projects. While the majority of scientists protested or even boycotted the development of nuclear weapons, plenty of them agreed to cooperate. Many more work on technologies of war every day. Without a doubt, scientists can make mistakes or lose sight of their scientific integrity as easily as anyone else.

If the world ends due to global warming, even if we get off lucky and it results merely in catastrophic climate change that causes billions to suffer, we will all be complicit in the great failure of our generation. However, scientists must bear special responsibility in our failure to act on global warming. The blame is not for producing the technologies that generate greenhouse gases, but for their failure to assume their unique responsibility to push back more strongly against belief-based thinking and government policies.

For generations, scientists have played nicely in their own little sandboxes. With few exceptions, they have refused to ruffle feathers, failed to respond when statistics are misused or scientific facts are ignored. When a talk show host creates the illusion of a comparable legitimacy between evolution and creationism, the science guest who accepts this without protest deserves part of the blame.

Scientists have allowed science, fact, and reason to be manipulated and ignored by belief-based thinkers for many decades, and their cowardice has helped modern society to slide to the brink of another dark age of belief-based thinking. Knowledge is power, and as Spider-Man often points out, with great power comes great responsibility.

Scientists have great knowledge, but they have arguably shirked their responsibility to educate, to stand against misinformation, and to ensure the factual integrity of public policy. Scientists individually and science collectively can and should do better. We must do better.

Our Scientific Journey

🗣 *Most of us cannot hope to become scientists.*

That may be true, but we can become more scientific.

One way to do better is to appreciate our collective journey as a species away from belief-based thinking toward a more scientific way of thinking. It is only in the last few hundred years that we have been on this road, and we have made astounding progress.

But it has not been a quick transition. It didn't happen overnight. We as a superorganism of sorts have progressed in fits and starts with lots of hard-earned lessons along the way. Even today, many of us have not caught up with where we need to be individually in order to achieve the success we require collectively.

Each of us can, within ourselves, follow, emulate, and reaffirm the collective journey that has led us to where we are; the journey that has led us out of a much darker time into an age of relative wonder.

Following is just a very selected few stories of individual scientists who have advanced our collective progress toward a society based on facts and reason. I selected their stories not because of their particular contributions to science, but because of their role in shaping *how* we think and behave as scientists. This includes the lessons learned from their limitations and mistakes.

Eratosthenes (276–194 BCE)

A key part of science is careful observation. Scientists must be very good at pattern recognition, to see order in seemingly chaotic data, but they must also be good at rejecting false patterns and spotting anomalous data. Not only must they notice the unusual, they must also have a burning curiosity to explain observations rather than just accept them.

One great story to illustrate the power of observation is the true tale of Eratosthenes. He served as Chief Librarian at the Great Library of Alexandria during the Greek Classical periods, two hundred years before Christ and even longer before the tenure of Hypatia.

Eratosthenes happened to read an account that, in the city of Syene, about 500 miles to the south, on the day of the summer solstice, the sun was directly overhead, causing pillars to cast no shadow and the bottom of a deep well to be evenly lit.

For most people this would hold absolutely no interest. What possible use could such a trivial fact offer? But Eratosthenes noticed it, and he also thought to confirm it. But he found that, on the same day of the year in Alexandria, pillars cast a shadow and the water at the bottom of wells was not evenly lit as expected.

What is one to make of this? Again, most people would simply ignore it as having no importance, or they would discount the report from Syene as obviously incorrect.

But Eratosthenes confirmed that report, and then he asked himself how this could possibly be true. He hypothesized that the only thing that would explain such a phenomenon would be if the surface of the Earth were curved. Greek scholars as far back as Pythagoras had suggested that the Earth might be spherical, but this was certainly not a widespread belief. Plato and Aristotle argued the case, but the evidence was not generally compelling or persuasive.

Eratosthenes however went further than just speculating that the Earth is spherical. He made measurements. He actually hired a man to pace off the exact distance from Alexandria to Syene. Based on that measurement, he used geometry to calculate the predicted circumference of the Earth.

Eratosthenes calculated the circumference of the Earth with over 99 percent accuracy. Not bad for a guy who had nothing except his brain, eyes, two legs (albeit someone else's legs), and a great passion for knowledge, unfettered by the prevailing beliefs of the time.

In his *Cosmos* series, Carl Sagan recounts the story of Eratosthenes with far greater storytelling ability than my own. I invite you to watch the series and hear his telling of this inspiring tale.

Roger Bacon (1219–1292)

During the Middle Ages, scholars gradually revived interest in Greek Classical knowledge. Some thinkers began to openly discuss intellectual issues, but this was largely relegated to translating and studying the classic literature that they held in awe and felt could not be improved. Despite the very real threat of Inquisition, some spoke out about the need for rational inquiry.

One notable example was an English Franciscan friar who lived in the early 1200s named Roger Bacon. Bacon is considered a harbinger of science by his advocacy of experimentation, an idea that would not take hold for 300 more years.

It is important to recognize that Europe was never the entire world. Asia, India, and the Middle East all have their unique histories of intellectual advancement. Bacon's advocacy of empirical thinking was influenced by the works of Muslim scientists.

Bacon put forth the idea that science is the handmaid of religion, not a challenge to it. In a written work, he proposed a principle of religious openness toward intellectual inquiry.

That kind of blasphemous proposition could not be voiced without friends in high places to provide protection. Bacon benefited from having a close friend in Pope Clement IV, who officially requested the opinion to protect his friend.

But Bacon was too far ahead of his contemporaries. After Pope Clement died, he was promptly imprisoned by his fellow Franciscans for his radical idea that one should consider facts in coming to know truth. Nevertheless, since that day, most popes, and the Dalai Lama, have held the official position that science is a useful tool to purge religious teachings of mistakes.

Nicolaus Copernicus (1473–1543)

After about 1400 CE scholars began to lose their awe of Greek and Roman classical knowledge and started to question and form their own thoughts. Although they did not use scientific methods, they ushered in the Age of Reason. Mostly devout Christians, they set forth the view that a study of the natural world honored God, rather than blasphemed.

Nicolaus Copernicus was a Polish astronomer and clergyman. More a philosopher than scientist, he actually made few observations, performed no experiments and expected no testing of his ideas. Most of his ideas came from a study of the classics.

He theorized a more elegant heliocentric model of the solar system than Ptolemy. In questioning the teachings of one of the icons of classical knowledge, he became one of the first people to break from an unquestioning acceptance of classical thinking.

Copernicus correctly placed the known planets, Mercury through Saturn, in proper order, proposed that the planets orbit the sun, that the Earth rotates, and that long-term fluctuation of the axis of spin accounts for the observed precession of the equinoxes.

He completed his ideas in 1510 but did not publish until the year of his death in 1543. His decades-long delay was probably not due to fear of church reprisals. In fact, he presented his ideas to Pope Clement VII and other clerical leaders at the Vatican, and they received it well, urging him to publish the work.

He was hesitant to publish his work because of the many questions left unanswered, such as why the planets don't fall into the sun and why the Earth's movement does not cause great winds.

Good scientists don't rush to publish incomplete theories. Copernicus wasn't interested in acclaim; he was interested in getting it right.

But Copernicus didn't get everything right. Although he questioned many prevailing beliefs about the universe, he wasn't immune to accepting some of them as givens. He adopted the assumption that the sun is the center of the universe. This is an example of a scientist allowing widespread beliefs to lead to unsupported conclusions.

Leonard Digges (1515–1559)

Leonard Digges was an English astronomer and a prominent Protestant. He was one of the few people of his time who recognized the importance of Copernicus's work. He invented the first telescope in 1550 in order to pursue his studies. In 1576 he expanded on the ideas of Copernicus by writing a book that proposed that the universe is infinite, with stars extending into infinity. The commonly held view at the time was that the universe was finite with a fixed number of stars.

Of course, we now know that the universe is finite with a fixed (although constantly changing) number of stars. But it is far bigger than his contemporaries imagined, and Digges was essentially correct. Like most everyone else, however, Digges also continued to adopt the assumption that our sun is at the center of the universe. Leonard Digges pioneered the cooperative spirit of science in his efforts to build upon the work of another scientist and to popularize science.

Andreas Vesalius (1514–1564)

Andreas Vesalius was a Swiss surgeon who is considered the father of modern anatomy. He was the first to continue the classical work of the Greek physician Galen in any meaningful way. Around 1536, a judge supplied him with the cadavers of executed criminals to study. Vesalius took them home for dissection. He did the dissections himself and employed top artists for his illustrations. His "hands-on" approach elevated the practice of surgery which previously had been seen as beneath the physician.

In 1543, he published the landmark work entitled *De humani corporis fabrica* (On the Structure of the Human Body), which provided extremely accurate and detailed drawings of human anatomy.

Vesalius set a precedent that one must see for oneself rather than simply rely upon the knowledge passed down from previous generations. His passion to make observations and measurements even drove him to perform unseemly dissections himself rather than rely upon the reports of his surgeons.

William Harvey (1578–1657)

William Harvey, an English physician, was the first to seriously expand upon the study of blood circulation undertaken by the Greek Galen 1,400 years earlier. Harvey proved that the heart is only a pump and not the wellspring of blood. Up until then it was assumed that the blood was produced in the heart. Harvey not only disputed this based on logic but he proved it. He measured the amount of blood pumped through the heart and proved that it was far too great to be produced there.

Through his experiments and tests, he also proved that blood circulates; it isn't merely produced in the heart and consumed by the body. He proved that the circulatory loop is completed through tiny almost invisible capillaries.

The contributions of Harvey cannot be understated. He not only hypothesized, but he went on to use experiments to prove his hypotheses and urged that observations should not be discounted because we cannot explain them. Harvey significantly raised the bar for what was considered sufficient scientific proof of a proposition.

Tycho Brahe (1546–1601)

Tycho Brahe was a Danish astronomer. In 1560, fourteen-year-old Tycho heard that a full solar eclipse was expected. When it happened exactly as predicted, it inspired him to study the heavens.

Brahe was a skilled observer of the planets and stars and an even more meticulous record keeper. He accurately documented over 777 fixed stars, producing his own cutting-edge instruments to locate celestial bodies.

In 1572, Brahe discovered a new star, a supernova, proving that stars are not permanent and unchanging as previously assumed.

In 1577, he discovered a near earth comet, again shattering assumptions that the universe is fixed and unchanging.

But Brahe did not have the theoretical imagination or mathematical skills to analyze his own data. Kepler did. Brahe was nevertheless highly protective of it and refused to turn it over to Kepler who only received it after the death of Brahe.

Although a clever inventor with a passion for recording data, Brahe did make many conceptual mistakes. He believed the Earth, not the sun, was the center of the universe and all else revolved around it. He thought it was a "physical absurdity" that the Earth should move. If it did, he argued, an object would veer to one side when dropped.

Brahe showed the importance of careful observation and record-keeping, providing fundamental data for many scientists to follow. His mistaken application of "commonsense logic" also cautions against biasing knowledge according to what seems clearly rational at the time, rather than trusting in facts.

Johannes Kepler (1571–1630)

Johannes Kepler was a German astronomer who has a wonderful story to tell. Kepler was a brilliant theoretician. Because of poor eyesight caused by smallpox as a child, Kepler did not make his own observations of the stars. He collected no data of his own. Instead, he relied upon the data of others like Tycho Brahe. He studied data of celestial movement and analyzed them with the tools of mathematics and geometry to theorize their actual behavior, something Brahe could not do himself.

Kepler spent most of his life pursuing a false hypothesis. In a moment of what he thought was divine inspiration, he envisioned the solar system as a heavenly manifestation of perfect geometry. He hypothesized that in the orbits of the five known planets, God expressed each of the five perfect geometrical solids as put forth by Pythagoras. Surely, he felt, any work of God would be one of geometrical artistry and perfection.

He spent much of his life looking for data that would allow him to fit the orbit of the planets into these shapes, proving his hypothesis.

After the death of Brahe, Kepler finally gained access to his data and eagerly analyzed it, confident he could finally fit it to a perfect geometrical scheme that would proclaim the elegant symmetry of God's creation.

But the data didn't fit the hypothesis into which he had invested so much of himself. In the end, his scientific integrity forced him to abandon his life-long vision of a solar system based on perfect geometric solids for a circular orbital model.

But even the elegance of perfect circular orbits didn't fit. When he found just two points in Brahe's data that didn't fit the aesthetically pleasing notion of perfect circles, he abandoned that as well.

He could have simply dismissed those two points as bad data. Most people probably would have done just that. But Kepler's faithfulness to the data, to facts, forced him to arrive at the correct answer in the end—that the planets follow elliptical orbits, not circular ones.

Through his faithful analysis of the data, Kepler went on to discover the three fundamental laws of planetary motion:

1.   *The planets move in elliptical orbits.*

2.   *Planets sweep through equal areas in equal time periods.*

3.   *The square of planetary orbits is equal to the cube of their solar radius.*

Kepler made many other contributions to science and also contributed in other areas.

He earned a living to pay for his scientific work by serving as an astrologer to royalty and nobility. His work in astronomy gave him inherent credibility in making predictions based on the position and movement of the stars.

Did he actually believe that the stars control human destiny? Definitely not. According to his own writings, he simply made-up astrological predictions to earn a living, trying to direct the believers in the best way he could by claiming his advice was written in the stars.

Kepler knew religious persecution as well. During his time, it was commonplace for a village or town mayor to simply dictate that all residents must follow a certain religion. If the mayor was replaced, the new mayor might well simply mandate that all residents must henceforth follow his religion or move out.

Since he was unwilling to compromise his religious beliefs, Kepler was forced to pack up his home and family and move many times.

What a cautionary tale against the slippery slope one stands upon when there is no separation of church and state!

Kepler also has the unique distinction of having written the first science fiction novel. He penned a fanciful tale about a traveler to the moon. He wrote of how this traveler built a ship that flew him to the moon, and he described his view of the Earth from the lunar surface.

As a result of that book, his mother ended up being jailed for witchcraft. It was "reasoned" that Kepler could not have written such a story unless his mother were a witch who used her magical powers to actually whisk him up to the moon and back. Kepler spent many years trying to free her from prison.

Kepler was a key figure in scientific history. While not yet integrating the complete scientific method, he was the first to use imagination and theoretical models to fit empirical data. He demonstrated the critical ability of scientists to put aside even their most deeply held ideas when the facts do not support them.

Although not a full-fledged scientist, and despite engaging in a bit of charlatanism to keep his lanterns burning, Kepler exemplifies scientific integrity.

William Gilbert (1544–1603)

In the early 1600s, the term "scientist" had not even been coined yet. Like their predecessors, those who studied the natural world were almost all firstly religiously trained and most held highly respected positions in the church.

They were also mostly wealthy, titled, educated, and held high public offices and lands. Each of them studied many different disciplines, including astronomy, mathematics, classics, philosophy, religion, art, physical sciences, and most every other field of knowledge. Most all of them knew and corresponded with their contemporaries.

William Gilbert was an English physician and amateur physicist. He is considered by many to be the first true scientist because he was the first to combine observation, hypothesis, and experimentation into a deliberate methodology to arrive at facts. Galileo was strongly influenced by his work and called him the father of the experimental method of science.

Gilbert displays the wide range of interests of thinkers of his time. He served formally as physician to the queen. But in all his spare time he studied alchemy until he concluded that transmuting lead into gold was a fantasy.

He took up physics and studied magnetism and electricity, a field left untouched since the work of Greek philosophers two thousand years earlier. He discovered laws of magnetic attraction and repulsion and disproved myths about magnetism. He showed that the Earth worked like a giant bar magnet. He coined the terms North and South Pole, attraction, and others.

As a result of his studies of magnetism and electricity, he published *De Magnete* in 1600. That publication stood for 200 years as the definitive work in the field until Michael Faraday came along to expand upon it.

In astronomy, Gilbert proved that precession of the equinoxes is caused by a wobble in the Earth's rotation (roughly suggested earlier by Copernicus) and suggested that the stars are at different distances and might have their own planets.

Gilbert was not only the first person to define science as a complete methodology, he also demonstrated a willingness to discard fields of inquiry, such as the transmutation of lead to gold, that are unfounded—no matter how attractive they might seem.

Galilei Galileo (1564–1642)

Galilei Galileo is a household name, but few people appreciate the extent of his contributions to science. He was an Italian astronomer and mathematician who championed Gilbert's method of experimental science.

He argued that hailstones of different sizes fall at the same speed, although it was widely believed that heavier ones fall faster and must be formed higher up in order to reach the ground at the same time.

He used ramps to study acceleration and to prove that heavier objects fall at the same rate. No one had ever bothered to test the assumption that heavier objects fall faster than light ones. The story of Galileo dropping balls from the tower of Pisa to prove this is most likely a myth, although that experiment was attempted later.

Similarly, everyone assumed that a pendulum with a heavier weight would swing faster than a lighter one. In timing swinging chandeliers with his pulse while bored in class, Galileo found that the period of swing is only based on the length, not the weight or size of the arc.

Galileo showed how a pulley works and proved they don't give you something for nothing; rather you do the same work by pulling a smaller effective mass over a proportionally longer distance.

He attempted to produce the first bulb thermometer and marketed the first mechanical calculator.

He wrote a book on the mechanics of inertia and motion. It proved that projectiles follow parabolic paths, with a vertical motion governed by gravity and a horizontal motion governed by inertial motion. He put forth equations to mathematically define trajectories.

One famous story tells of how Galileo challenged a bitter rival to prove by experiment the false claim that ice floats because of shape and not because it is less dense than water. On the day of the challenge, the rival failed to appear to prove his case.

Galileo had heard of the telescope but could not obtain one, so he built his own better one in a single day. By 1609 he made a model with 20x power and sent one to Kepler. In 1610 Galileo used it to discover the four brightest and biggest moons of Jupiter. He also used it to recognize that the Milky Way is made of individual stars and that the moon is covered by craters. He estimated the crater height quite accurately from the length of their shadows.

He studied Kepler's supernova and proved it did not move, suggesting it was in fact a star and arguing against the immutability of stars.

His book *The Starry Messenger* was translated into many languages, including Chinese, and made him extremely famous.

He dispelled doubts of the Copernican model. By finding the moons of Jupiter, he showed that our moon can orbit the Earth even though the Earth is orbiting the sun at the same time.

He also confirmed that Venus does show phases, proving it orbits the sun as well. This is a perfect example of observation confirming an earlier hypothesis. He noted that Saturn had distortions that would later be shown to be rings, and he noticed sunspots, although others had noted this, unbeknownst to him.

Although all his work supported Copernicus, Galileo was careful never to say so directly for fear of reprisals by the church. For the most part, he was on good terms with the clergy and protected by supporters in the Vatican. Despite his friends in high places, he had close brushes with heresy.

His most severe falling-out happened when he was commissioned by the pope to write an unbiased comparison of Ptolemy and Copernicus. He did so in dialogue form, in a witty book of that name, in which the advocate of Ptolemy is named Simplicus. The name communicated the clear message that the supporter of Ptolemy was dim-witted. He went too far this time and was charged with heresy— and therefore had to be convicted. He was never jailed or tortured, thanks to allies in the clergy who negotiated that he be held in relative luxury at a friendly estate.

Given the breadth and depth of his many accomplishments, it would still be surprising if Galileo never made a mistake. Although he pioneered inertia, he erroneously thought that inertia was circular. It seems silly and petty to even point out such a relatively minor technical mistake over such an amazing lifetime of accomplishment.

Robert Recorde (1512–1558)

Robert Recorde was a Welsh physician who made many important contributions to mathematics. His work in the early 1500s served as the basis of mathematics for over 100 years. He invented the plus, minus, and equal signs that we still use today.

He also worked as comptroller of the mint. In that capacity, he refused to allocate funds to put down a workers' rebellion. His political sense and ethical integrity resulted in his being jailed for treason. He also accused a superior of malfeasance. As a result, he died in debtor's prison after struggling to pay the costs of a libel action against him.

Recorde is an example of a scientist whose passion for the truth extended beyond the realm of scientific fact, into the domain of public policy and integrity. Although his whistleblowing landed him in prison, his is an example that more scientists should follow today.

Edward Tyson (1651–1708)

Edward Tyson was an English physician. His name alone earns him a place in this book, but his contributions are important as well. At the Bethlem Hospital (infamously known as Bedlam), Tyson was the first physician to strongly advocate for the humane treatment of psychiatric patients, forcing science to grapple with ethical considerations and human costs.

He is considered the father of anatomy. Tyson dissected a porpoise (with Robert Hooke illustrating) and showed that it was actually a mammal. His dissection and comparative study of chimpanzee anatomy demonstrated that they are remarkably similar to humans. His treatise of 1699, *The Anatomy of a Pygmie*, firmly established humans as a part of the animal kingdom and laid the foundation for centuries of anatomical work to follow.

Charles Darwin (1809–1882)

And then there was this fellow named Charles Darwin. Since the 1600s, when Hooke discovered the fossil record, since Tyson compared animal anatomy, researchers in every field of study were calling the belief in creationism into question. Many were hypothesizing that some process like evolution must be occurring. But Charles Darwin, a young English naturalist, was shocked when it was suggested that humans and animals might share a common ancestry. Although an agnostic with regard to religion, the notion disturbed his sensibilities.

But Charles did have an inquisitive mind and his classmates nicknamed him "Gas" because of his persistent dabbling in chemistry.

At age twenty-two in the year 1831 Charles signed up for a two-year expedition aboard the ship HMS *Beagle*. It lasted for five years. His job was to gather information in his capacity as a naturalist. What he accomplished must have exceeded the very wildest expectations for that modest post.

By the end of the voyage, Charles had written 770 pages of diary with 1,750 pages of notes. He had compiled twelve illustrated catalogs detailing almost 5,500 biological samples. Based on this data and his field observations, he concluded that there was a systematic process of change at work in nature. He went on to make sense of all his information in the form of a world-changing book called *On the Origin of the Species by Means of Natural Selection.*

Although it contained arguably the most important and powerful concept ever produced by humankind, Darwin had little interest in publishing his book. He knew the controversy, the outrage, that it would generate, and he had no stomach for it.

It had been 300 years since Copernicus, and people were only just finally coming around to fully accept his proposition that the Earth is not the center of the universe. Darwin knew that his proposition was far more inflammatory than even that!

So, he waited—twenty years—to publish his work. When he did so, in 1859, he lobbed it at the world like a bomb, retreating to the safety of an island to quietly live out his days studying molds and slimes. He preferred to let others fight the battle. And today, more than 160 years later, the explosion it caused is still reverberating.

Darwin died of a heart attack in 1882 and was buried at Westminster Abbey with full ecclesiastical honors.

People usually misunderstand Darwin's contribution. He didn't discover or invent evolution. Scientists had long suggested that such a process must be occurring in nature. But what he did was to put forth a logical and comprehensive description of the actual mechanism of evolution. Even if you suspect something exists, someone must discover exactly how it works before that idea can be fully embraced by science.

Gregor Mendel (1822–1884)

Many of us learned about Gregor Mendel in general science class. An Austrian botanist and the father of genetics, Mendel built upon Darwin by drilling deeper into the genetic basis of inheritance. He showed how specific traits are inherited or not inherited by offspring and put forth general theories to explain observed inheritance.

Although many historians question the actual quality of Mendel's research, he is typically presented as a role model for scientific inquiry for having employed sound scientific research methods and for having applied statistics to his analysis.

Regardless of whether all the credit he receives is fully deserved, he produced groundbreaking work and presented it to a largely uncomprehending audience in 1865. Few understood the importance of his work or its profound significance. Not many biologists had any training in statistics, and his results went largely unnoticed.

His work had little impact on science and would have to await rediscovery much later by Thomas Hunt Morgan before its importance would be fully understood and he would be rediscovered as the father of modern genetics.

James Clerk Maxwell (1831–1879)

James Clerk Maxwell was a Scottish physicist who easily ranks in the same league as Newton and Einstein. Building on the work of Faraday, he originated the concept of electromagnetic radiation. In 1864, he completely described electromagnetism in four immensely important equations named after him.

Before Maxwell, there were two things known as electricity and magnetism. After Maxwell, there would only be electromagnetism, one of the most important and fundamental forces of our universe.

But Maxwell contributed not only to the knowledge of science but to the very practice and philosophy of science. He put forth that "scientific truth should be presented in different forms and regarded equally true." This established the concept of scientific models.

The concept of a scientific model is confusing for non-scientists. Detractors often exploit that confusion to discredit science.

Maxwell's proposal of models helped to understand electricity and magnetism. Models explained how they can be so different but actually be the same thing.

Another perfect example of models is the duality of light, a concept that would not be understood fully until Einstein came along much later. One can conduct experiments to definitively prove that light is a wave. But you can also perform conclusive experiments to prove that light is a particle. Does this mean one is wrong? Does this mean you can't trust science? Does this call the very legitimacy of science into question?

It turns out that light is both a particle and a wave. In some situations, it displays wave-like behavior and in other situations it displays particle-like behavior. In one situation, its behavior can be predicted exactly by using a wave model, and in other situations its behavior can be predicted exactly using a particle model.

This was a critical change in worldview for scientists. Maxwell forced scientists to make the paradigm shift that would enable them to understand complex behaviors of the universe yet to be revealed.

Thanks to Maxwell, today's scientists are perfectly comfortable with adopting models that describe one facet of the gem of the cosmos.

Robert Millikan (1868–1953)

Robert Millikan was an American physicist and quantum experimentalist. Like many scientists, he refused to believe Einstein's prediction of the photoelectric effect. He set out determined to prove Einstein wrong. But eventually, after long and difficult experimentation, he was the one to prove Einstein correct.

He later wrote:

> *"I spent ten years of my life testing that 1905 equation of Einstein's and contrary to all my expectations, I was compelled in 1915 to assert its unambiguous verification in spite of its unreasonableness."*

As part of that work, he obtained an accurate value of Plank's constant. For this and for accurately measuring the charge of an electron, Millikan won the Nobel Prize in Physics in 1923. Millikan represents the best part of science. Science recognizes no gods—not even Einstein.

A legitimate and expected activity of science is to prove the other guy wrong. But, as Millikan demonstrated, when the facts speak, you must listen—even if they seem unreasonable to you and even if you have invested ten years and an immense portion of your scientific credibility trying to disprove them.

Thomas Hunt Morgan (1866–1945)

Just as Millikan spent years trying to disprove Einstein's photoelectric effect only to prove it correct, Thomas Hunt Morgan spent years trying to prove that the genetic theories of Mendel were not generally applicable. In the end, he proved exactly the opposite.

Morgan was an American zoologist who decided to work with drosophila, the common fruit fly, to disprove Mendel. As a result, he published "The Mechanism of Mendelian Heredity and the Theory of the Gene," which earned him the Nobel Prize in Physiology or Medicine 1933.

His paper established the chromosome theory of heredity by saying that genes are lined up in series on chromosomes and that they are responsible for identifiable hereditary traits. Morgan's determination to disprove Mendel resurrected the stillborn field of Mendelian genetics.

Stephen Hawking (1942–2018)

Stephen Hawking was one of our most famous living scientists. He is best known for his theoretical work in understanding the big bang and the early stages of our universe as well as the properties of black holes.

His ability to conceptualize physical realities that are extraordinarily far from our range of everyday experience was arguably unprecedented in human history. He possessed an almost preternatural ability to envision far back and far ahead in time and far off into subatomic worlds where our reality does not even apply.

Hawking long cautioned that the greenhouse effect causing global warming is likely to make the Earth uninhabitable. Yet, somehow, climate science deniers maintain that his opinion on this matter is not worthy of any measure of credibility.

Carl Sagan (1934–1996)

The American astrophysicist Carl Sagan made many significant contributions to the field of planetary astronomy and was instrumental in the success of our manned and unmanned space missions. He authored many books on science, science fiction, reason and logic, and ethics. But most notable about Carl Sagan was his unique ability to communicate, to popularize science, and influence others. His *Cosmos* series inspired a generation to take a closer look at the universe as revealed through science.

He didn't shirk from his social responsibilities as both a humanist and as a scientist. He was active in opposing nuclear proliferation, raising environmental consciousness, fighting global warming, and promoting space exploration. His was one of the most influential voices countering continual lobbying by Edward Teller for the wider use of nuclear bombs. Sagan simultaneously investigated paranormal phenomenon and cautioned against pseudoscientific thinking.

From Eratosthenes to Sagan and beyond, each of these scientists contributed not only to their particular fields of study, but have helped train our collective neural networks to think about and investigate the universe more scientifically.

I hope that this highly abbreviated glimpse into some of our most influential scientists illustrates how scientific thinking evolved over many lifetimes and how it can evolve within each of us during our own lifetime.

CHAPTER 8: FUTURES

🗣 *So how do we move forward toward a more fact-based society?*

Carl Sagan had been known to comment that if we humans should be so foolish as to destroy ourselves, it would be a terrible waste of six billion years of evolution.

We can reverse this current pandemic of delusion. We have the intellectual capacity to solve whatever challenges we face. But it would be so easy to fail. Untold numbers of species have gone extinct before us when the traits that made them successful up to that point ceased to serve them well in a changing environment.

Nature offers humans no special treatment. Our powerful ability to rationalize belief is no longer an advantage in the modern world that we have produced for ourselves. We have transformed it dramatically since the days when belief was, on balance, beneficial. Through our technologies we have increased populations, strained our planetary ecosystem, and created a malignant climate change catastrophe.

Our proclivity for belief is now a grave threat, one that has exploded through the vectors of technology into a global pandemic of delusion. Irrational beliefs indirectly undermine and actively block rational efforts to solve the challenges we face.

The temptation to just give up on humanity in the face of this pandemic of delusion is almost overwhelming. One might conclude that humanity has simply outgrown its petri dish, that we are the tragic victims of our own success, that we simply do not have the intellectual capacity to overcome our evolved limitations. Perhaps the most sensible response is to just party on and drink up all the champagne we can before our Titanic sinks into oblivion.

But as Naomi Klein urged, we cannot give into that kind of defeatism.

We have to proceed on the assumption that we can set down our champagne glasses and get to work saving our planet.

There is some basis for optimism.

Back in the thirteenth century, contemporaries of Roger Bacon quite probably looked at their situation and came to the same dire prognosis. History up to that point might have convinced many people that their relatively dismal existence was all that mankind would ever be capable of achieving.

They would have been so very wrong. Unbeknownst to them, they were standing on the precipice of unimaginable growth. The important growth here was not merely technical, but in how we humans think about the universe and go about finding solutions. So maybe the pessimist in me is wrong today as well. Maybe we can surpass our own pessimistic expectations.

There are other reasons for cautious optimism. As we have repeatedly pointed out in this book, our neural networks can learn better patterns of thinking, analysis, and decision-making. We clearly do possess the capacity to put aside beliefs and address our challenges in a more fact-based manner.

It's all up to our will and our intellect. We must improve our neural network training as individuals so that more fact-based behavior can emerge and manifest in our collective behavior.

Information technology has proven to be an extremely dangerous amplifier of delusion, but it also represents our greatest hope. It's not enough that it merely stops causing harm. If we are to succeed, it must play an active role in helping to retrain our neural networks to think more rationally.

We can do better. We can reverse this pandemic of delusion that threatens our very existence.

The alternative would be a tragic waste of six billion years.

Parting Words

Hey, you know what? I didn't agree with everything you said, but it was interesting!

It is gratifying to hear that coming from you, my imaginary friend and critic. I am truly gratified that you stayed with me through to the end of our journey together. I truly hope that you found it to be a fun, stimulating, and even thought-provoking experience.

Keep the ideas we shared here in mind as you go about your everyday life, and I'd wager that you'll see evidence of many of the things we discussed in your own experiences.

Beyond that, do try to implement some of the suggestions and insights presented here in your own life. Go read a good book on the history of science next, minimize your exposure to beliefs, and don't neglect to review the list of logical and ethical fallacies presented in the appendix at your leisure.

And again, thanks. The fact that you made it here is encouraging evidence that we can improve our ability to think about, and hopefully engage in, ever more effective fact-based thinking.

APPENDIX

Fallacies are general types of arguments that are based on flawed or manipulative logic. These almost invariably lead to fallacious, or false, conclusions. In our modern life we are inundated by fallacious arguments, wielded either by ignorance of sound logic or in an intentional effort to mislead.

To become better consumers of information, to prevent ourselves from being misled or manipulated, we need to learn to recognize these types of arguments. Fallacious arguments should always be dismissed or at least considered with appropriate skepticism.

The good news is that we can learn to quickly and even automatically recognize these types of arguments. They are essentially fill-in-the-blank arguments that are put forth where the blank is filled in with whatever conclusion one is trying to sell. It is just a matter of familiarity before you begin to find them blatantly and even laughably obvious.

You can start to train your neural network to recognize fallacious arguments just by reviewing and considering the following examples. After that, you can return to this section as a reference when you suspect a fallacious argument is being presented but cannot quite place it.

Logical Fallacies

Following are examples of just some of the logical fallacies that people will use to try to convince you of things that are not true. By learning to recognize them, you will become far better able to sniff out bad arguments or those contrived to convince you to believe a falsehood.

Although lengthy, this overview is not meant to be exhaustive. It merely reviews some of the many, many ways people will seek to fool or convince you.

For each, I contrive a representative sample argument from a hypothetical global warming denier. Just keep in mind that since fallacious arguments can violate many different rules of logic, many examples provided could violate other rules as well.

Ad Hominem

You can't trust Dr. Jones about the dangers of global warming because he is a racist.

This does nothing to argue against global warming but simply attempts to discredit the speaker with an attack that has no bearing on his knowledge of global warming.

Anecdote (Plural of)

Global warming simply isn't a fact because many researchers are measuring stable carbon dioxide levels.

This argues that because persons have a similar anecdotal experience this is proof of a given theory. This is a fallacy because it is subjective and heavily reliant on uncontrolled and possibly biased sources. Science requires statistical validation.

Arguing to Absurdity

So, then who is really to blame for global warming? How can you know for sure? What guarantee do we have? Who says that we can do anything to reverse it?

This is the tactic of carrying on the argument until it becomes absurd.

Arguing to Nausea

How do you know carbon dioxide causes global warming? Why should we believe carbon dioxide causes global warming? But is there total agreement that carbon dioxide causes global warming?

This tactic attempts to repeat the same argument so many times in so many different ways that the challenger eventually tires and gives up defending it.

Authority (Appeal to)

The case on global warming is closed because the commission set up by the president concluded that it is not a threat to man.

This argues that a position is settled based solely on the (supposed) opinion of an authority. We hear this all the time when someone wants to end debate without putting forth arguments or taking personal responsibility for doing so. At home we hear "Sorry, Jimmy, but your dad said so." At work we hear "Sorry, Jim, but that came from the CEO."

Bandwagon (Invoking the)

People all across the country are sick of all this nonstop harping about global warming.

This fallacy unfairly purports to speak for a large number of people. It attempts to entice others to adopt the supposedly popular position.

Beard (Argument of the)

Carbon dioxide levels have been increasing for decades and we have not seen a corresponding rise in species extinction rates.

This assumes that because things exist along a spectrum, different points of the spectrum are identical. In the case of global warming, we don't expect to see proportional correlation. Rather we predict threshold points at which catastrophic environmental collapse will occur.

Begging the Question

We must educate people about the myth of global warming.

This states the position one is trying to argue as an implicit assumption within the statement itself.

Circular Reasoning

Global warming is a natural occurrence. Natural occurrences cause global warming.

This is always fallacious because it makes two statements, each supposedly proving the other.

Common Sense Fallacy

Obviously if greenhouse gases were a problem, big business would see it in their own best interest to solve it.

This makes an unfounded appeal to common sense. Common sense isn't always correct, and people don't always follow their own common sense.

Confusing Correlation and Causation

Many crackpot environmentalists were present at the global warming rally.

This assumes that because one event is found to a given degree in the presence of another, that one of the events causes the other. This fallacy also occurs when causation is assumed simply because one event precedes another.

Conversion (Argument from)

I used to believe in global warming, but I've studied it in depth and have come to realize that it is unfounded hysteria.

This attempts to convince by testifying to a personal enlightenment. It is the "I was once a fool like you but now I'm smarter than you" argument. One's personal conversion is no evidence that they have learned the truth and have not in fact become mistaken.

Ignorance (Argument from)

You have offered no proof that global warming might not prove to be a good thing.

This argues that an unprovable position is true because it cannot be disproven. This is one of the most common and basic errors in logic and is never valid.

Conflict (Inflation of)

Scientists can't agree on the specific effect of carbon dioxide on global warming.

This attempts to create the illusion of legitimate disagreement among experts. Often this fallacy is based on specifics and not the core issue. This is a fallacious tactic regularly used to confuse evolution.

Conspiracy (Fallacy of)

Those global warming nuts have a hidden agenda to justify and advance their liberal policies.

This fallacy can work both ways. It can attempt to make the case that there is some hidden truth out there, known by very few, in order to prove one's position. Or it can also be invoked in such a way as to mock and dismiss legitimate evidence of collusion.

Deductive Fallacy

Scientists dispute global warming; therefore, we can rest assured that Dr. Smith will not agree with any action at this time.

This assumes that what is true for a group in general is true for a particular member of that group.

Discredit the Source

Where did you get those statistics on global warming, off the internet?

This tactic attempts to call into question the source of information. We see this used against the internet every day. Even though the internet has proven to be our most reliable source of unfiltered information, any information from the internet is continually made to seem suspect.

Dishonesty

No one has definitively shown that global warming is the result of human activity.

This knowingly or unknowingly puts forth incorrect information as if it were true. It is obviously never valid.

Elitism (Argument by)

Who are you to lecture me about global warming? I have been a leader of environmental policy for over 20 years.

This claims that one individual is somehow inherently more correct than their opponent by virtue of their status or experience. One must consider the relevance of their experience and the weight of facts before deciding how much weight to give their opinion.

Emotion (Appeal to)

Those people who cry about global warming are the same people who put their causes like the spotted owl before you and your children.

This tactic uses specific arguments in an attempt to raise emotions to the point at which the rational arguments become secondary.

Fallacy Fallacy

The research supporting global warming was not conducted over a sufficiently long period of time.

This ignores the possibility that a flawed argument might still have reached the correct conclusion.

False or Anonymous Authority

World-renowned experts disagree with the predictions of global warming proponents.

This fallacy is committed when a false authority is cited or a claim is cited from anonymous or unknown sources. Never allow someone to cite anonymous or invalid sources of information, especially as a sweeping generalization that is difficult to verify.

False Choice

What do you prefer—that we spend our money fighting global warming or fighting cancer?

This presents only two possible alternatives or two possible outcomes when in reality there are more.

False Causation

All this concern over global warming only started after crazy environmentalists lost their influence in Washington.

This presumes that because one thing preceded another that it was the cause.

False Equation

Carbon dioxide is essential to life, so therefore more carbon dioxide in the atmosphere can only be a good thing.

This tactic draws a false conclusion.

Future (Argument to the)

In twenty years, we will have forgotten all about this global warming scare.

This makes the claim that an argument will be proven at some future point in time. This "history will judge me favorably" claim is an argument that President Bush used many times to justify his policies. It should never be acceptable.

The Galileo Gambit

Everyone said Copernicus was wrong, so who is to say that the one scientist who denies global warming isn't the one who has it right?

This attempts to prove an unpopular position as true by comparing it to some famous person who was later proven to have been right. New Age thinkers use this one a lot.

Gallery (Argument to the)

Why are Americans always the ones who have to suffer to solve problems like global warming?

This argues to the sympathies of the particular audience. This is another argument that appeals to emotion rather than directly addressing the proposition.

Hermetic Fallacy

What do you know about global warming? You're a geologist, not a meteorologist!

This argues that one's position must be wrong because it originates in a different field of study. It may call credentials into question if an argument is being made on the weight of authority but has no bearing on the issue directly.

Illogic (Appeal to)

Science can't pretend to have all the answers; we can solve the global warming crisis through the power of prayer.

This makes an argument that is not supported by any logic; it normally involves citing unprovable, unknowable, and untestable propositions.

Inconsistent Application

> *The American government strongly condemns the Chinese government for failing to take proper measures to prevent global warming.*

It selectively applies criticism to one party while ignoring the same behavior in others. This statement reflects outright hypocrisy.

Inductive Fallacy

> *The case against global warming has not been made sufficiently to convince Dr. Smith; therefore, scientists dispute the theory.*

This assumes that what is true for one member of a group is true for all.

Intuition (Fallacy of)

> *I've seen lots of phony scares like global warming before, and my experience tells me that this is no different.*

This argues that one's personal experience gives one the intuition to make a judgment without any need for facts. This should only be given any credence in very limited situations.

Irrelevant Conclusion

> *Nature is self-correcting; it can adjust to handle changes in the atmosphere.*

This presents a conclusion that does not argue to the question at hand.

Magical Thinking

> *I can't tell you why global warming is a hoax—I just know it.*

This argues that one can simply know the answer in the complete absence of evidence to support it. Magical thinking should never be accepted as valid.

Moving Goalposts

> *Yes, carbon dioxide levels increased as predicted by global warming proponents last year, but we need to go out at least another decade to be sure.*

This sets a goal at a certain level for proof and then moves the goal farther away when that level is reached.

Non Sequitur

> *We don't really know if man is causing global warming. Why all this concern over some polar bears?*

This means "does not follow" in Latin. It creates a relationship between statements that have no logical connection.

Not Invented Here

The Kyoto treaty wasn't drafted by Americans, so it can't be in our best interests.

This argues that an idea that came from anyone other than "us" must be inherently flawed. It is another appeal to emotion and ego.

No True Scotsman

Dr. Jones believes in global warming; therefore, he cannot be a legitimate scientist.

This argues that because an individual has a particular trait, they cannot be a member of a given group.

Numbers (Argument from)

Most people don't believe that global warming is a serious threat.

This claims that an argument is valid simply because many people believe it to be true. The number of people who share a belief has no bearing on its truthfulness. In science, it is not numbers alone that are important, but that a sufficient number have subjected the proposition to independent objective verification.

Origin (Fallacy of)

You can't give a credible opinion on global warming because your nation is one of the worst offenders.

This claims that due to one's origin, one's argument is invalid. This is an attempt to discredit the other party, not a valid argument against the proposition.

Past Mistakes (Appeal to)

Science cried the alarm about ozone but we're still here. Why should be jump when they shout about global warming?

This tactic attempts to call into question current efforts by pointing to past mistakes, or in the case of ozone, a previous crisis averted because action was taken.

Pity (Appeal to)

I'd love to support efforts to curb global warming, but just think of all the poor children who could go hungry when their parents lose their jobs.

This attempts to argue simply by making an appeal to sympathy. It may have some bearing on how we choose to respond to the facts, but no bearing on the facts themselves.

Psychogenetic Fallacy

You liberals only believe in global warming because you hate the free market system.

This attempts to discredit a proposition by inferring some unfounded psychological motivation. Motive is not only difficult to ascribe but does not necessarily invalidate a position.

Red Herring

We can't address global warming until we first address the problem of judges legislating from the bench!

This is simply the tactic of changing the subject so that the focus is directed somewhere else.

Regression toward the Mean (Ignoring)

Many locations haven't shown increases in mean temperature.

This fails to recognize that most outliers tend to shift toward the mean over time. It ignores trends.

Rhetorical Question (Argument by)

How could efforts to halt global warming not destroy our economy?

This tactic attempts to terminate debate and make the proposition seem intractable by posing an unanswerable or excessively broad question.

Ridicule (Argument by)

OK, so we have carbon dioxide in the atmosphere. It's so wonderful that we have scientists spending all our money to tell us that!

This attempts to argue simply by mocking the proposition. It makes no real argument and should always be seen as evidence of a bankrupt position.

Rod (Argument by the)

Anyone who makes claims that gasoline engines contribute to global warming could face lawsuits from the oil and auto industries.

This argues merely by making an appeal to force and coercion. It may intimidate people from speaking the truth but does not invalidate the truth.

Samaritan Intent

The president doesn't support the global warming treaty because he only wants to protect the average American.

This denies responsibility for harm by claiming good intentions. Even if these intentions are true, the road to hell is paved with good intentions, and they have no bearing on the truth of a matter.

Slippery Slope

> *If we let them mandate carbon dioxide emission standards, then the government will try to control every aspect of our lives.*

This makes the case that an action should not be taken because it will lead to some other undesirable action, even if there is no reasonable likelihood of that happening. Sometimes a slippery slope argument can be reasonable, but often it is simply employed as a scare tactic. One should examine the reasonableness of the particular claim.

Statistics (Appeal to)

> *We hear all these statistics thrown around about global warming, but who can we really trust?*

This tactic attempts to discredit an argument by raising suspicions about statistics in general.

Strawman Argument

> *If global warming nuts have their way, they'll soon be telling you that you aren't allowed to grill out in your backyard anymore!*

This attempts to weaken a position by altering it in a way that no one would agree with. This is one of Sean Hannity's favorites and should never be acceptable.

Sweeping Generalization

> *Everyone who believes in global warming is uninformed about the research.*

This makes an argument based on a broad generalization that is not based on fact. Generalizations can be true, but they must be supported. Too often they are made in the absence of evidence.

Texas Sharpshooter

> *Studies show that global warming would actually have a beneficial effect on many arid communities. We should be studying those environments.*

This attempts to focus attention and effort on a particular favorable subset of the population. It essentially tries to focus your evaluation on an anecdotal exception rather than on the overall population.

Tradition (Argument by)

We Americans have a long history of putting our faith in the marketplace to solve problems like global warming.

This claims that because a course of action is accepted as customary, it is the best one. Having made the same mistake a thousand times does not make that a good thing the next time or the fact that it worked before does not assure it will work again.

Truth Lies

Carbon dioxide level have increased in our atmosphere naturally in the past.

This is perhaps the most often used logical fallacy in our post-factual Trump era. These are statements that are crafted to be technically true in a very narrow sense, but overall have the intention and result of perpetuating a greater lie.

Two Wrongs Make a Right

Why should we curb greenhouse gas emissions? China is putting out more greenhouse gases than we do!

This argues that, since someone else is guilty of the accusation, that absolves you of any responsibility. This is often used by children, but never excusable when used by adults.

You Also

Who are you to preach against global warming? You took an airplane to this conference, didn't you?

This attempts to discredit the argument by accusing the other person of the same thing. It may expose hypocrisy, but never has any bearing on the issue.

Weasel Words

Global warming theorists are the only people who take it seriously.

This is the extremely popular technique of choosing words that communicate an underlying hidden message. For example, the word theorist draws immediate comparisons to crackpot conspiracy theorists without saying that outright. The tactic of weasel words has been turned into an art form by conservatives in the last few decades.

Wishful Thinking

We should not overreact to global warming; science will certainly find a solution. It always does.

This diminishes the severity of a problem by expressing unfounded optimism. It should never be accepted as the only result is to delay any resolution of the problem until it may be too late.

Let me end with one additional fallacy of my own.

One of the Above

> *Climate change may be caused by man, or it may be caused by cattle, or it may be a totally natural process.*

This fallacy is most frequently invoked when people argue over causation or contributing factors. It suggests that there is only one answer and if one is right the others must be wrong. More often than not, the real answer is actually "all of the above."

Ethical Fallacies

In addition to logical fallacies, I'd like to suggest that there is also such a thing as **ethical fallacies**. In fact, in our national politics we seem to be ceaselessly deluged by ethical fallacies. Here is one:

"I've Got Mine"

> *Sure, we might spend a lot of money on global warming, but how does that put food on your table?*

This tactic appeals to the selfishness of the listener by pointing out that the argument won't help them personally.

Note that it is with deliberate intent that I speak of ethical fallacies and not moral fallacies. Morality is itself a form of ethical fallacy. The reason I make that distinction is because moral thinking is typically based on ethical fallacies including **"Appeal to the Bible."**

Note that a related and no less dogmatic form of ethical fallacy is **"Appeal to the Constitution."** In fact, many of the same people who would like to bind us to their interpretation of the Bible would also like to turn the Constitution into another Bible, binding even secular individuals to their particular religiously based interpretation of yet another literal and unassailable scripture.

Two related ethical fallacies are **"Appeal to the Majority"** and **"Appeal to Individual Rights."** Sometimes these are valid arguments, but often they are not. When some argue that "a majority of Americans support the death penalty," that does not constitute a valid ethical argument. Likewise, when some argue that we should not restrict any gun sales because it is an individual right, clearly this is insufficient ethical justification. Politicians and advocates often similarly appeal to federal versus state rights inconsistently and arbitrarily when it serves their narrow interests.

Another set of ethical arguments that are often invoked are fallacies of **"Time and Space."** Just because something may have been accepted or considered ethical in biblical times, or even in Revolutionary War days, does not mean it is ethical today. And just because something may be ethical in one place does not ensure that it is ethical in another. Note that religious people have great trouble with this concept. It is too complicated and messy for them. It requires too much thought. They disparage this kind of ethical thinking as "situational" and therefore immoral. They prefer universal and immutable dogma.

Note that just because something is lawful does not make it ethical either. **"Invoking the Law"** is therefore another possible fallacy. Of course, we do our best to create ethical laws, but just because something is law does not make it ethical in all situations. Laws should be fluid enough to ensure fairness in individual situations. This concept is antithetical to some religious thinkers who have trouble with anything beyond simple dogmatic thinking. Ironically, they are most likely to insist the law be adhered to by others while allowing themselves to override the law when they can rationalize that it is contradicts their faith.

There are other fallacies related to belief. Many of the same people are most likely to invoke the **"Fallacy of Sincerity."** Just because a belief is "sincere or heartfelt" does not make it any more or less ethical. Similarly, there is sometimes an **"Appeal to Intent or Ignorance."** These may be extenuating factors, but neither of them makes an action any more or less ethical.

Another is the **"Ethical Proximity"** fallacy. This is the fallacy used to grab all benefits for those in closest proximity to us while shifting all blame away to those farthest from ourselves or our group.

And then there is the **"Personal Responsibility"** fallacy. This version of ethical proximity is used to argue that those who are farthest away or the least powerful must take personal responsibility for their actions while those closest to us or in the most powerful positions in our society are merely victims of "the system."

And then there is the **"Character versus Issues"** fallacy. When we are talking about the flaws in an opposing politician, pundits focus on their basic character failings. But when forced to respond to character flaws in their own candidate, advocates insist that we should instead focus exclusively on "the issues."

Another ethical fallacy that is constantly used, particularly during elections or during the aftermath of a ginned-up march to war, is the **"Water Under the Bridge"** fallacy. This is frequently invoked by those guilty of past failures or even crimes, to insist that all of that is simply water under the bridge—over and done with—and that we must instead look forward. However, when an opponent has similar past failures, they insist that we must never, ever forget.

Probably the most hypocritical ethical arguments is the **"Forgiveness Fallacy."** This is typically invoked by Christians, particularly evangelical Christians, to serve as both a shield and a sword. Whenever one of their own is guilty of wrongdoing, they insist that we must forgive and that only God can judge. However, when the guilty party is not one of them, they insist that only God can forgive and that we must never forget nor forgive. Seems to me that those who most need forgiveness are the ones who advocate for it most strongly, but only when it benefits them.

There is a theme here. We tend to selectively use one set of ethical arguments to rationalize away problems with those in closest proximity to us, and a different and entirely contradictory set of ethical arguments to attack those we disagree with, often for completely unrelated reasons. This is called spin by some, advocacy or good debate tactics by others, and bald-faced hypocrisy by most objective observers. Yet we see and hear these and other fallacious ethical argument all the time.

But this is the thing. Just because almost every line of rhetorical attack or defense in our public discourse is some manifestation of these basic tactics, doesn't mean we should just tune out. That is simply not an option. Rather, just as with logical fallacies, by learning to quickly recognize the general forms of ethical fallacies, we can instead tune *past* all the nonsense intended to obscure and deflect and see through to the heart of contentious issues that are critically important to all of us.

GLOSSARY

Following is a glossary of terms as they are used in this book:

Facts

Assertion: A statement that has not been verified to be true. It may or may not be a fact.

Fact: An assertion that has been *validated or* is true in reality but is not verifiable.

Purported fact: An assertion that is claimed to be a fact but has not actually been validated.

Unsupported fact: Used to point out that an assertion lacks any logic or evidence to support it.

Validated fact: An assertion that has been actively proven to be true either through evidence or logic.

Symbolic fact: Something that exists, but only in our minds.

Logical fact: A fact that is validated by logic.

Probability fact: A fact that is expressed as a statistical probability.

Hard fact: Emphasizes that the fact has been verified.

Alternative fact: A euphemism for a lie or untruth, first popularized by Kellyanne Conway in a sincere attempt to muddy facts.

Fuzzy fact: A very vague and imprecise assertion.

Fuzzy logic: Vague and imprecise logic.

Opinion: A personal assertion of belief or fact.

Mistake: An unintentional misrepresentation.

Lie: An intentional misrepresentation, including assertions that willfully ignore evidence to the contrary.

Beliefs

Belief: An assertion that has been disproven by evidence, lack of evidence, or logic.

Benign belief: A belief that is purported to be harmless or beneficial but nevertheless causes harm to one's neural network integrity.

Deeply held belief: A belief that is purported to be particularly strong, often used as a ploy to exempt it from criticism.

Faith: Complete and absolute certainty that a belief is a fact, especially when that belief is wildly unbelievable.

Delusion: A belief that is unsupported or disproven by evident facts to the contrary. It is differentiated from a belief, which may be based on ignorance or some mistaken assessment of plausibility.

Bizarre delusion: A delusion that is so divorced from reality as to raise it to the level of a particularly acute delusion.

Conspiracy: A secretive action conducted through the overt or effective cooperation of multiple individuals or organizations.

Conspiracy theory: A reference to a particular conspiracy, most often used in a dismissive manner to discredit and delegitimize.

Generalization: A mostly justified appraisal of behaviors associated with particular traits.

Stereotype: A largely unjustified generalization.

Prejudice: A stereotype that is based in part at least on particular prejudicial traits.

Pseudoscience: A belief that is presented as logical and factual, often with a facade of scientific plausibility.

Cult: An organized structure of beliefs that has acquired a body of followers but still insufficient to be accepted as mainstream.

Religion: A cult that has attracted sufficient followers to become institutionalized as mainstream.

New Age: Used in this book to encompass all nonreligious forms of magical thinking.

Evidence

Evidence: Verified facts that support an assertion.

Direct evidence: Evidence that supports an assertion without any inferences being required.

Anecdotal evidence: Reports that are not verified, replicable, or statistically valid.

Conclusive evidence: Evidence that proves a proposition.

Fallacy: An argument that invokes invalid logic.

Thinking

Attitude adjustment: A sudden change in thinking and perspective. Can occur in the form of a *Revelation*.

Learning: The term used to describe what is the process of neural network training.

Education: The way we normally train our neural networks through repeated exposure to new facts.

Socialization: The process of learning the norms and conventions of our various social groups.

Marketing: Repeated exposure to messages through stealth techniques. Recognizes that we do not need to be aware of stimuli to be affected by them.

Indoctrination: The process of teaching a person or group to accept a set of beliefs uncritically, especially by a governing body. It typically entails saturation with repeated messages and the overt suppression of contradictory information.

Brainwashing: The technique of modifying the feelings and thinking of an individual through intensive behavior modification.

Compartmentalization: The separation of mutually incompatible thinking in the brain. This is achievable to some degree but is largely an invalid rationalization for belief.

Backfire effect: The idea that repeatedly exposing people to information can cause them to be more entrenched in their thinking. This is an incomplete characterization at best.

Rationality

Rational thinking: Fact-based thinking that is based on true evidence and sound logic.

Rational: A person who is a typically rational thinker or is thinking rationally about a particular question.

Rationality: An assessment of the rational capacity of a person generally or as pertains to a particular question.

Rationale: An argument or justification arising from a particular rationalization.

Rationalization: The mental process of coming up with a rationale to support a particular belief or conclusion or to reconcile rationally incompatible ideas.

Rationalize away: A particular type of rationalization in which we produce some explanation to ignore or dismiss evidence that does not support our beliefs or conclusions.

Reason (noun): The cause, explanation, or justification one gives to support their actions or conclusions.

Reason (verb): To think rationally.

Reasonable: Our ability to be fair, moderate, and accommodating.

Superrational: A subtle and complex concept used to describe a recursive type of decision-making in which individuals consider the behavior of others in their mental calculations.

Suprarational: Used to describe a level of thinking that transcends logic and reason. This can be used to describe anything from simple intuition to psychic powers.

People

Kool-Aid drinker: A person who accepts ridiculous assertions if they come from sources that they trust.

Conspiracy theorist: A person who tends to see events as related even when they are independent.

Coincidence theorist: A person who tends to deny causation and rather assert that related events are unrelated.

Healthy skeptic: A person who generally does not believe assertions, regardless of the source, if they do not pass reasonable tests of logic and evidence.

Scientific skeptic: A person who generally does not accept testable assertions that have not be subjected to the scientific method of validation.

Fact-based: A person who generally bases their decisions on validated facts.

Belief-based: A person who often bases important decisions upon beliefs in spite of logic or evidence to the contrary.

Belief-tolerant: A person who, while they may be generally fact-based, are reluctant to criticize the beliefs of others.

Humanist: A person who lives by an affirmative set of secular ethical principles.

Atheist: A person who does not believe in any god.

Agnostic: A person who is "99 percent" sure that God does not exist but is willing to acknowledge some possibility.

Absolute atheist: An atheist who asserts that there is simply no chance whatsoever that any god exists.

Nones: People who are not affiliated with any religious group but may or may not believe in a god.

Spiritual: People who distance themselves from any religious group but nevertheless wish to identify a having supernatural beliefs.

New Age: People who believe in unscientific "New Age" principles. Slightly dated, but generally used in this book to include any people who have "magical" thinking unrelated to religion.

Science

Speculation: A tentative hypothesis suggested to explain a particular phenomenon.

Hypothesis: An unproven but testable explanation for a given phenomenon.

Experiment: A test to prove or disprove the validity of a hypothesis.

Theory: A tested and verified explanation of all known evidence related to a given phenomenon.

Law: A theory that represents fundamental universal truths.

Science: Encompasses both a methodology for arriving at truth a body of validated knowledge.

Hard science: Fields of study that deal with objective phenomenon that can be validated by unambiguous experimentation.

Soft science: Fields of study, largely dealing with complex human behaviors, that are not easily studied or understood.

Scientific method: The systematic procedure followed to find truth.

Scientist: A person who practices the scientific method.

Spectroscopy: A set of tools that allow scientists to observe direct evidence of distant or minute phenomenon that lie beyond normal human perception.

Model: A scientific construct, like an analogy, that correctly represents and predicts at least a portion of a complex phenomenon.

Basic research: Research performed for the sake of expanding human knowledge in new and unanticipated ways.

Applied research: Research conducted to find and refine the principles discovered through basic research.

Cosmos: A description of our universe, our reality, as a knowable, predictable set of phenomena.

General

Intuitive: The feeling that a proposition is rational and obvious arising largely from the strength of the associated neural network connection. Can be true or false, sensible or crazy.

Common sense: An intuitive feeling or self-evident conclusion that many people claim to share.

Morality: A form of ethical reasoning that is based largely upon dogmatism and punishment.

Ethics: A code of moral behavior based upon evolved humanistic principles.

Gullibility: Neural network programming that fails to filter out or properly assess factual information and arguments.

Pattern recognition: A primary function of our neural network that involves recognizing patterns or exceptions to patterns.

False positive: The identification of a pattern when it does not actually exist in the data.

False negative: The failure to identify a patter that exists in the data.

Training fact: A set of information that creates a pathway in our neural networks from inputs to associated conclusions.

Swarm behavior: The collective behavior of organisms when they coordinate their individual behaviors to emulate one larger organism.

Emergent behavior: Expresses the aspect of swarm behavior in which a collective behavior "emerges" from seemingly unrelated individual primitives. For example, bridge-building is an emergent behavior unique to certain ant species.

REFERENCES

Facts

Beswick, K. (2011). "Knowledge/beliefs and their relationship to emotion." In K. Kislenko (Ed.), *Current state of research on mathematical beliefs XVI: Proceedings of the MAVI-16 Conference.* Tallinn University of Applied Sciences, June 26–29, 2010.

Cushman, F. (2020) "Rationalization is rational." *Behavioral and Brain Sciences,* 43, e28: 1–59.

Gottlieb, M. S. (1998). "Discovering AIDS." *Epidemiology,* 9(4), 365–367.

Harmon-Jones, E., & Harmon-Jones, C. (2007). "Cognitive dissonance theory after 50 years of development." *Zeitschrift Fur Sozialpsychologie,* 38, 7–16.

Isaacs, L. L. (2007). "Evaluating anecdotes and case reports." *Alternative Therapies in Health and Medicine,* 13(2), 36–38.

Kruger, J., & Dunning, D. (1999). "Unskilled and unaware of it: How difficulties in recognizing one's own incompetence lead to inflated self-assessments." *Journal of Personality and Social Psychology,* 77(6), 1121–1134.

Gore, A. (2007). *Assault on Reason,* (New York, Penguin Press, 2007), pp.1–2.

Beliefs

Bowdring, M. A., & Sayette, M. A. (2018). "Using placebo beverages in group alcohol studies." *Alcoholism, Clinical and Experimental Research,* 42(12), 2442–2452.

Brown, W. (1994). "Placebo as a treatment for depression." *Neuropsychopharmacology,* 10, 265–269.

Cushman, F. (2020) "Rationalization is rational." *Behavioral and Brain Sciences,* 43, e28: 1–59.

Harmon-Jones, E., & Harmon-Jones, C. (2007). "Cognitive dissonance theory after 50 years of development." *Zeitschrift Fur Sozialpsychologie,* 38, 7–16.

Zhong, W., Cristofori, I., Bulbulia, J., Kreuger, F., & Grafman, J. (2017). "Biological and cognitive underpinnings of religious fundamentalism." *Neuropsychologia,* 100, 18-25.

Confusion

Airenti, G., Cruciani, M., Plebe, A., eds. (2019). *The Cognitive Underpinnings of Anthropomorphism.* Lausanne: Frontiers Media.

Bode, S., He A. H., Soon, C. S., Trampel, R., Turner, R., et al. (2011). Tracking the unconscious generation of free decisions using ultra-high field fMRI. PLoS ONE, 6(6), e21612..https://doi.org/10.1371/journal.pone.0021612

Conway, M. A. & Loveday, C. (2015). "Remembering, imagining, false memories & personal meanings." *Consciousness and Cognition*, 33, 574–581.

Cromwell, H. C., Mears, R. P., Wan, L., & Boutros, N. N. (2008). "Sensory gating: a translational effort from basic to clinical science." *Clinical EEG and Neuroscience*, 39(2), 69–72.

Cushman, F. (2020) "Rationalization is rational." *Behavioral and Brain Sciences*, 43, e28: 1–59.

Di Giorgio, E., Lunghi, M., Simion, F., & Vallortigara, G. (2017). "Visual cues of motion that trigger animacy perception at birth: The case of self-propulsion." *Developmental Science*, 20(4).

Granovetter, M. (1978). "Threshold models of collective behavior." *American Journal of Sociology*, 83(6), 1420–1443.

Hamlin JK, Baron AS (2014) Agency attribution in infancy: Evidence for a negativity bias. PLoS ONE, 9(5), e96112.

Hinchey, M. G., Sterritt R, & Rouff C (2007). Swarms and swarm intelligence. Computer, 40(4), 111–113. https://doi.org/10.1109/MC.2007.144

Jarcho, J. M., Berkman, E. T., & Lieberman, M. D. (2011). "The neural basis of rationalization: Cognitive dissonance reduction during decision-making." *Social Cognitive and Affective Neuroscience*, 6(4), 460–467.

Lak, A., Hueske, E., Hirokawa, J., Masset, P., Ott, T., Urai, A. E., Donner, T. H., et al. (2020). "Reinforcement biases subsequent perceptual decisions when confidence is low, a widespread behavioral phenomenon." eLife, 9, [e49834]. https://doi.org/10.7554/eLife.49834

Law, C. T., & Gold, J. I. (2009). "Reinforcement learning can account for associative and perceptual learning on a visual-decision task." *Nature Neuroscience*, 12(5), 655–663.

Levine D. S. (2009). "Brain pathways for cognitive-emotional decision making in the human animal." *Neural Networks*, 22(3), 286–293.

Maij D. L. R., van Schie H. T., & van Elk M (2019) "The boundary conditions of the hypersensitive agency detection device: An empirical investigation of agency detection in threatening situations." *Religion, Brain & Behavior*, 9(1), 23–51.

Proctor R. N. (2012). "The history of the discovery of the cigarette-lung cancer link: Evidentiary traditions, corporate denial, global toll." *Tobacco Control*, 21(2), 87–91.

Rai, A (2020). "Explainable AI: from black box to glass box." *Journal of the Academy Marketing Science*, 48, 137–141.

Scholl, B. J., & Gao, T. (2013). "Perceiving animacy and intentionality: Visual processing or higher-level judgment? "In M. D. Rutherford & V. A. Kuhlmeier (Eds.), *Social Perception: Detection and Interpretation of Animacy, Agency, and Intention* (pp. 197–229). MIT Press.

Schuetz P. N. (2021). "Fly in the face of bias: Algorithmic bias in law enforcement's facial recognition technology and the need for an adaptive legal framework." *Minnesota Journal of Law & Inequality*, 39(1), 221–254.

Soon, C. S., Brass, M., Heinze, H. J., & Haynes, J. D. (2008). "Unconscious determinants of free decisions in the human brain." *Nature Neuroscience*, 11(5), 543–545.

Varella M. A. C. (2018) "The biology and evolution of the three psychological tendencies to anthropomorphize biology and evolution." *Frontiers in Psychology*, 9,1839.

Wardle, S. G., Taubert, J., Teichmann, L. et al. (2020). "Rapid and dynamic processing of face pareidolia in the human brain." *Nature Communication*, 11, 4518.

Davis, R. L., Xhong, Y. (2017). "The Biology of Forgetting—A Perspective." *Neuron*, 95(3), 490-503.

Manassi, M., Whitney, D (2022). "Illusion of visual stability through active perceptual serial dependence." *Science Advances*, 8.

Steinberg, J. R., Finer, L. B., (2012). "Coleman, Coyle, Shuping, and Rue make false statements and draw erroneous conclusions in analyses of abortion and mental health using the National Comorbidity Survey." *Journal of Psychiatric Research*, 46, 407-411.

Delusion

Bortolotti, L., Cox, R., Broome, M.R., & Mameli, M. (2012). "Rationality and self-knowledge in delusions and confabulations: Implications for autonomy as self-governance." In L. Radoilska (Ed.), *Autonomy and Mental Disorder*, Oxford University Press.

Cushman, F. (2020). "Rationalization is rational. Behavioral and Brain Sciences, 43, e28: 1–59.

McKay, R. T., & Ross, R. M., (2021). "Religion and delusion." *Current Opinion in Psychology*, 40, 160–166. https://doi.org/10.1016/j.copsyc.2020.10.002

Clarity

Cialdini, R. B., (2001). "Harnessing the science of persuasion." *Harvard Business Review*, 79(9), 72–79.

Crapse, T. B., & Sommer, M. A. (2012). "Frontal eye field neurons assess visual stability across saccades." *Journal of Neuroscience*, 32(8), 2835–2845.

DiSpenza, J (2008). *Evolve Your Brain: The Science of Changing Your Mind*. Simon & Schuster.

Distler, C., & Hoffmann, K. P. (2003). "Development of the optokinetic response in macaques: a comparison with cat and man." *Annals of the New York Academy of Sciences*, 1004, 10–18.

Enke, B. (2010). "Kinship, cooperation, and the evolution of moral systems." *The Quarterly Journal of Economics*, 134 (2), 953–101.

Giles J. (2005). "Internet encyclopaedias go head to head." *Nature*. 438(7070), 900–901.

Hertwig, R., & Gigerenzer, G. (1999). "The 'conjunction fallacy' revisited: How intelligent inferences look like reasoning errors." *Journal of Behavioral Decision Making*, 12(4), 275–305.

Jemielniak D. (2019). "Wikipedia: Why is the common knowledge resource still neglected by academics?" GigaScience, 8(12), 139.

Johnson, S. P. (2020). "Development of the visual system." In J. Rubenstein, P. Rakic, B. Chen, K. Y. Kwan, *Neural Circuit and Cognitive Development*. 2nd ed, (pp. 335–358). Academic Press.

Nishida, S., Sasaki, Y., Murakami, I., Watanabe, T., & Tootell, R. B. (2003). "Neuroimaging of direction-selective mechanisms for second-order motion." *Journal of Neurophysiology*, 90(5), 3,242–3,254.

Ramachandran, V. S. (1995). "Anosognosia in parietal lobe syndrome." *Consciousness and Cognition*, 4, 22–51.

Rougier, N. P., Noelle, D. C., Braver, T. S., Cohen, J. D., & O'Reilly, R. C. (2005). "Prefrontal cortex and flexible cognitive control: rules without symbols." *Proceedings of the National Academy of Sciences of the United States of America*, 102(20), 7,338–7,343.

Tarczy-Hornoch K. (2012). "Accommodative lag and refractive error in infants and toddlers." *Journal of AAPOS*, 16(2), 112–117.

White, C. J. M. & Norenzayan, A. (2019). "Belief in karma: How cultural evolution, cognition, and motivations shape belief in supernatural justice." In J. M. Olson (Ed.), *Advances in Experimental Social Psychology*, Academic Press.

Science

Blackmore, S. *The Meme Machine*. New York: Oxford University Press, 2000.

Skinner, B. F. (1938). *The Behavior of Organisms*. Appleton-Century.

ABOUT THE AUTHOR

I am a native of Wisconsin, educated in the UW system and a Badger fan. My degrees were in chemistry and in secondary education, although I spent some time as a psychology major as well.

I spent two years living in India, where I taught primary school, and then returned to the United States to teach high school. I returned to UW for my doctorate in inorganic chemistry, for which I qualified, but left before my thesis research was complete to take a job as a computer specialist at a paint and coatings research center.

That turned out to be a great decision. During college, I discovered that I had more natural talent for computer programming than for mixing chemicals and I was able to focus on building hardware and software to support other coatings researchers who worked with beakers and test tubes. My innovative research work earned me the extremely prestigious identification as a "global corporate asset."

I eventually left research to start a consultancy in software development. I completed over a hundred highly successful software projects and became known as the go-to guy to turn around struggling and failing software projects. During that time, I also taught computer science at the college level.

My independent work structure allowed me to travel quite a bit. I have lived, worked, or traveled extensively in over seventy-five countries, depending on how you count them. I worked in England, taught in India, served in the Peace Corps in South Africa, spent a year circumnavigating Central and South America, motorcycled and hitchhiked around North America, hiked across the Borneo rainforest and the Gobi Desert, rode on horseback through Zimbabwe, jeeped across the Outback, was snowed in at an Everest base camp, and canoed up the Zambezi, to name only a handful.

I've published a number of scientific articles and contributed to technical books, ghost-written for a major computer book series, published my own books on computer programming, and also self-published a book on managing high performers in the workplace called *Intangible Management*. I even tried my hand at a fantasy novel called *The Resonant Aura*. I have produced over 200 articles on my blog, www.figmentums.com.

To be totally transparent about my worldview, I am an absolute atheist and a humanist. My primary interest, however, is not advancing atheism or renouncing religion, although I engage in both. My focus is advancing fact-based thinking. In my view, the way to a healthier society is by helping people to be more fact-based in their thinking. To "take away" belief without first creating a foundation of fact-based thinking is to simply invite another belief system to replace it. I trust that when fact-based thinking predominates, religion will just fade away on its own.

While living in New York City I was a frequent speaker on various topics related to fact-based thinking. Nowadays I live with my wife Beth on the Puget Sound in Washington State. Beth is a medical doctor, an epidemiologist, and a researcher.